This is a Flame Tree Book
First published in 2003

01 03 05 04 02

1 3 5 7 9 10 8 6 4 2
Flame Tree Publishing
Crabtree Hall, Crabtree Lane, Fulham,
London, SW6 6TY, United Kingdom
www.flametreepublishing.com

Flame Tree is part of
The Foundry Creative Media Company Limited

ISBN 1 904041 47 7 trade edition
ISBN 1 904041 98 1 plc edition

A copy of the CIP data for this book is available from the British Library

Printed in China

TRUE CRIME

A SOURCE BOOK

Jon Sutherland & Diane Canwell

INTRODUCTION: BARRY PRITCHARD

**FLAME TREE
PUBLISHING**

CONTENTS

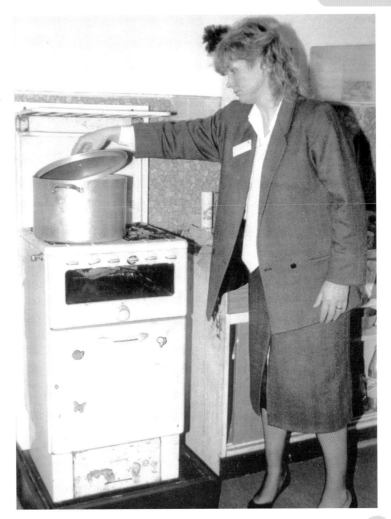

INTRODUCTION

True Crime is a collection of tales about all aspects of the criminal world. It brings together cases, both notorious and little known, to offer an enthralling compendium of true crime.

There has always been a universal fascination with stories of crimes and criminals. Who knows the cause? Maybe it is to do with law-abiding citizens' curiosity into how others have flouted the conventions of society in a way they would never do, or because they provide an insight into human psychology and behaviour. Perhaps it is an escape from everyday life: as a species we are curious, and who could not fail to feel the slightest twinge of intrigue at the details of the latest murder trial covering the front pages of our morning newspaper?

Prior to stories of true crime being printed in books and newspapers, accounts of sensational crimes of the day were spread through other

◀ LEFT: The clothes worn by Charles Lindbergh Jr at the time of his kidnapping are shown in court.

media. Verses and ballads from the sixteenth to nineteenth centuries gave gory details of crimes with moralistic overtones, and occasionally criminals would write 'true confessions' themselves. The advent of the daily newspaper meant that information about criminal activity could be spread easily to a wide audience, a practice which continues unabated today. When the judicial process shifted to trial by evidence rather than confession, there were a whole new series of events to include in the newspaper accounts: the search for evidence, interviewing of witnesses, locating the suspect and the trial itself, at which evidence is displayed and witnesses are presented. When police forces were first formed the detective became the main investigators in criminal cases. From then on many accounts, both fictional and real, were based upon their work.

Today, people are more interested in the workings of the criminal mind than ever: countless films and books are based on real crimes, and many criminals, such as Bonnie and Clyde, Myra Hindley, and Fred and Rosemary West, are virtually household names. Turn on the television, and you will see 'real life' criminal investigation programmes, drama

◀ LEFT: Detectives discover yet another Yorkshire Ripper victim.

series based on actual events, and re-enactments of crimes as an attempt to solve cases, both old and new. No day goes by without some kind of criminal activity being reported on our news bulletins. We live in a world where people are highly aware of the types of crime that go on around them, and are fascinated and fearful in turn.

True Crime embraces the scope of the criminal world. It is divided into ten sections, each of which deals with a particular aspect of crime, and looks at the most notorious or celebrated cases within each category over time. In organising the book in this way, the authors succeed in showing how crime has evolved over the last three or four hundred years, and in many cases how frighteningly similar crimes committed today are to those committed three or more hundred years ago. Recent cases included are all too painful and familiar: the tragic case of the death of toddler James Bulger; the unbelievable extent of the murders committed by Dr Harold Shipman; the did-he-didn't-he intrigue of the O. J. Simpson case, and the seemingly random shootings of the Washington sniper. Looking to the past, it contains details of some notorious cases, including the cannibalistic Sawney Bean family and the elusive Jack the Ripper. Organised crime plays an increasingly large role in today's society, and the book includes a section on the organised crimes committed by gangsters over the past hundred years or so. Mass murderers, serial killers and spree killers from the past three centuries all have a place in the book, as do crimes committed by women and children and cases which remain unsolved.

The methods used to catch criminals have changed as scientific techniques have advanced. Where once a case was unsolvable, the perpetrator can now be caught using incriminating evidence such as a speck of saliva or a hair, thanks to forensic science and DNA testing. Punishment, too, has changed over time. *True Crime* looks at different investigative techniques, and at the types of capital punishment that have been meted out, past and present.

What one must not forget is that behind each of the stories in this book there lies a human tragedy – the death of the victim, the grief of those left behind, or even a miscarriage of justice for the accused. *True Crime* does not seek to glorify crime in any way; instead, by gathering together stories of real events from around the world, it presents a sickening and, at the same time, engrossing account of what drives people to commit crimes.

Barry Pritchard
Former Superintendent Operations, Salisbury

ASSASSINS AND MASSACRES

DAMIENS, ROBERT FRANÇOIS (1757)

In 1757, a half-witted crank named Robert Damiens made an attempt on the life of Louis XV of France. The French had already lost two kings to assassins: Henry III, who was stabbed to death in 1589, and Henry IV in 1610. These had been murders motivated by religion, but Damiens was simply crazed. He attacked the king with a blunt knife, failed to take the monarch's life, and was eventually torn to pieces by four horses – a fate reserved for those guilty of treason.

See Zhelyabov p. 15

THE MURDER OF PC GRANTHAM (1830)

The first English policeman to lose his life while in uniform was PC Grantham, on 29 June 1830. Grantham was on duty in North London that evening, when he intervened in a fight between two Irishmen. The two men, and a woman who was with them, stabbed Grantham until he fell to the ground and then violently kicked him several times. He died soon afterwards and the perpetrators were never brought to justice.

See The Murder of PC Blakelock p. 33

MCNAGHTEN, DANIEL (1843)

In 1843, Daniel McNaghten, a Scottish woodworker, attempted to kill the British prime minister, Robert Peel, but instead assassinated Peel's secretary, Edward Drummond. McNaghten believed that the government was plotting against him. In a landmark case, the defendant was acquitted on the grounds that he was insane, the opinion of nine experts. McNaghten was committed to the Bethlehem Hospital (Bedlam) and later to Broadmoor. This case pioneered the idea that while all defendants are considered sane at the outset of their trials, if this is later proved otherwise, they cannot be deemed responsible for their actions. The concept was later adopted by most Commonwealth countries and some states in America. The crucial point in such cases was the defendants' incapacity to understand the severity of their actions – in other words, a diminished responsibility for what they had done.
See John Warnock Hinckley Jr p.31

WILKES BOOTH, JOHN (1865)

John Wilkes Booth, from Baltimore in Maryland, was a Confederate and operated as a spy and smuggler during the early years of the American Civil War, using his occupation as a touring actor for cover. In 1864, he began plotting the kidnap of Abraham Lincoln – the leader of the northern US states during the war – hoping to seize and exchange him for Confederate prisoners and munitions. The plan had to be abandoned in March 1865, however, when Lincoln changed his itinerary. Booth began again, though, only this time he and his fellow conspirators planned to assassinate Lincoln, his vice-president Johnson and the secretary of state, Seward, on the night of 14 April 1865.

◄ *LEFT: The execution, by quartering, of Robert François Damiens in 1757.*

Lincoln was attending a performance at the Ford Theatre in Washington, occupying the State Box with his wife and two close friends. Booth shot Lincoln in the head and then leapt down on to the stage, breaking a bone in his leg. Nonetheless, he effected his escape. Elsewhere, Seward was badly wounded but the attack on Johnson failed to materialise.

On 26 April, the conspirators were cornered at a firm in Port Royal, Virginia, and in the confrontation Booth was mortally wounded. On 29 June, his co-plotters were found guilty and sentenced to hang on 7 July. Among them was Mary Surratt, the first African-American woman to be executed.

See Charles Guiteau p. 16

▶ RIGHT: The body of fatally wounded Tsar Alexander II is hurried back to the palace.

THE KILLING OF JUAN PRIM (1870)

An unknown assassin shot Juan Prim, the Spanish prime minister, in December 1870, as he was leaving the Madrid government chamber. Prim was a Liberal and a monarchist, and was known to have innumerable opponents in the more reactionary right-wing side of Spanish politics. There is little doubt that clandestine reactionary forces were behind the assassination and that this assisted in ensuring that the killer was never identified.

See Gavrilo Princip p. 20

ZHELYABOV (1881)

Zhelyabov had attempted to assassinate Tsar Alexander II of Russia in February 1880, and even though this failed he continued to plan the downfall of the monarch. Zhelyabov was captured at the end of February 1881, but over the ensuing days his anarchist followers struck again, using a bomb. The blast shattered the Tsar's legs and he died several days later. The anarchists had taken no chances this time, planting assassins along all the rail routes out of St Petersburg.

See Yakob Yurovsky p. 21

◀ LEFT: A drawing of Abraham Lincoln's assassination at Washington's Ford Theatre.

GUITEAU, CHARLES (1881)

Charles Guiteau was something of a religious crank, but this did not prevent his entry into US politics. He was part of the unsuccessful campaign for the Democrat presidential candidate, Horace Greely, in 1872. In 1880 he supported Ulysses S. Grant, who also lost. Guiteau then switched his allegiance to the successful James Garfield and firmly believed that the new president should reward him with a political post. For some months after Garfield's election, Guiteau pestered staff at the White House, certain that Garfield would reward his loyalty. At first he was seen as something of a joke, but soon he gained a reputation as a pest. When no post was forthcoming, Guiteau became frustrated and determined to eliminate the man who was hindering his political career. He shot Garfield on 2 July 1881. Garfield lingered between life and death for several months, and finally died on 19 December. Still basking in the limelight, Guiteau was executed in June 1882.

See Leon Franz Czolgosz p. 17

▶ RIGHT: Leon Czolgosz shoots US President McKinley at the Pan-American Exposition in Buffalo.

◀ *LEFT: An illustration of Guiteau's trial for the murder of President Garfield in 1881.*

RAVOCHOL (1892)

In 1892, Ravochol, or François-Cladius Koeningstein, took action against the French government after the suppression of a labour rally in Clichy. He planted bombs at the homes of the presiding judge and prosecutor in the case, then bombed the Lobau Barracks in Paris; there were no deaths from the bombings. Identified at a Paris restaurant by a waiter and sentenced to life, Ravochol was later executed for two earlier killings. The restaurant was subsequently bombed by other anarchists.

See Robert François Damiens p. 12

CZOLGOSZ, LEON FRANZ (1901)

Polish-American Leon Czolgosz was fascinated by the newspaper accounts of Gaetano Bresci's assassination of King Humbert I in July 1900. Czolgosz was determined to gain for himself the same degree of fame. He bought himself a pistol and headed off to the Pan-American Exposition in Buffalo, with the intention of killing the president, William McKinley.

On 6 September 1901, Czolgosz joined a queue of people waiting to shake hands with McKinley. When he reached the head of the queue, he shot McKinley in the abdomen and chest. Arrested immediately, Czolgosz refused to speak and remained silent throughout his trial. He was sentenced to death by electrocution; acid was then poured into his coffin to destroy his body. Czolgosz was the first assassin to be executed by electrocution.

See Charles Guiteau p. 16

▶ RIGHT: London police line Sidney Street in Houndsditch with shotguns at the ready.

THE TOTTENHAM OUTRAGE (1909)

In 1909, two Eastern European anarchists attempted to snatch the payroll from a factory in Tottenham, London. The wage clerk refused to cooperate and shots were fired. Soon the gunmen were being chased through the streets by unarmed policemen. The gunmen fired back at the policemen, missing their targets but killing a young boy. When they reached Chingford Road, the gunmen jumped on a passing tram. During

the ride they shot and wounded one of the passengers and, as they leapt off the tram, they also injured a milkman. They then made off on a horse-drawn grocer's van, chased by policemen on bicycles and armed with cutlasses. Both men were later cornered, but committed suicide after the two-hour chase, which had covered six miles. The incident had cost the lives of one policeman and a child, as well as seven police and 14 civilians wounded.
See The Houndsditch Killings and the Sidney Street Siege p. 18

◀ LEFT: Anarchists hijack a tram in Tottenham; police pursue them in another tram.

THE HOUNDSDITCH KILLINGS AND
THE SIDNEY STREET SIEGE (1910)

The Sidney Street Siege, or the Battle of Stepney as it was also known, was the culmination of a series of armed burglaries in the Houndsditch area that had claimed the lives of three policemen. The desperados – Latvian and Russian nationals – were cornered in a house in Sidney

Street in December 1910 and were besieged until 2 January 1911. Attempts to seek a peaceful resolution were met with a hail of gunfire. At one point, operations were directed by the home secretary, Winston Churchill. Eventually, the revolutionaries set the house on fire. Two bodies were found and four other members of the gang were arrested. It was established that the two dead men had been the Houndsditch killers and the other four were later released.

See The Tottenham Outrage p. 18

SCHRANK, JOHN (1912)

US presidential candidate Theodore Roosevelt's short-sightedness and his habit of delivering long-winded speeches undoubtedly saved his life in 1912. John Schrank, a psychotic New York barkeeper, attempted to kill Roosevelt during a stop in Milwaukee as part of his presidential election campaign. Schrank had aimed for Roosevelt's head, but a bystander spoiled his aim at the last second. Roosevelt did not even realise he had been shot until someone noticed a hole in his overcoat. The bullet had passed through a double-folded 50-page speech script and his spectacle case before entering his body, lodging in his chest wall. The assassination attempt ruined Roosevelt's chances of election and he lost to William Taft. Schrank was committed to a mental institution in Wisconsin, where he died in 1943 without ever having received a visitor.

See Giuseppe Zangara p. 21

◀ *LEFT: Gavrilo Princip, assassin of Archduke Franz Ferdinand in Sarajevo.*

PRINCIP, GAVRILO (1914)

Gavrilo Princip was a Bosnian Serb who assassinated Franz Ferdinand, Archduke of Austria and the heir to the Austro-Hungarian throne. The attack took place on 28 June 1914 and was undoubtedly one of the key events that led to the outbreak of World War I. Earlier in the day, there had been a Serbian bomb attack on the archduke, which had killed the driver and wounded the passengers in the car behind him. The archduke was heading for the hospital to visit the victims when Princip seized his chance and shot Franz Ferdinand's wife Sophie in the head, and the archduke in the chest. Franz Ferdinand bled to death before the wound could be tended.

The Austrians demanded to be allowed to investigate the conspiracy in Serbia and just one month later World War I began. Princip was a member of the pro-Serbian Young Bosnia Group, supplied by a secret organisation known as the Black Hand, which had links with the Serbian government and military.

Princip was given 20 years imprisonment for the murder of Franz Ferdinand and his wife on that fateful day in Sarajevo. Princip died of tuberculosis in prison on 28 April 1918.

See Claus Von Stauffenberg p. 22

YUROVSKY, YAKOB (1917)

Yakob Yurovsky's father was a criminal who had been deported to Siberia, and Yurovsky himself had joined the Bolsheviks in 1905. By 1918, he had become a leading member of the Bolshevik party and in early July he had been assigned the task of guarding the Russian royal family, who were being held prisoner.

In July 1917, in the company of 10 militia, Yurovsky read the death sentence to Tsar Nicholas II in the basement of a house on the outskirts of Ekaterinburg. He shot the tsar and then his wife, Alexandra. The other members of the firing squad despatched the rest of the family – the tsarevich Alexei and his four sisters – and their servants. The bodies were first left in an abandoned mine, but they were later reburied along a road when the truck carrying their corpses got stuck in mud.

This massacre was the culmination of a bitter struggle between the Bolsheviks and the White Army, still loyal to the Romanov royal family and the events of the night of 17 July 1918 saw the end of the Russian monarchy. Yurovsky, a hero of the revolution, finally died after a long illness in 1938.
See Zhelyabov p. 15

ZANGARA, GIUSEPPE (1933)

Italian-born Giuseppe Zangara blamed American president Franklin D. Roosevelt for privations suffered during the Depression. On 15 February 1933, while the president was visiting Bayfront Park in Chicago, Zangara pushed his way into the crowd, armed with a revolver. Being short, he had to stand on a chair. Zangara missed Roosevelt, but hit the Chicago mayor and four onlookers. Although Zangara was initially sentenced to 84 years imprisonment, this was changed to the death sentence after the mayor succumbed to his injuries and died. Zangara was executed on 20 March 1933.
See John Schrank p. 19

VON STAUFFENBERG, CLAUS (1944)

By the summer of 1944, the fortunes of Nazi Germany had turned irrevocably for the worse. For some time there had been a smouldering resentment against Adolf Hitler and his leadership. It was therefore decided amongst certain circles of the German officer class to rid the country of its führer. Claus von Stauffenberg placed a bomb in a briefcase inside Hitler's command bunker in Rastenburg, Prussia; the weapon had been provided by German intelligence. The bomb failed to kill Hitler and the plot to seize power failed. Von Stauffenberg was shot and many of the conspirators were slowly put to death, their agonies filmed for Hitler's later delight. It has been estimated that some 20,000 people were killed or sent to concentration camps as a result of Hitler's purges after the attempt.

See Gavrilo Princip p. 20

TORRESOLA, GRISELIO AND OSCAR COLLAZO (1950)

These Puerto Rican nationalists attempted to assassinate President Harry Truman on 1 November 1950. Truman was staying at a nearby house while the White House was being renovated. The nationalists approached from different directions and engaged in a running gun battle with police and agents. Torresola was shot and killed, along with one policeman. Collazo was sentenced to death but Truman

◀ *LEFT: Claus von Stauffenberg, who attempted to assassinate Adolf Hitler in 1944.*

commuted the sentence to life imprisonment, and he was released in 1979. He died in Puerto Rico in 1994.

See John Warnock Hinckley Jr p. 31

SECRET ARMY ORGANISATION (1962–65)

The Secret Army Organisation, or the Organisation de l'Armée Secrète was a right-wing group that decided to take direct action against French moves to give Algeria independence. They first tried to blow up President Charles de Gaulle in Aube, but the roadside bomb failed to explode. In January 1962 they killed one and wounded 13 when they exploded a bomb in the Foreign Ministry in Paris. On 22 August 1962 they carried out a machine-gun attack on the car carrying de Gaulle in the suburbs of Paris. He escaped unscathed and most of the former French soldiers who had carried out the attack were arrested. They made two more attempts in March 1963 and five more in 1964, followed by three others in 1965.

See Carlos the Jackal p. 29

OSWALD, LEE HARVEY (1963)

Lee Harvey Oswald was the alleged assassin of President John F. Kennedy. He was a former US Marine and had lived in the Soviet Union between 1959 and 1962, where he had married a Russian national. He returned to the US and became involved in pro-Castro Cuban politics. Officially at least, he shot Kennedy from the sixth floor of the Texas Schoolbook Depository, where he was employed, in Dallas at around 12.30 p.m. on 22 November 1963.

Shortly afterwards he was arrested and from the outset he denied that he had shot anyone. Two days later, whilst being transferred to another prison, Oswald was assassinated by Jack Ruby. This act only sought to muddy the waters even further, as it is widely believed by many that Oswald did not, in fact, fire the fatal shots and that Ruby had killed Oswald to prevent the truth ever being disclosed.

The Warren Commission was set up in November 1963 to investigate the assassination, but to this date their findings have remained secret, simply fuelling the belief that Kennedy was assassinated as the result of some elaborate conspiracy. Officially, Oswald remains the prime candidate, but many believe that one day the truth will be revealed.
See Jack Ruby p. 24

RUBY, JACK (1963)

Two days after Oswald had been arrested for assassinating President Kennedy, this Dallas nightclub owner assassinated the assassin. Ruby was of Polish extraction and had been involved in organised crime from a fairly young age. He habitually carried a gun and claimed that his assassination of Oswald was a spur-of-the-moment decision. The actual

assassination was broadcast live on American television. Ruby initially claimed that he had killed Oswald to save Jacqueline Kennedy the trauma of testifying at the trial, but many believe that Ruby was part of a larger mafia conspiracy and his task was to silence Oswald.

On 14 March 1964 Ruby was found guilty of Oswald's murder, but the conviction was overturned and before he could be retried, he died of cancer in prison on 3 January 1967.
See Lee Harvey Oswald p. 23

◀ LEFT: *Nightclub owner Jack Ruby, seconds before shooting Lee Harvey Oswald in the stomach.*

RAY, JAMES EARL (1968)

James Earl Ray assassinated the civil rights leader Martin Luther King Jr on 4 April 1968 at the Lorraine Motel in Memphis, Tennessee. Witnesses had placed Ray at the scene of the assassination, and suspicions about his guilt were compounded by the fact that he fled the country immediately after the event. He was apprehended at Heathrow Airport in London on 8 June. His fingerprints were found on the rifle and on a pair of binoculars that had been found at the scene of the crime, and he admitted to buying a similar rifle. He claimed that he had given the weapon to a man called Raoul; this man has never been traced. It was always believed that Ray had not acted alone.

In court the following year he pleaded guilty to the assassination, but just three days after he had been convicted of the killing and sentenced to 99 years, he withdrew his confession. Martin Luther King's son Dexter continually supported James Ray's demand for a re-trial. He believed that his father and Ray were victims of a broader conspiracy. Ray died from a kidney disease in 1998, as a result of receiving a blood transfusion following a stabbing incident in prison. To date, further investigations have proved inconclusive.

See Lee Harvey Oswald p. 23

SOLANAS, VALERIE (1968)

Valerie Solanas was a militant feminist during the 1960s. In 1967 she had written a play entitled

▶ *RIGHT: James Earl Ray, Martin Luther King's killer, is escorted to a cell in Memphis, Tennessee.*

The Scum Manifesto, which rounded on men and expressed her opinion of their desire for power and money. She had asked the Pop artist Andy Warhol to produce her play in 1967, but he had never responded to this request. She demanded the script's return from him; Warhol told her he had lost it and she began demanding money instead. On 3 June 1968 she entered his studio in New York and shot him three times, for which she received three years for attempted murder. Solanas became a drug addict and a prostitute after serving her prison sentence and died at the age of 52 in San Francisco.

See Mark Chapman p. 30

> ▶ RIGHT: *Damage to a department store following an arson attack by Baader Meinhof terrorists.*

BAADER MEINHOF (1968–77)

The Red Army Faction (RAF) was led by Andreas Baader and Ulrike Meinhof and was one of three terrorist groups active in West Germany between 1968 and 1977. At least in principle, the Baader Meinhof gang wished to overthrow capitalist society, yet they had a strange mixture of political ideals that were difficult to determine.

Following the siege of the West German Embassy in Stockholm in April 1975, the bulk of the gang were finally rounded up. They were placed on trial in 1976; it lasted two years, the longest and most expensive trial in West German history.

Baader and Meinhof committed suicide in prison along with the other two founders of the group, Gudrun Ensslin and Jan-Karl Raspe. In all, 26 of the group were tried, most receiving long sentences. Even while the main gang leaders were in prison, other members were still active,

kidnapping and hijacking in order to make demands for the release of the others. All attempts failed; all they had achieved was to make the West German government more powerful. The group formally ceased operations in 1992. Over they years they were responsible for a multitude of kidnappings, assassinations, robberies, arson attacks and bombings.
See The Weathermen p. 27

THE WEATHERMEN (1970S)

During US involvement in the Vietnam War, a number of civil rights groups and students were involved in protests against government policy. A group known as the Weathermen was a far more radical faction that planted bombs in its attempt to convince America to change its policies. The group set off a series of bombs in the New York area, including one that exploded prematurely, claiming the lives of three of the Weathermen group. After this incident they tended to bomb empty buildings, but when America's involvement in the Vietnam War ended, the reason for their existence also stopped. The Weathermen group gave way to a more violent organisation with links to the Black Panthers and the Black Liberation Army, who would carry out a series of robberies, including the Brinks robbery in 1981.
See Baader Meinhof p.26

SKINGLE, ARTHUR AND PETER SPARROW (1971)

On the evening of 27 June 1971, Detective Constable Ian Coward stopped a car

▶ *RIGHT: Three women from the militant Weathermen organisation are handcuffed together.*

containing two men in Reading on suspicion of drunk driving. As the policeman approached the vehicle, Skingle shot him nine times. Coward died a month later. Skingle had just been released from prison and Sparrow also had a criminal record. Witnesses identified them from mug-shots and they were picked up, tried and sentenced to life terms for the murder.

See Joseph Guerin p. 28

GUERIN, JOSEPH (1971)

One evening in 1971, Mike McNeil, a police sergeant in New York, pulled in a car driver whose license did not match the car's registration number. As he was questioning the man, the other three occupants of the car drove off. McNeil caught them, searched them then climbed into the driver's seat. Guerin had a concealed revolver and shot McNeil several times in the head. Guerin ran off, but the other occupants remained to give evidence. Guerin had been wanted for robbery and was sentenced to life imprisonment.

See Arthur Skingle and Peter Sparrow p.27

BREMER, ARTHUR (1972)

Arthur Bremer seemed doomed to anonymity. He was a poor shot, yet determined to be an assassin. Sometime in 1972 he decided to kill either Richard Nixon or George Wallace; his attempt to assassinate Nixon ended in failure, but on 15 May 1972 he shot Wallace at a presidential rally in Laurel, Maryland. He was sentenced to 53 years for attempted murder and will be 74 by the time he is released.

See Lynette Fromme p. 30

CARLOS THE JACKAL (1972–94)

Venezuelan-born Ilich Ramirez Sanchez, known as Carlos the Jackal, had a three-decade career of bombings, kidnappings, hijackings and assassinations. On 14 August 1994, living under an alias in Khartoum, Sudan, the Jackal was finally captured and transferred under heavy guard to Paris to face a catalogue of charges, including a car bombing in the centre of Paris in 1982. He was also charged with a grenade attack on an Israeli bank, being the mastermind behind the Munich Olympics atrocity in 1972, the seizing of hostages at the OPEC meeting in Vienna in 1975 and numerous other crimes. He was to spend three years in solitary confinement before being sentenced to life for the murder of two French security agents and a Lebanese revolutionary in 1975.

See Secret Army Organisation p. 23

BYCK, SAMUEL S. (1974)

Samuel S.Byck was a failed businessman who believed that the US political system was corrupt. He had begun threatening President Nixon by mail in 1972, but on 22 February 1974 he launched his plan 'Operation

◀ *LEFT: Carlos the Jackal (Ilich Ramirez Sanchez) and various arms belonging to him.*

Pandora's Box' with the intention of hijacking an airliner and crashing it into the White House. He shot his way on to a jet at the Baltimore-Washington airport. The plane was unable to lift off, so he shot the pilot and co-pilot; faced with capture he committed suicide.

See Arthur Bremer p. 29

FROMME, LYNETTE (1975)

Lynette Fromme was a disciple of Charles Manson. When Manson was sentenced to life imprisonment she feared he would be forgotten, so she determined to assassinate President Gerald Ford to remind people that Manson's 'family' still lived. On 5 September 1975 she attempted Ford's murder in Sacramento, but had not correctly loaded her gun and was wrestled to the ground. She was sentenced to life but escaped from a prison in San Diego. Since her recapture, she has been held in maximum-security prisons in West Virginia, Lexington and Florida.

See Charles Manson p.259

BULGARIAN SECRET SERVICE (1978)

Georgi Markov was a Bulgarian refugee who had fled the authorities and had been granted political asylum in Britain. He began working for the BBC World Service, broadcasting to Bulgaria, and incurred the wrath of those in power there. On 7 September 1978, whilst walking along The Strand, Markov was prodded in the thigh with an umbrella. He had been poisoned with ricin, delivered by a pellet with microscopic holes.

See Secret Army Organisation p. 23

CHAPMAN, MARK DAVID (1980)

Mark Chapman shot ex-Beatle John Lennon outside the Dakota Building in New York on 8 December 1980. Some people still believe that

Chapman was not just a disturbed stalker, as it was thought at the time, but that he may have been part of a broader conspiracy to murder the pro-peace musician. Chapman believed that the lyrics in Lennon's songs were directed at him and, as a paranoid schizophrenic, he apparently could not ignore these signals. Lennon's son, Sean, believed that shadowy government officials had ordered the execution of his father. Chapman was sentenced to 20 years imprisonment in 1980. He had his first parole request rejected in 2000 on the grounds that his killing of John Lennon was calculated and unprovoked.

See Valerie Solanas p. 25

▸ RIGHT: *President Reagan is helped into the Presidential Limousine after being shot in 1981.*

HINCKLEY, JOHN WARNOCK JR (1981)

Oklahoma-born John Hinckley was obsessed with the actress Jodie Foster, and equally fascinated with assassination. He was fined for possession of handguns whilst stalking President Carter in 1980, then determined to shoot the new president, Ronald Reagan, detailing the 'historic deed' in a letter to Foster. Outside Washington's Hilton, Hinckley fired six shots; one hit Reagan in the chest and three other people were wounded. Hinckley, not guilty due to insanity, was sent to St Elizabeth's Institution in Washington.

See Daniel McNaghten p.13

AGCA, MEHMET ALI (1981)

Agca attempted to assassinate Pope John Paul II on 13 May 1981, but only succeeded in wounding him. Agca claimed to be a member of the Popular Front for the Liberation of Palestine, but they denied his membership of their group. He then claimed to be backed by the Bulgarians, who had been forced by the KGB to launch an assassination attempt in response to the Pope's support for the Polish Solidarity Movement. No clear link or motive was ever established. Agca was sentenced to life, but in June 2000 he was pardoned by the Italian president, Carlo Azeglio Ciampi, and deported to Turkey, where he currently resides in prison for the murder of a newspaper editor.

See Mark David Chapman p. 30

THE MURDER OF PC YVONNE FLETCHER (1984)

In November 1999 the Libyan government agreed to pay compensation to the family of PC Yvonne Fletcher. Fletcher was a serving officer murdered outside the Libyan Embassy in London in 1984, whilst on duty at a demonstration against the Libyan leader, Colonel Gaddafi. The burst of fire had killed Yvonne Fletcher and injured 11 other people, mostly Libyan dissidents, after which there had been a tense 10-day siege before the 22 Libyan officials had been allowed to leave Britain. The police had been forced to allow the gunman and his accomplices to leave the Libyan Peoples' Bureau and fly to Tripoli because of their diplomatic immunity. To date, no one has been charged for the murder of the police woman.

See The Murder of PC Blakelock p. 33

◀ LEFT: *A memorial stone for PC Yvonne Fletcher in St James Square, London.*

THE MURDER OF PC BLAKELOCK (1985)

During the Broadwater Farm Riots in Tottenham, London in 1985, PC Keith Blakelock was hacked to death whilst trying to protect firemen who were dealing with a blaze. In 1987 Winston Silcott, Mark Braithwaite and Engin Raghip were all convicted of his murder, but the convictions were later overturned on appeal; it was felt that the police had fabricated evidence to implicate the three men. Silcott was later awarded punitive damages for the wrongful conviction, but nonetheless is currently serving a life sentence for the murder of a nightclub bouncer, Anthony Smith. Silcott's release has been continually delayed due to his refusal to acknowledge that he murdered Smith, claiming that the killing was an act of self defence.

See The Murder of PC Yvonne Fletcher p. 32

RYAN, MICHAEL (1987)

On 19 August 1987, Michael Ryan stalked the streets of Hungerford, Berkshire, shooting at will. He murdered 16 and wounded 14, eight of whom were seriously injured. Ryan was an unemployed labourer with a love of guns and weapons. He had begun the slaughter across the border in Wiltshire, with the cold-blooded killing of Susan Godfrey; he had then driven into Hungerford on the town's market day in order to find more victims.

▶ RIGHT: *Morning newspapers tell of the Hungerford massacre, 20 August 1987.*

As the firing started, one of the victims, a police officer, Roger Bereton, managed to contact another officer who called in firearms units and a helicopter. Bereton then died where he lay. After rampaging through the town, Ryan barricaded himself in a school and the police surrounded the buildings with snipers. Negotiators made contact with Ryan, who told them 'I have killed all those people, but I haven't got the guts to blow my own brains out'. Just after 7.00 p.m. Ryan found the courage and the police discovered him dead in one of the school's classrooms.

The massacre prompted the government to ban semi-automatic rifles in Britain under the Firearms (Amendment) Act of 1988. Ryan's chosen weapon, unlicensed, had been a Russian-designed AK47.

See Robert Sartin p. 34

SARTIN, ROBERT (1989)

During a 20-minute period on Sunday, 30 April 1989 in Monkseaton, Tyne and Wear, Robert Sartin killed one and wounded 14 others. Schizophrenic Sartin would later claim to have heard voices in his head compelling him to carry out the attacks. He had been obsessed with the Moors Murders committed by Myra Hindley and Ian Brady, and the poisoner Graham Young. He had also visited Hungerford, the site of Michael Ryan's massacre. Sartin habitually wore black, and liked to be known as Satan.

Sartin was just 22 when he strode around Monkseaton armed with a shotgun, discharging the weapon at anyone he saw. When he stood trial in April 1990 he was deemed 'unfit to plead' and was subsequently confined to a psychiatric unit for an indefinite period.

See Michael Ryan p. 33

THE ÉCOLE POLYTECHNIQUE MASSACRE (1989)

On 6 December 1989, Marc Lépine ran riot through this educational institution in Montreal, Canada, murdering 14 women. Lépine blamed women – feminists in particular – for his failed application to be accepted on to an engineering course. Another motive for the killings was the fact that Lépine's pregnant girlfriend intended to have a termination. Lépine began his slaughter by storming into an engineering class and declaring his hatred of feminists, before opening fire on the women in the room. After his rampage, he calmly committed suicide.

The date is reserved as a memorial day for those who were killed at the Polytechnique and in 1998, largely as a result of the massacre, the Canadian government passed shotgun control laws.

See The Dunblane Massacre p. 35

THE DUNBLANE MASSACRE (1996)

Thomas Hamilton was obsessed with small boys and was a former scout leader whose behaviour had been brought into question. On 13 March 1996 Hamilton stormed into a primary school in Dunblane at Stirling in Scotland and fired over 100 rounds in three minutes, killing or wounding everyone present in the gym. Hamilton was well armed, with two pistols, Browning semi-automatics, two revolvers and over 700 cartridges.

◄ *LEFT: Dr Mick North (left), father of a Dunblane victim and Tony Hill (right), father of a Hungerford victim, at the 1996 launch of the 'Gun Control Network' pressure group.*

He claimed the lives of one teacher and 15 small children. Fifteen more children were wounded, as were three other teachers. One of the children was pronounced dead on arrival at hospital. After completing the massacre, Hamilton turned a revolvers on himself.

Apparently, some form of revenge for his dismissal as a scout leader was Hamilton's motive, and in his own mind it was the gym, in which he had run a boys' club, that was the focus of his rage. The entire massacre lasted no more than three minutes, but the pain and the anguish caused by Hamilton's act will live long in the memory of the small Scottish community. The tragedy prompted the government to impose further restrictions on firearms, particularly since Hamilton possessed the weapons legally.

See The École Polytechnique Massacre p. 35

THE SANAA MASSACRE (1997)

On 30 March 1997, Mohammad Ahmad Al-Naziri launched an attack on two schools in Sanaa, Yemen. He was armed with an assault rifle and fired indiscriminately into two crowds of pupils, killing six children and two adults. There did not appear to be any specific reason for the attack and the Yemeni court sentenced him to death the following day; the execution was duly carried out by firing squad just a week later.

See The Tadjena Massacre p. 36

THE TADJENA MASSACRE (1998)

On 9 December 1998, Islamic militants perpetrated a massacre at Tadjena, 200 km (60 miles) to the west of Algiers in Algeria. They slit the throats of 42 people. These attacks, which have recurred with growing

▸ *RIGHT: Floral tributes are laid out in memory of the Erfurt Massacre victims.*

frequency, are part of the insurgency difficulties in Algeria. In 1992 the elections were cancelled after the Islamic Salvation Front was poised to win. The army took over and since then more than 100,000 people have died in the escalating violence.

See The Erfurt Massacre p. 37

THE ERFURT MASSACRE (2002)

On 26 April 2002, Robert Steinhäuser, dressed like a Japanese ninja, burst into a school in Erfurt, Germany, and murdered 13 teachers, two students and a police officer. Steinhäuser had been recently expelled from the school for truancy. He chose the day deliberately as his former classmates were sitting examinations. He burst into a classroom armed with a

pump-action shotgun and a pistol and began indiscriminately picking off members of staff. Shooting at anyone who moved, he roamed around the school. The police took around 10 minutes to respond and Steinhäuser killed the first of them to appear. A history teacher managed to push him into one of the classrooms, after ripping the mask he wore from his face. With the police arriving in ever-increasing numbers, Robert turned the gun on himself.

See The École Polytechnique Massacre p. 35

CHILDREN OF CRIME

YORK, WILLIAM (1748)

Ten-year-old William York lived in a workhouse in Eyke, near Bury St Edmunds in Suffolk, where he shared a bed with five-year-old Susan Mayhew. One morning in 1748 William woke to find that Susan had wet the bed. He took her outside, cut her wrists and elbows, then slashed open her thigh; the little girl bled to death. William was given the death sentence, but chose a career in the navy as a reprieve.

See Mary Flora and Nora Bell p. 48

ALLNUTT, WILLIAM (1847)

William Allnutt was a sickly and dishonest child, who drove his family to distraction. On 20 October 1847 his grandfather, Samuel Nelme, finally lost his temper and hit the boy. William determined to get even with the old man and began lacing his sugar bowl with arsenic. Nelme died in agony a week later. On investigating the death, police discovered that William had stolen a watch and 10 sovereigns from his grandfather. The 12-year-old was initially sentenced to death, but this was commuted to life imprisonment.

See Lizzie Borden p. 43

DANCEY, ALFRED (1850)

Alfred Dancey, a slum boy from Bedminster, Gloucestershire, was the object of persistent bullying from two older boys. In 1850, the 14-year-old could stand it no longer and shot one of the bullies dead with a pistol. Alfred was tried and found guilty of murder.

◀ LEFT: An 1867 cartoon of a bully 'that must be put down' – as Alfred Dancey did quite literally.

He was transported to Australia for 10 years. Bullied children, who live in fear of their tormentors, are prime candidates for suddenly striking back, a trend that has been repeated in many cases since Alfred Dancey's.

See The Browood County Seven p. 56

FITZ, ALFRED (1855)

Alfred Fitz, a nine-year-old slum dweller from Liverpool, lost his temper whilst playing with his friend James Feleeson. Fitz killed the boy using a broken brick, then he and another friend threw James's body into a canal to avoid detection. They were identified, however, and found guilty of manslaughter in August 1855. They were sentenced to 12 months in Liverpool prison.

See Robert Thompson and Jon Venables p. 53

▸ *RIGHT: Boston's Old State House around the time of the Jesse Pomeroy killings.*

POMEROY, JESSE (1871–74)

Jesse Pomeroy started his reign of terror in the Boston area of the United States at the tender age of 12. Between December 1871 and February 1872, he abducted, tortured and probably raped several young boys. He was quickly identified and sentenced to an 18-month spell in a reform school. He was released in February 1874, but it seems he had not learnt his lesson. In April of that year a young girl, Mary Curran, disappeared, quickly followed by four-year-old Horace Mullen. When police found Horace's body, it showed around 30 stab wounds and the head had almost been severed. The subsequent investigation uncovered a blood-stained knife and muddy shoes in Pomeroy's room; Curran's decomposed body was later found in the cellar.

On 10 December 1874 Pomeroy was sentenced to death, but as he was only 14 this was commuted to solitary imprisonment for life. In 1883, after fracturing a gas pipe, Pomeroy blew open his cell door; he was seriously injured and three other prisoners were killed. Pomeroy died, still incarcerated, at the age of 72. Despite claims at the time that he had murdered up to 27 children, it seems likely that Curran and Mullen were his only two killings, although he was certainly guilty of numerous assaults and rapes.

See Marie Schneider p. 42

◀ *LEFT: The late-nineteenth-century outskirts of Berlin, where Marie Schneider lived.*

SCHNEIDER, MARIE (1886)

From an early age, Marie Schneider showed signs of extreme disobedience and a tendency to bully other children so she could steal from them. As she grew older, however, she also acquired a taste for torturing them. In 1886, at the age of just 12, Marie took the final step and committed murder. She took a three-year-old girl to the second storey of a building and, after stealing her earrings, ordered her to sit on the windowsill. Marie then pushed the child to her death. Apparently, she wanted to sell the earrings so she could buy sweets. She was sentenced to eight years imprisonment.

See Jesse Pomeroy p. 41

BORDEN, LIZZIE (1892)

Young Lizzie Borden was convinced that her father's new wife, Abby, had married him for his money. On the morning of 4 August 1892, Bridget Sullivan, the maid at their home in Fall River, Massachusetts, was awoken by Lizzie's cries that someone had killed her father. When the police arrived they found the bodies of Andrew and Abby Borden, which had been mutilated with an axe. They immediately questioned Lizzie about her movements prior to her parents' deaths and although they could not initially connect her with the murders, she contradicted herself during the inquest and suspicion fell on her again. She was forced to stand trial in June 1893.

There was only circumstantial evidence against Lizzie: she had been seen burning a dress shortly before the police arrived to search the house (she said the garment had paint on it); she had also attempted to purchase prussic acid several days before the murders took place. She had become a wealthy young lady on the death of her father and stepmother. However, the jury at her trial were told: 'To find her guilty, you must believe she is a fiend. Gentlemen does she look like it?' The jury clearly did not think so and found her not guilty. Lizzie died in 1927, but not before Bridget had retired to Ireland, with a sizeable chunk of the fortune.

See William Allnutt p. 40

▶ *RIGHT: Axe murderer Lizzie Borden, who killed her father and stepmother.*

LEOPOLD, NATHAN AND RICHARD LOEB (1924)

Nathan Leopold and Richard Loeb, law students at the University of Chicago, wanted to commit the perfect crime. It was the summer of 1924 and the two bored young men hired a car under false names and drove to a private school, where they offered 14-year-old Robert Franks a ride. They had written a ransom note even before knowing who they would kidnap, and this was delivered to Franks' distraught father, Jacob, the following morning. Before Franks could deliver the $10,000 ransom that afternoon, the body of his son was found in a culvert 30 km (20 miles) south of Chicago.

Near the corpse was a pair of spectacles that were quickly linked to Leopold. The boys' alibi was thin and they broke down and confessed to murder. Loeb had intended to knock Franks unconscious with a chisel, but the blow had been too hard. A bloodstained rental car was retrieved, Loeb's typewriter matched the ransom note and the spectacles provided irrefutable evidence. The boys' defence counsel entered a plea of guilty on the grounds of temporary insanity to reduce the sentence from mandatory execution to a prison sentence. Loeb died in prison in 1936 and Leopold was released in 1958.

See Serology p. 169

▶ *RIGHT: Nathan Leopold and Richard Loeb, kidnappers and murderers, are escorted by police.*

MCDONALD, ROLAND (1924)

Fifteen-year-old Roland McDonald from Amhurst, Maine was convicted of shooting schoolteacher Louise Gerrish in 1924. After 34 years in prison, he took a lie-detector test that suggested he may have been innocent after all. Nonetheless, his parole request was turned down. In many countries, the treatment of juvenile offenders was as harsh as that of adults; they were expected to display the same degree of maturity.

See Lie Detectors and Polygraphs p. 166

STINNEY, GEORGE JUNIUS JR (1944)

On 24 March 1944, George Stinney Jr, a 14-year-old illiterate boy, murdered young girls. Betty June Binnicker and Mary Emma Thames's skulls had been smashed with a railroad spike. The tiny community of Alcolu in Clarendon County, South Carolina, was stunned. Stinney had been seen with the girls and, after an hour's questioning, he confessed to the crime. Since he had already confessed, his trial was only a formality; under South Carolina law Stinney was considered an adult, and the jury took just 10 minutes to decide on his guilt. On 16 June 1944 Stinney became the youngest person to die in the electric chair.

See Mary Flora and Nora Bell p. 48

YOUNG, GRAHAM (1962–72)

From an early age, Graham Young had been fascinated with poisons and with death. He became a prolific reader of accounts of the Moors Murders and of Adolf Hitler's activities. He began experimenting with poison on his family at the age of 13, trying out belladonna on his sister, Winifred. Mercifully, the dose was insufficient to kill her; Young claimed he had put it in her tea by mistake. Throughout 1962 several members of the Young family fell ill, as did a school friend of Graham's. At Easter that year his stepmother, Molly, died. His father took a turn for the worse and hospital tests showed arsenic and antimony poisoning. Young was sent to Broadmoor. He spent nine years there, and on his release he began his new life working in Hertfordshire.

In November 1971, two of his workmates died of thallium poisoning and two more were seriously ill from the effects of Young's experiments with poisons. Young described himself as 'your friendly neighbourhood Frankenstein' and the police were well aware of his criminal background. Young, always an outsider, verbally vicious and willing to turn to poison if someone crossed him, was sentenced to life in 1972.

See William Allnutt p. 40

KEMPER, EDMUND (1964)

Kemper committed his first murders at the age of 15, when he killed his grandparents on their farm in August 1964. He was judged insane and was released from an institution in 1969. He then became interested in the girls living

◀ *LEFT: Edmund Kemper, who turned himself in to the police and confessed to several murders.*

◄ LEFT: *Mass-poisoner Graham Young, who was found guilty in 1972.*

on the Santa Cruz campus of the University of California. In 1970 Kemper began giving the girls rides in his car, and in April 1973 he called the police to inform them he had killed six girls who had gone missing over the previous three years. He confessed to the murders, mutilation, necrophilia and cannibalism and also stated that he had killed his own mother with a hammer and strangled her friend; he had decapitated his mother and used her head as a dartboard. He was sentenced to life imprisonment.

See William Allnutt p. 40

THE MURDER OF SYLVIA MARIA LIKENS (1965)

On 26 October 1965, Indianapolis police found the body of Sylvia Likens, covered in wounds, many of them cigarette burns. Much of her skin had been peeled off her body and the words 'I am a prostitute and proud of it' had been burned into the skin. Sylvia and her sister Jenny worked and travelled with a carnival and they had been left in the care of a woman named Gertrude Baniszewski – a woman they barely knew. Over a period of several months, a group of children as young as 11, led by Gertrude and her daughter Paula, and including Jenny, had tortured Sylvia.

Gertrude, the only adult, and four of the children stood trial for Sylvia's murder; charges against the other children were dropped. Due to the ages of the younger defendants, many received care orders rather than prison sentences. Gertrude received the heaviest sentence: she was found guilty of murder and sentenced to life. She was paroled on 4 December 1985. She changed her name to Nadine van Fossan and moved to Iowa, where she died of cancer in 1990.

See Laurie Tackett and Melinda Loveless p. 52

BELL, MARY AND NORMA BELL (1968)

In May 1968, three children stumbled upon the corpse of youngster Martin Brown. A few days after Martin's death, someone broke into his nursery school and scribbled on a wall in crayon 'I murder so that I may come back'. Handwriting experts were sure it was the work of a child.

In August 1968, three-year-old Brian Howe was found strangled near the same school and the Newcastle police began interviewing all of its 1,200 underage residents. The police made two arrests based on their enquiries: Mary Bell and Norma Bell; although neighbours, the two 11-year-olds were not related. During interviews, each accused the other of 'squeezing' Brian Howe's throat, but both denied having anything to do with the murder of Martin Brown.

The girls were tried between in December 1968. Mary bragged in court that she wrote the graffiti 'for giggles' and confidently stated that 'murder isn't that bad ... we all die someday anyway'. Norma was quieter and seemed more fragile; she was to receive three years' probation. Mary was sent to a detention centre, then prison, and was released in 1980 at the age of 23.

See William York p. 40

See William York p. 40

◀ LEFT: Child killer Mary Bell, who was released from prison in 198

BOSKET, WILLIE (1978)

Fifteen-year old Willie Bosket committed his first murder on 19 March 1978 in New York. He was no stranger to the courts; in fact he had been living a life of crime since the age of nine. His father had been an armed robber and in one attack had stabbed two men to death, earning him a life sentence. Willie followed in his father's footsteps and killed again on 27 March. He was soon picked up, and his gun was linked to the latest murder and a wounding a few days previously.

Willie stood trial on two counts of murder and one of attempted murder; he faced a maximum of five years imprisonment because of his age. The outrage caused in America by this lenient sentence brought about the Juvenile Offenders Act of 1978, which allowed for the prosecution of children as young as 13.

After serving four years, Willie was at liberty for just 100 days, in which time he attempted to rob a man and attacked a court official. Back in prison, he then attempted to murder a guard; an act that ensured he remained in prison for the rest of his life.

See John Travers and His Gang p. 50

SPENCER, BRENDA (1979)

Brenda Spencer was the inspiration for the Boomtown Rats' hit single 'I Don't Like Mondays', as this was, in her own words, the reason why she murdered two people and wounded nine on a Monday morning in January 1979. Spencer was just 16 at the time, but had been given a rifle and considerable amounts of ammunition by her father as a Christmas present. Spencer was an epileptic and suffered from bouts of depression. In court, she blamed her father for having sexually abused her for several years.

Her home was across the street from San Diego's Grover Cleveland Elementary School. She shot the principal and another male worker at

▶ RIGHT: *The memorial stone commemorating the victims of Brenda Spencer's shooting spree.*

the school, then wounded eight pupils and a police officer who tried to intervene. She pleaded guilty to murder and assault and was sentenced to two life sentences. Spencer remains in prison and to this day is considered a threat.

See Nathan Ferris p. 51

COLLIER, CINDY AND SHIRLEY WOLF (1983)

Cindy Collier (15) and Shirley Wolf (14) used their youth and gender to con their way into peoples' California apartments in order to rob them. They knocked on doors at random and on one occasion an elderly woman, Anna Brackett, let them in and they chatted to her for a while, planning how best to steal her belongings. Suddenly, Wolf grabbed the woman by the neck and Collier ran into the kitchen and brought in a knife. Wolf then stabbed Anna Brackett 28 times. The killers were soon picked up by the police and they openly confessed that they had enjoyed killing the woman and would undoubtedly kill again. They were given the maximum sentence for children of their ages and were both released at the age of 27.

See Nathaniel Abraham p.67

TRAVERS, JOHN AND HIS GANG (1986)

On 3 February 1986 Anita Cobby disappeared from Sydney, Australia. Her body was found the following day; she had been abducted, raped, extensively beaten, dragged through a barbed-wire fence and then her throat had been cut to the point of decapitation.

John Travers led a gang who preyed on women, and between them its members had over 50 convictions for robbery, drug dealing, car theft,

PRESENTED BY THE STUDENT BODY
IN MEMORY OF
BURTON WRAGG & MIKE SUCHAR
WHO DIED IN THE SERVICE OF HELPING OTHERS
JANUARY 29, 1979

assault and rape. The police quickly rounded up the gang and Travers, Michael Murdoch, Michael Murphy, Gary Murphy and Leslie Murphy were all tried and sentenced to life. Travers was just 17 and had first been arrested at the age of 12. The others who were older, all had long criminal records. The savagery of this murder made this one of Australia's most notorious crimes.

See The Murder of Sylvia Maria Likens p. 47

FERRIS, NATHAN (1987)

Twelve-year-old Nathan Ferris from Missouri suffered much teasing from his peers because he was overweight; so much so that one day he decided that the next indignity would be met with ultimate force.

He had warned a school friend of his intentions and told him not to come to school on the fateful day of 2 March 1987. Nathan shot and killed the first classmate to make fun of him – and then shot himself.

See Alfred Dancey p. 40

SHERMAN, TIMOTHY SCOTT (1987)

Early in the morning of 12 October 1987, Ann and Stevenson Sherman were shot and killed while asleep in their bed. When the police arrived, the Shermans' 18-year-old son Timothy was in the house with his maternal grandfather, William Gibson. Timothy told the officers that he had heard gunshots and had run to his grandfather's nearby home. The two of them returned to the Sherman house, where Gibson called the police.

In Timothy's bedroom, police discovered a box of 12-gauge shotgun shells stuffed under the mattress of his bed. Two shells were missing. The hidden gun was also found and had Timothy's fingerprints on it. In 1988, a Maryland jury convicted Sherman of killing his mother and adoptive father, and sentenced him to two consecutive terms of life.

See Lizzie Borden p. 43

TACKETT, LAURIE AND MELINDA LOVELESS (1992)

On the night of 10 January 1992, lesbians Melinda Loveless (16), Laurie Tackett (17), Hope Rippey (15) and Toni Lawrence (15) abducted and murdered 12-year-old Shanda Sharer in Madison, Indiana. Shanda had been dating Loveless's former girlfriend, Amanda Heavrin. They took her to an abandoned house, where they tortured her and then threw her into the back of a car, hitting her with a tyre iron every time she made a noise. They then drove her to another isolated spot, where they poured petrol over her, setting her on fire while she was still alive.

The girls were quickly identified and Loveless pleaded guilty to murder, arson and imprisonment, and was sentenced to 60 years. Tackett received the same sentence. Rippey was given 60 years, with 10 years suspended and 10 years of probation. Lawrence, less active in the torture and murder, was given 20 years. In November 1998 Lawrence was eligible for an early release, but the parole board turned down her request. She was finally paroled in December 2000.

See Diane Zamora and David Graham p. 57

THOMPSON, ROBERT AND JON VENABLES (1993)

On 12 February 1993, 10-year-olds Robert Thompson and Jon Venables murdered James Bulger – who was just two years old – in a case that shocked the nation.

The two boys had found James playing inside a shopping centre in Liverpool, while his mother was in a shop. They took him on a long walk that ended at the railway tracks. Here they splashed him with blue paint, then battered him with bricks and an iron bar. He was still alive, so they draped him over the train track and waited for the inevitable. There was also evidence that the child was sexually abused.

On 18 February, Thompson and Venables were arrested and subsequently charged with murder, after Venables broke down during interview and admitted his part in the killing. It was to be several years before Thompson confessed his guilt.

Thompson and Venables were granted release on parole in 2001, after being provided with new identities. They had spent just eight years, four months and 10 days in secure local care homes, a few miles from the Bulger home, for the horrific murder.

See The West Memphis Three p. 55

THE WEST MEMPHIS THREE (1993)

On 5 May 1993, three eight-year-old boys left the Weaver Elementary School, near West Memphis, Arkansas after an ordinary day. They were never seen alive again. The following afternoon, their bodies were found in a creek area known as Robin Hood Hills; they were naked and had been beaten and tied. One had been repeatedly stabbed in the groin and then castrated. Police believed that the deaths were the result of some bizarre satanic ritual and already knew of a boy who was interested in such things – Damien Echols.

There was no evidence to connect Echols to the crime, yet he and his two friends, Jason Baldwin and Jessie Misskelley, were tried and found guilty of the murders, primarily the result of the testimony of a local woman who was determined to earn a reward. She told her son to say that he had seen Echols in the area and approached Misskelley, a 17-year-old mentally impaired boy, to fabricate an eye-witness account. The police manipulated his evidence, which served to corroborate their suspicions, but in doing so he incriminated Baldwin and himself. The three young men are still in prison, fighting for a fair retrial.

See Robert Thompson and Jon Venables p. 53

⬆ *ABOVE: A Wicca ceremony, the cult said to have been behind the West Memphis Three killings.*
◀ *LEFT: Police restrain a man from throwing a rock at the van carrying James Bulger's killers.*

THE BROWOOD COUNTY SEVEN (1993)

For years, Bobby Kent terrorised his high-school classmates in Fort Lauderdale, Florida, with cruel acts of psychological, physical, and sexual abuse. Eventually, his victims had enough, and on a summer night in 1993, seven of them lured Bobby to the edge of the Everglades with a promise of sex and drugs, and made the tormentor pay for his crimes with his life. They left his body to rot in the swamp. Some of the teenagers took an active part in bludgeoning and stabbing Kent to death, whilst others seemed to be simply along for the ride. The court sentenced the seven teenagers involved to various sentences from three years to life. It was a brutal, premeditated murder perpetuated by suburban teenagers from good, middle-class homes.

See Alfred Dancey p. 40

◀ *LEFT: A baseball bat was the weapon used in the Bobby Kent murder.*

ROUSE, JAMIE AND STEPHEN ABBOT (1995)

On 15 November 1995, Jamie Rouse carried out an attack at Richland High School in Lynnville, Tennessee, that claimed the lives of teacher Carolyn Foster and student Diane Collins. In November 1997, despite pleas of insanity, Rouse was sentenced to life. Abbot, who had helped him plan the attack, was given 40 years. Rouse was suffering from depression and the motive seems to have been poor grades given by his teachers.

See Evan Ramsey p. 59

ZAMORA, DIANE AND DAVID GRAHAM (1995)

Teenagers Diane Zamora and David Graham started dating in August 1995, but in November of that year Graham was unfaithful to Diane. When he confessed his infidelity, Diane told him he must kill the girl he had betrayed her with, Adrianne Jones.

On 3 December, in their home town of Grand Prairie, Texas, David arranged a date with Adrianne. Together they drove out to a secluded spot where Diane, hidden in the car, smashed her victim's head in with a dumbbell.

The body was found the next day and David was interviewed and cleared, but in August the following year Diane confessed to two friends, who promptly contacted the authorities. On 17 February 1998 Diane was convicted and received a life sentence. In July of that year David was also convicted and sentenced to life. Neither will be eligible for parole for 40 years.

See Laurie Tackett and Melinda Loveless p. 52

LOUKAITIS, BARRY (1996)

Barry Loukaitis entered his classroom at Moses Lake, Washington, on 2 February 1996 dressed as a western gunfighter. The 14-year-old had two pistols, a high-powered rifle and nearly 80 rounds of ammunition. He shot and killed three and wounded several others; he then took hostages. The siege was finally ended when a teacher disarmed him. Although Loukaitis claimed that he had been suffering

◄ LEFT: *Unable to break her love rival's neck, Diane Zamora struck Adrianne Jones with a dumbbell.*

from severe mood swings, one of his classmates told the police that Loukaitis had told him that it would be fun to kill and that it was all planned. According to eye witnesses, Loukaitis had shot without any emotion, apparently choosing targets at random in the class. Loukaitis was found guilty on all counts and sentenced to spend the rest of his life in prison.

See Dylan Klebold and Eric Harris p. 65

DUBOSE, DAVID JR (1996)

On 25 September 1996, David Dubose Jr shot his English teacher, Dr Horace P. Morgan, four times. He obeyed when a school official told him to put the gun down and slide it to him. Dubose was just 16 and had been at the DeKalb Alternative School in Scottsdale, Georgia, for less than a week. He was committed indefinitely to a state mental hospital. Dubose continues to have delusions and hallucinations.

See Michael Carneal p. 61

FERRELL, RODERICK (1996)

Roderick Ferrell, aged 16, from Murray in Kentucky, led a vampire clan whose members often cut their arms open to suck each other's blood. One day, Ferrell led the group to Eustis in Florida, where he killed the elderly parents of a former girlfriend, Heather Wendorf. Heather had remained with two other girls while Ferrell took Howard Scott Anderson with him to the Wendorf home. Inside, he clubbed the sleeping Richard Wendorf with a crowbar and then stabbed Naoma to death. On Richard's chest, Ferrell burned the shape of a 'V' with some cigarettes.

The others implicated in the attack, Dana Cooper and Charity Keesee, will not be released until 2014 and 2007 respectively, while Ferrell and Anderson are serving life sentences. Heather was cleared of all charges.

In March 2003, Ferrell began a request for a retrial claiming he had an inadequate defence in 1996.

See Luke Woodham p.59

MANZIES, SAM (1997)

In 1997, 15-year-old Sam Manzies murdered 11-year-old Eddie Werner. Eddie was fundraising for school and Manzies invited the boy in, then raped and strangled him. Manzies, from New Jersey, and himself the victim of child abuse, had been showing signs of depression and paranoid schizophrenia. His parents had reported to a doctor that he was becoming violent. Manzies was sentenced to 70 years and Manzies' molester was sentenced to five years.

See Marie Schneider p.42

RAMSEY, EVAN (1997)

On 19 February 1997, 16-year-old Evan Ramsey walked into his Bethel High School in Alaska and murdered a pupil, Josh Palacios, and the art teacher, Reyne Athanas. Ramsey had warned school friends of his intentions and stated that his primary purpose was to commit suicide. Nonetheless, Ramsey surrendered to the police and was subsequently sentenced to 200 years in prison. He will not be eligible for parole until he is 75 years of age.

See Barry Loukaitis p.57

WOODHAM, LUKE (1997)

On 1 October 1997, youngster Luke Woodham slit his mother's throat, then concealed a rifle in his coat and drove to Pearl High School in Mississippi. He opened fire on his school friends, killing two and wounding seven.

Woodham was a member of an adolescent demonic cult called 'Croth', and the other six boys in the group were charged with conspiring to help Woodham carry out the attack. Woodham claimed that he was under the spell of one of the others, Grant Boyette, who had caused him to be possessed by demons. On 5 June 1998, however, Woodham was found guilty of murdering his mother and sentenced to life. On 13 June he was given two further life sentences and 20 years for the murder of two of his classmates.

See Roderick Ferrell p. 58

O'CONNELL, CHAD (1997)

On 2 November 1997, teenagers David Moreno and Justin Pacheco aided a friend, Alvarez English, who was being attacked in a street fight in Vacaville, California. During the scuffle, English was stabbed repeatedly by Chad O'Connell; he immediately confessed but walked free on probation. Moreno and Pacheco were accused of provoking the situation and convicted of the murder of their friend. On 5 November 1998 they were sentenced to long prison terms, but were freed on appeal in February 2000.

See the West Memphis Three p. 55

▶ RIGHT: *Following the Kentucky shooting, students hang a poster reading 'WE FORGIVE YOU MIKE!'.*

CARNEAL, MICHAEL (1997)

At the age of just 14, Michael Carneal murdered three of his fellow students and wounded five others when he opened fire in a morning prayer meeting at Heath High School in Paducah, Kentucky on 1 December 1997. He was armed with a handgun, two rifles, two shotguns and plenty of ammunition that he had stolen from a neighbour's garage. He had warned friends that something big was going to happen, but the young atheist, who had been the victim of bullying, had not disclosed his intentions.

Carneal pleaded guilty and was sentenced to be detained in a juvenile centre on the grounds of mental illness. In August 2000 the families of the three girls he killed agreed to a $42 million settlement, setting a legal precedent for school shootings in America.

See Dylan Klebold and Eric Harris p. 65

GOLDEN, ANDREW AND MITCHELL JOHNSON (1998)

On 24 March 1998, cousins Mitchell Johnson (13) and Andrew Golden (11), dressed in camouflage gear, opened fire from woodland near their school in Jonesboro, Arkansas, while their classmates were engaged in a

◀ LEFT: *The Woodham family home, where Luke Woodham allegedly murdered his mother.*

fake fire drill initiated by the two boys. In a few brief moments they had gunned down 12-year olds Natalie Brooks, Paige Ann Herring and Stephanie Johnson and 11 year-old Brittany Varner. Ten other pupils were wounded and a teacher, Shannon Wright, later died from her injuries. Significantly, all the victims were female; Johnson and Golden's targets were girls who had refused to date them. One of the wounded was Johnson's 11-year-old former girlfriend, Candace Porter, who had broken up with him the previous day.

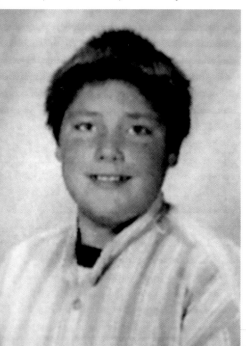

In court, both the boys were found guilty of murder and of attempted murder, but under Arkansas law they could only be tried as juveniles, which means that they will both be released when they reach 21. Johnson's lawyers claimed that their client had become disturbed since he had been molested at the age of six, whilst Golden's defence was a plea of insanity.

See Charles Whitman p.229

WURST, ANDREW J. (1998)

Andrew Wurst was a small and sullen boy who attended

James W. Parker Middle School in Edinboro, Pennsylvania. On 24 April 1998, Wurst shot and killed his science teacher, and wounded another teacher and two pupils at a school graduation dance. Experts suggest he may have suffered from paranoid delusions. Wurst will not be eligible for parole until he is 45 – a considerable wait for a boy who committed murder when he was just 14 years old.

See David Dubose Jr p. 58

KINKEL, KIPLAND (1998)

On 20 May 1998, 15-year-old Kipland Kinkel was expelled from Thurston High School in Springfield, Oregon, for having brought a loaded gun into class. That night he murdered his own parents, booby-trapped the house with bombs, stole a car, and the following morning drove to school, heavily armed with a rifle, two handguns, a knife and pepper spray. Kinkel walked into the school cafeteria and indiscriminately opened fire. The attack was only brought to a halt when a wounded student forced Kinkel to the ground. Two students were killed and 22 others were wounded as a result of the attack. It was amazing that so few had been hit or killed – over 400 people were in the cafeteria when Kinkel opened fire.

Kinkel came from a privileged background, yet had developed an interest in bomb-making and killing small animals; he was also an expert marksman. Even after his arrest, when he was being searched, Kinkel tried to stab a police officer and use his pepper spray. Kinkel was sentenced to 112 years in prison. In 2007 he will be transferred to an adult prison.

See Evan Ramsey p. 59

◀ *LEFT: The yearbook photograph of Mitchell Johnson, a teenage spree killer.*

PHILLIPS, JOSHUA (1998)

In 1998, 14-year-old Joshua Phillips from Florida battered his eight-year-old neighbour, Maddie, with a baseball bat and then hid her body under his bed. Phillips' mother found the corpse seven days later and Phillips confessed that he had hit Maddie with a baseball by accident, then hit her with the bat and stabbed her 11 times. Phillips was convicted of first-degree murder and sentenced to life imprisonment.

See Sam Manzies p. 59

KLEBOLD, DYLAN AND ERIC HARRIS (1999)

Dylan Klebold and Eric Harris became known as the 'Trench Coat Mafia' and were responsible for a horrific attack on the Columbine High School in Littleton, Colorado on 20 April 1999. Klebold was 17 and Harris 18. They revelled in everything German and were obsessed with the Nazis. There were eight other members of the Trench Coat Mafia, all of whom listened to Goth-rock music, wore swastikas, believed in white supremacy and considered themselves to be suburban terrorists.

The attack began at 11.30 a.m. and they rampaged through the school for four hours, combing the classrooms and corridors in a systematic manner, seeking out victims in a hideous version of hide-and-seek. Students and teachers hid wherever they could. In total they slaughtered 12 students and a teacher, and wounded 24 others, five of whom were critically injured. When several SWAT teams arrived on the scene in an attempt to bring the attack to an end, the two boys turned the guns on themselves in the library. They left 50 explosive devices around the school and in their cars and homes.

See Barry Loukaitis p. 57

◀ LEFT: *High-school killer Kipland Kinkel in a photograph of his fifth grade football team.*

◄ *LEFT: A girl puts 13 crosses into the ground to signify the victims of the Columbine shooting.*

SOLOMON, THOMAS J. JR (1999)

On 20 May 1999, Thomas Solomon Jr opened fire on his classmates at the Heritage High School near Conyers in Georgia. He shot and wounded six, but mercifully none of the victims was badly injured. Solomon had intended to commit suicide after the attack, but he was talked out of doing so by the school's vice-principal. It is believed that at the time Solomon was suffering from depression after breaking up with his girlfriend, and that he had been prescribed Ritalin and anti-depressants. Solomon, who was 15 at the time of the attack, claimed he had been inspired by the Columbine massacre. The defence claimed he was mentally ill. Tests continue, and if Solomon is found sane he will face 351 years imprisonment as a result of the 21 charges brought against him.
See Dylan Klebold and Eric Harris p. 65

ABRAHAM, NATHANIEL (1999)

In 1999, 11-year-old Nathaniel Abraham was placed on trial for the random shooting of a stranger, Ronnie Greene, aged 18, outside a store in Pontiac, Michigan. Abraham had stolen a rifle and had told friends he was going to shoot someone, boasting about it after the event. When arrested he claimed it was accidental, but was convicted of second-degree murder, the youngest defendant ever to stand trial for murder in Michigan.
See Nathan Ferris p. 51

TATE, LIONEL (1999)

Lionel Tate was just 12 when he was indicted for the murder of six-year-old Tiffany Eunick. Two years later, a jury found him guilty of first-degree murder, a conviction which, in Florida, carries a sentence of either execution or life without parole.

The murder took place on 28 July 1999, when Tiffany was taken to the home of childminder Kathleen Gossett-Tate for the night. Kathleen went to bed at 10 p.m. Forty minutes later Tiffany was dead; she showed evidence of 32 different injuries, consistent with punching, kicking and other physical violence.

Had Tate admitted to the attacks, he would have received three years and a period of probation, but he chose not to and was sentenced to life. His mother, Kathleen, said 'how do you accept a plea for second-degree murder when your child was just playing?'

See Joshua Phillips p. 65

TULLOCH, ROBERT AND JAMES PARKER (2001)

In February 2001, teenagers Robert Tulloch and James Parker were charged with the murders of husband-and-wife Dartmouth College professors, Half and Susanne Zantop. The stabbings had taken place in Hanover, Vermont on 27 January 2001. They were arrested at an Indiana truck stop two days after fleeing Vermont, where they had voluntarily given fingerprints.

In the six months before the murders took place, Tulloch and Parker went to four other randomly chosen homes, planning to talk their way in, find the residents' ATM cards and PIN numbers and then murder them. According to friends and neighbours, the pair did everything together – and that included murder, it seems. A fingerprint found on a knife sheath left at the scene matched Parker's, and bloody footprints also linked Tulloch to the crime. In April 2002, they were both sentenced to life.

See Cindy Collier and Shirley Wolf p. 50

▶ *RIGHT: James Parker is led to the Henry County Courthouse, suspected of killing two profe*

WILLIAMS, CHARLES ANDREW (2001)

Charles Andrew Williams was just 15 years old when he launched his own mini-version of the Columbine massacre. He had suffered from bullying and hated the discipline enforced at the Santana High School in Santee, California. The attack took place on 1 March 2001, and a the end of it two students were dead, 11 were wounded and two teachers had also been seriously injured.

Williams was charged with two counts of murder and 26 counts of attempted murder; he is currently being held in a juvenile facility. Under Californian law he will be eligible for parole at the age of 65. Had he been tried as a juvenile, he would have been released at the age of 25.

see Dylan Klebold and Eric Harris p. 65

DEADLIER THAN THE MALE

BLANDY, MARY (1752)

One of the most famous crimes in eighteenth-century England was that of Mary Blandy and her married lover, Captain William Henry Cranstoun. Mary's father Francis was reputedly a man of wealth and, although Cranstoun was already married, Francis still offered him a dowry of £10,000 for his daughter. Mary and Cranstoun had their sights set higher than this, though, and planned to poison Francis and inherit all his money. They systematically fed arsenic to the old man, but their activities aroused suspicion and they were reported to the authorities. Cranstoun fled to France, leaving Mary to face the trial alone. The case was heard at Oxford Assizes in February 1752 and

Mary maintained that she believed the poison was simply a drug to make her father approve of her lover. Despite this, she was found guilty and faced execution on 6 April 1752. When her father's estate was settled, it was revealed that he was not even worth the £10,000 dowry he had offered.

See Annette and Charlene Maw p. 92

◀ LEFT: *Mary Blandy pictured with Elizabeth Jefferies, with whom she corresponded from prison.*

NAIRN, KATHARINE (1765)

Katharine Nairn married Thomas Ogilvy in January 1765, but it was not long before she began a relationship with his brother, Patrick. The pair killed Thomas by spiking his tea with poison, but another brother, Alexander, was a doctor and insisted on a post mortem. Katharine and Patrick were charged with incest and murder. Patrick was hanged in

November 1765 but as Katharine was pregnant her sentence was deferred. Disguised as an officer, she escaped from prison and disappeared either to France or America.

See Susan Barber p. 95

BROWNRIGG, ELIZABETH (1767)

Elizabeth Brownrigg was undoubtedly one of the most sadistic psychopaths of the eighteenth century. She and her husband had 16 children of their own and took in many of the poor and disadvantaged women and children in their neighbourhood in Greenwich, London. Over several years she systematically tortured and imprisoned a number of girls and women charged to her care and is believed to have murdered at least 13 of her own children. The authorities investigated Brownrigg in 1767 after numerous accusations of cruelty to her 'apprentices'. The Brownriggs fled but were arrested in Wandsworth and subsequently tried at the Old Bailey. Elizabeth Brownrigg was found guilty of murder and sentenced to death, but her husband, James, and son John were acquitted and given just six months imprisonment for acts of cruelty. On 14 September 1767, before being taken to Tyburn to be executed, Elizabeth confessed her crimes to a clergyman. There were enormous crowds lining the streets and the hangman immediately carried out the sentence for fear that she would be lynched before he could accomplish his task. After the execution her body was dissected and her skeleton was hung in the Surgeon's Hall.

See Amelia Dyer p. 79

> ▸ *RIGHT: Elizabeth Brownrigg, who treated her apprentices with terrible cruelty.*

MANNING, MARIA (1849)

Maria and Frederick Manning met their end by hanging at Tyburn on 13 November 1849 in front of a record crowd of 50,000 people. They had been found guilty of the premeditated murder of Maria's lover, Patrick O'Connor. Maria was born in Switzerland but had moved to England as a teenager. In 1846 she had struck up a relationship with O'Connor but had then met Frederick, and the latter had proved to be a better financial prospect. The couple married and set up business with a beer shop in Hackney, but it quickly became apparent to Maria that she had married the wrong man. Nonetheless they resolved to murder O'Connor and relieve him of his railway bonds and ready cash. The murder took place on 10 August 1849 – Maria herself shot O'Connor in the head and Frederick finished him off with a chisel.

See Hanging p. 180

KENT, CONSTANCE (1860)

Constance Kent may have been the victim of a miscarriage of justice that cost her 20 years imprisonment, for despite the fact that she pleaded guilty to the murder of her three-year-old half-brother, Francis, the evidence suggests that she was not the perpetrator of the crime.

Constance's father had remarried shortly after the death of his first wife and the new Mrs Kent – Miss Pratt, a former governess – soon gave birth to a son. Young Francis disappeared from the family home near Trowbridge, Wiltshire on 30 June 1860 and his body was later discovered in an outside privy; his throat had been cut so deeply that his head was nearly severed. Suspicion fell on Constance, who had been badly treated by her stepmother and was known to have resented Francis's arrival. The evidence was circumstantial, though and Constance was never charged. Surprisingly, however, on 25 April 1864, she confessed to the crime. Her description of how she had killed the boy contradicted police observations: she claimed to have cut his throat with a razor, but the child had been suffocated and then the wound inflicted. It seems possible that the murder was carried out by her father, with the help of the governess and nurse, Elizabeth Gough, although no motive could be established. Constance was released from prison in 1885 and changed her name to Ruth Emilie Kaye, emigrating to New South Wales, where she died in April 1944.

See Susan Smith p. 99

EDMUNDS, CHRISTIANA (1871)

The case of Christiana Edmunds is one of unrequited love. In 1871 Christiana was a 42-year-old spinster living in Brighton, when she met and fell in love with Dr Beard, who was already married. Their relationship began with the exchange of passionate letters, but things soon became out of hand as Christiana endeavoured to poison Beard's wife by filling chocolate creams with strychnine. Beard suspected what was going on but, fearing a scandal, he simply forbade Christiana from seeing him.

Devastated by the end of the affair, Christiana embarked on a new career as the 'Chocolate Cream Poisoner'. She bought several more batches of chocolates, laced them with strychnine, and then returned them to the shop. Over the next few weeks several people fell seriously ill, and when Sidney Barker died Beard contacted the police and told them what he knew. Christiana was sent to Broadmoor, where she died in 1907.

See Jean Harris p. 94

> ▸ *RIGHT: Prolific poisoner Christiana Edmunds bought strychnine over the counter at a chemist's.*

WEBSTER, KATE (1879)

The Irish-born Kate Webster already had a criminal record for robbery when she committed murder in 1879. It is known that at some point she had been living with a man, by whom she had a son; by 1877 they had both abandoned her, and perhaps it was this that drove her to kill.

In January 1879 Kate moved to Richmond to take a position as maid to a wealthy retired schoolteacher named Julia Thomas. Less than two months later she ambushed the old lady at the top of the stairs, hit her and threw her down the stairs, then strangled her. She dragged the body into the kitchen, laid it on the table, removed the head with a meat saw and dismembered the body with a carving knife. She heated up a large copper pan of water to boil the body parts, then began selling Mrs Thomas's body fat as 'best dripping' to her neighbours.

Mrs Thomas's disappearance soon aroused suspicion, however, and Kate fled to Ireland; she was arrested there shortly afterwards. She denied any knowledge of the murder, but was found guilty and sentenced to death. She was hanged in Wandsworth Prison on 29 July 1879.

See Hanging p. 180

MAYBRICK, FLORENCE (1889)

James Maybrick, considered by many to be a Jack the Ripper suspect, met Florence, an Alabaman, onboard ship in March 1881. They married in July despite the fact that James, a successful Liverpool cotton broker, was a habitual drug user with a mistress and several children.

When Maybrick became ill the household nurse, Alice Yapp, and James's brothers, Edwin and Michael, became convinced that Florence was poisoning Maybrick because she was known to use fly papers containing arsenic as a way of removing facial skin blemishes.

On 11 May 1889 James lapsed into a coma and died. The post-mortem led to Florence's arrest, and the coroner's inquest in May of that year recommended that Florence be brought before the Liverpool Assizes.

Despite evidence that her husband had taken arsenic as well as other drugs, the jury were convinced of Florence's guilt and sentenced her to death. The public, however, demanded a reprieve. Finally, the Home Secretary transmuted her sentence to life imprisonment. Florence spent 15 years in prison, and was released in 1904. She died at the age of 79 whilst living as a recluse in Connecticut; she never accepted that her sentence was just.

See Alma Rattenbury p. 84

▶ RIGHT: Florence Maybrick, convicted of killing her husband in 1889.

PEARCEY, MARY (1890)

Mary Pearcey had been having an affair with the married Frank Hogg. On 23 October 1890 Mary invited Frank's wife Phoebe and their 18-month-old daughter to pay a visit to her house. Later that day a Hampstead policeman found a woman's body lying amongst rubble; her skull had been crushed and her head severed from her body. A bloodstained pram was found nearby. On 25 October the body of Frank Hogg's daughter was discovered; she had been suffocated.

The police learned of Mary's affair with Frank and a search of her house revealed a poker covered with hair and blood, and a bloodstained knife, as well as blood on the kitchen walls, ceiling and Mary's

underwear. Throughout their search, Mary played her piano and sang. She denied seeing Phoebe on the day of the murder. Further investigation revealed that the child had been alive when it left Mary's house, but had probably been suffocated by the weight of her mother's body when it was dumped into the pram.

Mary was tried at the Old Bailey, her defence claiming insanity, but the jury were unconvinced and she was hanged on 23 December at Newgate Prison. Mary's last request was for a mysterious advertisement to be placed in a Madrid newspaper, which read 'M.E.C.P. Last wish of M.E.W. Have not betrayed.'

See Yvonne Sleightholme p. 97

◀ *LEFT: Mary Pearcey's house in Camden Town, where she murdered her lover's wife.*

FORD, CLARA (1894)

Clara Ford desperately hated male attention and so she often wore men's clothes in an effort to avoid it. In 1894, when Benjamin Westwood made improper advances towards her, she shot him. Life for this mixed-race woman in turn-of-the-century Toronto had been difficult and despite her colour the jury was impressed with her independence and indignation. She was cleared of the charge and it transpired that Westwood had previously seduced Clara's daughter.

See Margaret Allen p. 89

▶ *RIGHT: A public hanging at Newgate Prison, where Amelia Dyer was executed.*

DYER, AMELIA (1895)

Amelia Dyer's sinister baby-farming activities emerged at her trial in 1896. Bristol-born Dyer, a mother and respected member of the Salvation Army, left her husband and started baby-farming in Long Ashton, but she was discovered, imprisoned, and remained in a workhouse until June 1895. She then moved to Reading, where she began to advertise herself as a child-minder in the local paper.

On 30 March 1895 a bargeman pulled a brown-paper parcel from the Thames and in it discovered the body of a baby girl. The child had been strangled with tape and a brick had been used to weigh the corpse down. On 2 April a further two parcels were found stuffed into a carpet bag. Dyer – alias Mrs Thomas – had wrapped one of the children in brown paper that had her new name and address on it, and was arrested after two days. It became clear that many of the children barely lived 24 hours in Dyer's care. Evidence against her appeared daily and four other corpses were fished out of the Thames. The 57-year-old became known as the Reading Baby Farmer. She attempted suicide, but failed and was put on trial. The defence claimed insanity, but the jury passed a guilty verdict and Dyer was hanged on 10 June 1896 after confessing her guilt.

See Elizabeth Brownrigg p. 73

GUNNESS, BELLE (1908)

Norwegian-born widow Belle Gunness lived in Laporte, Indiana, with her three children and her lover, Ray Lamphere. In a bizarre practice, Gunness advertised in the Chicago newspapers for suitors to share her farm. When they arrived at the farm in Indiana, they were drugged, robbed, butchered and buried. Fourteen men were killed in this way.

When the farm went up in flames on 28 April 1908, investigators found the bodies of the three children and a headless female corpse, whom they believed to be Gunness; the discovery of some dentures seemed to corroborate this.

Lamphere was charged with the murder of Gunness and the children. In prison he confided that they had lured an unknown woman to the farm, killed her and planted the dentures. Gunness had disappeared with the proceeds of the robberies and murders, never to be seen again.
See Mary Wilson p. 91

FAHMY, MARGUERITE (1923)

Marguerite had worked as a prostitute, but on her marriage to Prince Ali Kamel Fahmy Bey she became a very wealthy woman, and Ali showered her with gifts. Once they were married, however, he expected her to be compliant with what she would later describe as 'unnatural lovemaking'. Events came to a head in July 1923, while the couple were staying at the Savoy Hotel in London. Marguerite had been forced to see a doctor after Ali had claimed his conjugal rights. She would later testify that she felt in fear of her life. In the early hours of the morning, in the hotel corridor, she shot him three times. Marguerite was cleared in court.
See Sheila Garvie p. 93

◀ *LEFT: Local officials look through the remains of Belle Gunness' burned-down house.*

TILFORD, LIZZIE (1929–35)

Between 1929 and 1935, Lizzie Tilford murdered two of her husbands by poisoning them with arsenic. Born in England, but then living in Canada, it was her accent that prompted a pharmacist to remember her and, when an inquest was opened on the death of her second husband, she was quickly implicated. She was found guilty of the second murder and hanged for her crimes in December 1935 at Oxford County Jail.

See Mary Wilson p. 91

DONALD, JEANNIE EWAN (1934)

Despite circumstantial evidence, Jeannie Ewan Donald was found guilty of the murder of eight-year-old Helen Priestly on 16 July 1934. Helen disappeared in Aberdeen on 20 April whilst running an errand. The following day a sack containing Helen's strangulated body was discovered in the tenement block. Someone had attempted to make the attack look like sexual assault, but investigations disproved this. Suspicion immediately fell on the Donalds, whose animosity towards the Priestly family was well-known. Mr Donald was questioned but his alibi held and the police moved to Jeannie Donald, whose own alibi was disproved. After fibre, hair, blood and dust analysis tests had been conducted, Jeannie was arrested. The judge sentenced her to death, but this was commuted to life imprisonment; she was released on parole 10 years later.

See Susan Smith p.99

◀ *LEFT: A magazine cover showing a dangerous, masked woman, from around the time of the Jeannie Ewan Donald case.*

BECKER, MARIE ALEXANDRINE (1934)

At the age of 53, the Belgian Marie Alexandrine Becker was unhappily married. She took a lover, Lambert Bayer and used the drug digitalis to rid herself of her husband. Bayer lasted until November 1934, when he too succumbed to digitalis. Becker then poisoned two elderly women, taking their possessions and life savings, but she was denounced by anonymous letters to the police. Convicted, she spent the rest of her life in prison.

See Mary Wilson p. 91

COO, EVA (1935)

Brothel-keeper Coo's scheme was to take out a $6,000 insurance policy on her handyman, Harry Wright, and then kill him, making it look like an accident. She and her cohort Martha Clift drove Harry outside New York and murdered him with a hammer. They then drove their car over his body. The police were not convinced of the accidental death pleas and Martha was sentenced to a minimum of 13 years. Eva went to the electric chair on 27 June 1935.

See Dorothea Waddingham p. 85

RATTENBURY, ALMA (1935)

In 1935 Britain was riveted by the Rattenbury Murder Case and the relationship between a woman in her mid-thirties and an 18-year-old chauffeur. It was all to end in great melodrama and tragedy.

At 2 a.m. on Sunday, 25 March 1935 police were called to the Rattenbury home in Bournemouth to find the distinguished Canadian architect Francis Rattenbury severely battered but still alive; he would die in hospital four days later. Alma immediately confessed, but so, too, did the chauffeur, George Stoner. They both then pleaded not guilty in court. Stoner was sentenced to hang but he refused to implicate Alma and she was cleared.

Three days after the trial ended, Alma travelled to Christchurch. She then sat down by a river bank, wrote a note and stabbed herself six times. Her death released Stoner from his vow of silence and he recounted that both he and Alma had been upstairs when they had heard a groan. They had come down to see Francis battered. His appeal was still turned down but he served just seven years, later becoming a distinguished soldier during World War II.

See Florence Maybrick p. 76

WADDINGHAM, DOROTHEA (1935)

A widow with five children, Dorothea Waddingham set up a nursing home in Nottingham, despite the fact that she had no nursing training. She and her lover, 39-year-old Ronald Joseph Sullivan, advertised locally for patients.

In January 1935, 89-year-old Mrs Baguley – senile and bedridden – and her daughter, Ada Louisa – aged 50 and suffering from disseminated sclerosis – arrived in Waddingham's care. After rewriting their wills in Waddingham's favour, both women were dead by May.

The Nottingham Medical Health Officer, unhappy with the circumstances, ordered post-mortems, which disclosed morphine in the

LEFT: A local newspaper reports on the Rattenbury case.

bodies. Waddingham and Sullivan were arrested and charged with murder. Sullivan was acquitted; Waddingham was found guilty and hanged at Winson Green Prison in Birmingham on 16 April 1936 after a failed appeal.

See Mary Creighton and Everett Applegate p. 86

BRYANT, CHARLOTTE (1935)

Charlotte Bryant was a drinker and a prostitute, known in their home town of Yeovil as 'Black Bess', 'Compton Bess' or 'Killarney Kate'. She began an affair with their lodger, Leonard Parsons, and after they moved to Sherbourne, Dorset, Frederick became ill. He died on 22 December 1935. Charlotte was damned by her neighbours. A post mortem revealed death by poisoning. She was hanged at Exeter Prison on 15 July 1936.

See Florence Maybrick p. 76

⬆ *ABOVE: Poison is the most popular murder method among women and was used by killers such as Charlotte Bryant and Anna Hahn.*

CREIGHTON, MARY AND EVERETT APPLEGATE (1936)

Mary Creighton may have been responsible for the deaths of three people, including her own brother. She and her husband John were arrested in 1923 after the death by poisoning of her brother Raymond. Creighton was the beneficiary of his estate, but she was acquitted of the charges. She was later arrested again on suspicion of the murder of her father-in-law, but again she was found not guilty.

In the 1930s Mary and John and their daughter Ruth moved into the home of the Applegate family. Mary began an affair with Everett Applegate and used arsenic to poison his wife Ada in September 1936. Mary and Everett went on trial in January 1937 and they were both found guilty of murder. They were executed at Sing Sing on 16 July 1937.
See Eva Coo p. 84

HAHN, ANNA (1937)

German-born Anna Hahn preyed on elderly men in the Cincinnati area in the 1930s, poisoning them with a mixture of croton oil and arsenic. She posed as an official nurse and seduced men to secure their inheritances before despatching them. She claimed two victims in one week in June 1937, prompting the police to exhume the bodies. The 'angel of mercy', as she called herself, was undone and was electrocuted on 7 December 1938.
See Electrocution p. 185

RANSOME, FLORENCE IRIS WOUIDA (1940)

Jealousy was the motive in a famous triple murder in Matfield, Kent, in July 1940. The victims were Dorothy Fisher, her daughter Freda and their maid, Charlotte Saunders. Dorothy had separated from her husband, Walter, who had moved in with Florence Ransome. After the murders, it transpired that Ransome had cycled to Dorothy's home and had shot the three of them in a frenzied attack, which she had tried to make look like a bungled burglary. She claimed to have no recollection of her movements on 9 July and was certified insane. Most damning had been the evidence of her own brother, Fred, who told the court that he had lent his sister a shotgun the day before the killings and she had returned it the day after.
See Jean Harris p. 94

BECK, MARTHA (1948)

Martha Beck and Raymond Fernandez became known as the Lonely Heart's Killers. Beck was an overweight, highly sexed individual who had several disastrous relationships before meeting Fernandez through a lonely heart's advertisement.

During the 1940s, they began to prey on other lonely hearts, using Fernandez's charm to seduce the women and persuade them to hand over their savings. By December 1948, the deceptions turned to death, with the murder of Janet Fay and, shortly after, Delphine Downing and her young child.

Fay's body was found in New York and Beck and Fernandez were charged with three murders and linked to a further 17. In court, Beck was candid about her sexual relationship with Fernandez, providing sensational headlines. They were electrocuted on 8 March 1951 in Sing Sing Prison.

See Raymond Fernandez p. 226

ALLEN, MARGARET (1948)

Pipe-smoking Margaret Allen, who preferred to be known as Bill, was in a long-term relationship with the more elderly Nancy Chadwick. Nancy's body was found in the early hours of 28 August 1948; she had been battered to death with a hammer. Margaret confessed, and in court she was found guilty and sentenced to hang. Allen's last words were 'it would help if I could cry, but my manhood stops my tears'.

See Gwendolyn Graham and Catherine Woods p. 96

▶ RIGHT: The death notice posted at Holloway Prison, London, after Styllou Christofi was hanged there.

CHRISTOFI, STYLLOU (1954)

Styllou Christofi was a 52-year-old Greek Cypriot who was hanged for the murder of her daughter-in-law. Styllou had moved into a ground-floor flat in Hampstead in July 1953 to live with her son Stavros and his German wife Hella, but the move was not a success and the two women did not get along. Eventually, Hella could take no more of her mother-in-law and insisted that Styllou return to Cyprus.

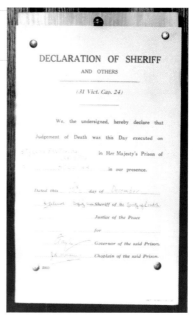

◀ LEFT: Raymond Fernandez (third from left) and Martha Beck in court, charged with two murders.

On 28 July 1954, after Stavros had left for work, Styllou hit Hella over the head with an ash-plate from the kitchen stove. She then strangled her, soaked her body in petrol and set fire to her in the back garden.

Styllou was brought to trial at the Old Bailey on 25 October 1954. She pleaded not guilty but had been advised to enter a plea of insanity. The jury returned a guilty verdict and the judge sentenced Styllou to be hanged. She was executed at Holloway Prison on 13 December 1954.

In 1925, when Styllou was a young woman, she had been acquitted of murdering her own mother-in-law in Cyprus, by ramming a burning torch down her throat.

See Ruth Ellis p. 90

ELLIS, RUTH (1955)

It was clear from the outset that Ruth Ellis was guilty of gunning down David Blakely at 9 p.m. on Easter Sunday, 10 April 1955. The possible motive, however, and the assistance of Desmond Cussen, were facts largely ignored by the court during her trial.

Ellis and Blakely had met in 1953 at the Steering Wheel Club in Brick Street, near Hyde Park Corner, and for the next two years they endured a tumultuous relationship, punctuated by bouts of violence, heavy drinking and overwhelming jealousy. In January 1955 Ellis fell pregnant with Blakely's child; he beat her and punched her in the stomach, causing her to miscarry. Although Ellis was certainly having an affair with Blakely's friend Desmond Cussen, the prospect of Blakely seeing another woman – as he had frequently threatened – was too much. On Easter Sunday, Ellis and Cussen drove Blakely to Hampstead and shot him. On the day before her execution a statement showed that Cussen had

▸ RIGHT: David Blakely, a racing driver, and Ruth Ellis, who murdered him in 1955.

provided the gun and taken her for gun practice in woods the day before the shooting. Ruth Ellis was hanged at Holloway Prison on 13 July 1955.

See Hanging p. 180

WILSON, MARY (1956)

Mary Wilson became known as the Widow of Windy Nook. Her 41-year marriage to husband John ended abruptly in July 1955. The Wilsons had taken in a lodger, John Russell, who was soon sharing Mary's bed. After poisoning her husband, Mary killed Russell in the same way in January 1956. She married Oliver Leonard in June the same year; he lasted just 13 days. Ernest Wilson lasted two weeks after their marriage the following year. Mary inherited little from each of the men.

Ultimately the police ordered the exhumation of the bodies and found that they all contained rat poison and phosphorous. In the Leeds Assizes in March 1958, she claimed that her elderly husbands had taken phosphorous as an aphrodisiac. Unconvinced, the jury found her guilty and she remained in prison until her death on 5 December 1962.

See Charlotte Bryant p. 86

RUMBOLD, FREDA (1956)

Freda and Albert Rumbold had a strange relationship. According to Albert's mother, 'Freda was a very odd person, particularly at the time of the full moon'. Odd sexual habits seem to have been the core of the problems and sometimes Albert would choose to sleep with his daughter instead. Freda shot Albert in the head with a shotgun on 25 August 1956 and despite claiming it was an accident, she was sentenced to life.

See Sheila Garvie p. 93

GARVIE, SHEILA (1968)

A complex sex life led to murder in Kincardineshire, Scotland, in 1968. Sheila Garvie found that her husband Maxwell's sexual demands were too overwhelming for her alone and in 1967 the couple began sharing their bed with Brian Tevendale and his sister, Trudy. Brian and Sheila made plans to run away together whilst Trudy, although married to an Aberdeen policeman, was quite content with Max. Nonetheless Sheila and Brian murdered Max and his body was not found until mid-August – in an underground tunnel at Lauriston Castle.

Sheila and Brian were found guilty of murder and sentenced to life imprisonment. An accomplice, Alan Peters, received a verdict of not proven. Sheila had been turned in by her own mother after she had confided her part in the murders.

See Marguerite Fahmy p. 81

MAW, ANNETTE AND CHARLENE (1979)

On numerous occasions Annette and Charlene Maw had seen their drunken and aggressive father viciously beat their mother, Beryl. On 27 March 1979, they too became the targets of their father's aggression and the girls determined that he would never touch them again. An argument broke out and in the running fight Beryl hit her husband over the head with a mirror. As the three women bent over Maw to see if he was unconscious, he grabbed Annette by the throat and, terrified, she stabbed him repeatedly.

In court nine months later, Annette and Charlene were found guilty of manslaughter and sentenced to three years. Their mother was not charged.

See Marie Witte p. 95

◀ LEFT: A crowd gathers outside Aberdeen High Court to hear the verdict of the Sheila Garvie trial.

HARRIS, JEAN (1980)

Jean Harris, the headmistress of an exclusive Virginian girls' school, murdered her lover, Dr Herman Tarnower, the creator of the Scarsdale Diet. Jealousy of Tarnower's affairs compelled Harris to drive for five hours in the rain to his home in Westchester, New York, and to shoot four times on 10 March 1980. She had intended to shoot herself, but instead she lived and was convicted of murder and sentenced to 15 years in prison. Harris was addicted to amphetamines and she claimed that she felt suicidal whilst suffering from withdrawal symptoms at the time of the murder. Harris wrote three books in prison and suffered two heart attacks, but in 1992 she was released and has subsequently become a prison reformer.

See Ruth Ellis p. 90

ENGLISH, CHRISTINE (1980)

Christine English had tried everything to combat her moods of depression, loss of memory and insomnia resulting from pre-menstrual syndrome. She and her boyfriend, Barry Kitson, had a tempestuous relationship as a result of her symptoms.

On 16 December 1980 Barry announced that he was going to meet another woman. English was determined to stop him but drove him to the pub; after 30 minutes Barry reappeared and they began fighting in the car. When Barry got out of the car Christine pushed the accelerator and hit

◀ *LEFT: Jean Harris arrives at court, charged with Dr Herman Tarnower's murder.*

him, leaving his right leg almost severed; he later died in hospital.

On 10 November 1981 she was brought before Norwich Crown Court and pleaded guilty to manslaughter on the grounds of diminished responsibility. The judge, recognising that pre-menstrual syndrome was a sufficient mitigating circumstance, let her walk free.

See Clara Ford p. 79

BARBER, SUSAN (1981)

Susan and Michael Barber lived with their three children in Westcliffe-on-Sea, Essex. On 31 March 1981 a cancelled fishing trip caused Michael to return home unexpectedly, where he discovered his 15-year-old friend Richard Collins in bed with his wife. He threw Collins out of the house and beat up his wife.

Michael began suffering from headaches, nausea and stomach pains. Despite antibiotics, he worsened and he was admitted to Hammersmith Hospital; he died there on 27 June and was cremated a few days later. A suspicious pathologist had retained some of Michael's organs, however, and further tests revealed paraquat poisoning.

Susan was charged with murder, conspiracy to murder and administering poison, and Richard was charged with conspiracy. Susan admitted that she had put poison in gravy which only Michael ate. Richard received two years and Susan life imprisonment. In July 1983, Susan remarried in prison.

See Charlotte Bryant p.86

WITTE, MARIE (1981)

Trail Creek, Indiana, was the location for two murders carried out by Butch Witte at the behest of his mother, Marie. In 1981 police were called to their home when Butch's pistol had accidentally gone off, killing his father. The police accepted these explanations but when retired Elaine Witte was absent from home for five months the police began to grow suspicious. They traced Marie and her two sons, Butch and Eric, to a trailer park in San Diego. They were forging and cashing Elaine's Social Security cheques. Although well-coached by his mother, Butch admitted to shooting his grandmother with a crossbow. Butch and Eric testified against their mother in court and she was sentenced to 90 years for murdering her mother-in-law, 30 for conspiracy and 50 for murdering her husband.

See Annette and Charlene Maw p. 93

DOWNS, DIANE (1983)

In May 1983, Diane Downs drove to a hospital in Oregon with her children, all badly wounded. One died within an hour of their arrival and the other two were permanently disabled. Downs claimed that a 'bushy-haired stranger' had shot her children, but during the investigation her story kept changing and police became suspicious. She told them of child abuse, rape, a failed marriage and a promiscuous lifestyle, but she was convicted and imprisoned. Downs will be eligible for parole in 2009.

See Susan Smith p. 99

GRAHAM, GWENDOLYN AND CATHERINE WOOD (1988)

Lesbian nurses Gwendolyn Graham and Catherine Wood worked together at the Alpine Manor Nursing Home in Michigan. They took to murdering elderly women in their care and making love whilst they washed the bodies. Six victims were claimed until Graham found a new lover and Wood told her ex-husband of the killings.

The police, using Wood as their star witness, succeeded in convicting Graham of six counts of murder, earning her life imprisonment without prospect of parole. Wood attempted to put the bulk of the blame on her ex-lover; despite explaining to the court that Graham had suffocated the victims and that she had taken a minor role in the killings. She received a minimum of 20 years at the conclusion of the trial in 1988.

See Margaret Allen p.89

SLEIGHTHOLME, YVONNE (1988)

When William Smith ended his 18-month relationship with Yvonne Sleightholme, she told him she was suffering from leukaemia and the guilt-ridden William took her back. Yvonne began planning their wedding, innocent of the fact that William had rekindled a relationship with a former lover, Jayne Wilford. Yvonne moved out when William told her he was to marry Jayne in May 1988. Soon after the couple began receiving threatening phone calls, suffered arson attacks on their farm and were sent a wreath. The police were called in, but nothing came of their investigations.

On 13 December Yvonne shot Jayne in the head and feigned a sexual attack on her. The police investigated Yvonne's relationship with William and carried out forensic tests on her car, positively identifying Jayne's blood on the upholstery. On 10 May 1991 Yvonne Sleightholme was jailed for life at Leeds Crown Court.

See Ruth Ellis p. 90

BRODERICK, BETTY (1989)

Betty married Daniel T. Broderick III in 1969 and the couple had five children. Betty supported Dan and their family while he trained to be a lawyer. He eventually became a multi-millionaire. The couple were rancorously divorced in 1989 and three months later Dan married again. After Dan's lawyers threatened Betty with contempt over the custody battle, she went to Dan's home and shot her ex-husband and his new wife.

Betty was tried twice; the first trial ended in a hung jury. In a second trial, she was convicted of two counts of second degree murder. The jury foreman said after the trial: 'We only wondered what took her so long to kill him.' She was sentenced to 32 years and will be eligible for parole in 2011.

See Yvonne Sleightholme p. 97

PHILPOTT, GILLIAN (1989)

Twenty-one-year-old Gillian Philpott's new husband, Graham, was a 45-year-old divorced father of three, as well as being her boss at the bank where she worked. Gillian's twin sister, Janet, accompanied them on their honeymoon and later lodged with them.

By December 1989, Gillian was convinced that her sister and her husband were having an affair and confronted them; Janet left the house. At New Year a drunken Graham asked for a divorce; Gillian's response was to strangle him with a dressing-gown cord. She tried to make it look like suicide by faking a note, before attempting to kill herself by driving her car to the edge of a cliff. The car pitched over, but Gillian only sustained superficial injuries.

She was found guilty of manslaughter in January 1991 and was sentenced to two years. Despite attempts to fake a suicide pact, forensic evidence pointed to murder.

See Betty Broderick p.97

SMART, PAMELA (1990)

In 1991 Pamela Smart was sentenced to life imprisonment for plotting the murder of her husband, Gregory. The New Hampshire trial, televised across the US, featured the 22-year-old Pamela and her 15-year-old lover William Flynn, whom she had met at the school where she worked. After

Gregory had discovered his wife's affair, she had convinced 'Billy' and three accomplices to fake a break-in and murder her husband.

The police soon linked Flynn with Pamela and he and two of the accomplices testified against her. The press nicknamed her the 'Ice Princess'. She was found guilty and sentenced to life with no opportunity of parole. The four young men were all sentenced to long prison terms for their involvement in the killing.

See Betty Broderick p. 97

▸ *RIGHT: Nicole Kidman star of* To Die For, *a film based on Pamela Smart's plot to murder her husband.*

SMITH, SUSAN (1994)

In 1994 in South Carolina, Susan Smith drowned her two small boys and then claimed that they had been kidnapped. She said that an African American hijacked her car, and for 10 days there was a massive police manhunt. She eventually confessed; her motive was that the children were getting in the way of her love life. In July 1995 Smith was sentenced to 30 years; she will be eligible for parole in 2025.

See Diane Downs p. 96

GLUZMAN, RITA (1996)

On the morning of 7 April 1996, a New Jersey police patrolman spotted a man taking bags out of the boot of two cars and throwing them into the river. He decided to investigate and found eight other bags. One contained blood-soaked clothing, and in the others a body later identified as Yakov Gluzman had been cut into 65 pieces. The policeman arrested the man, Vladimir Zelenin, on the spot.

Gluzman was a Russian-born millionaire microbiologist; in 1995 he had filed for divorce from his wife Rita on the grounds of mental cruelty. The divorce was acrimonious and in March of that year she approached Zelenin, her cousin, to help her kill Yakov. Knowing her husband's movements and having a key to his apartment allowed them to ambush, murder and dismember him. Zelenin had struck the first blow and Rita had finished Yakov off, beginning the dismemberment herself.

When Zelenin was interviewed, he readily implicated Rita, but she had disappeared. When she was eventually caught, she was charged under the 1994 Domestic Violence Statute, until that time never used against a woman. There was no physical evidence tying her to the crime, yet she was sentenced to life imprisonment. In 1999, the US Supreme Court refused to hear Rita Gluzman's appeal.

See Ruth Ellis p. 90

ROUTIER, DARLIE LYNN (1996)

On 6 June 1996, Darlie Routier's young sons, Damon and Devon, were stabbed to death in their home in Rowlett, Texas. Routier told police that an unknown intruder had entered their home and attacked her and the boys before escaping through the garage. Routier had been extensively injured during the attack and was hospitalised.

Routier was arrested two weeks later and tried in 1997 in Kerrville because of pre-trial publicity. The jury convicted her of the murders of her children, despite the stab wounds which she had suffered She remains on death row. Throughout the trial, and indeed since then, Routier has protested her innocence and has the continued support of her husband, who witnessed her injuries on that fateful night. Routier's defence attorneys believe that new forensic tests will help prove that she is innocent, including the blood on the nightshirt she was wearing, unknown fingerprints in the house and the presence of male pubic hair in the kitchen.

On the night of the killings, a chemical called luminol used by the crime-scene investigator revealed blood in the sink, indicating a clean-up. Had Routier butchered her sons, and then, while standing over the sink, slit her own throat? Clearly, the jury thought she had.

See Kristin Rossum p. 101

ROSSUM, KRISTIN (2002)

Australian Kristin Rossum was a toxicologist working in San Diego when she was convicted of murdering her husband. She told the police that he had taken a combination of old prescription drugs she bought in Mexico while she was trying to kick her addiction to methamphetamine. She had actually used fentanyl, an opiate given to cancer patients, 80 times more powerful than morphine. Fentanyl was the perfect poison: odourless, colourless and dissolvable. Rossum claimed that her husband had taken his own life as their marriage was near an end. She may have conspired with her lover, Michael Robertson, to kill him with drugs stolen from their office. They were both sacked when several doses were found to be missing after her husband's death. In December 2002, she was given life without parole.

See Forensic Entomology p. 173

◄ LEFT: Darlie Lynn Routier's husband speaks at a rally to end the death penalty in Texas.

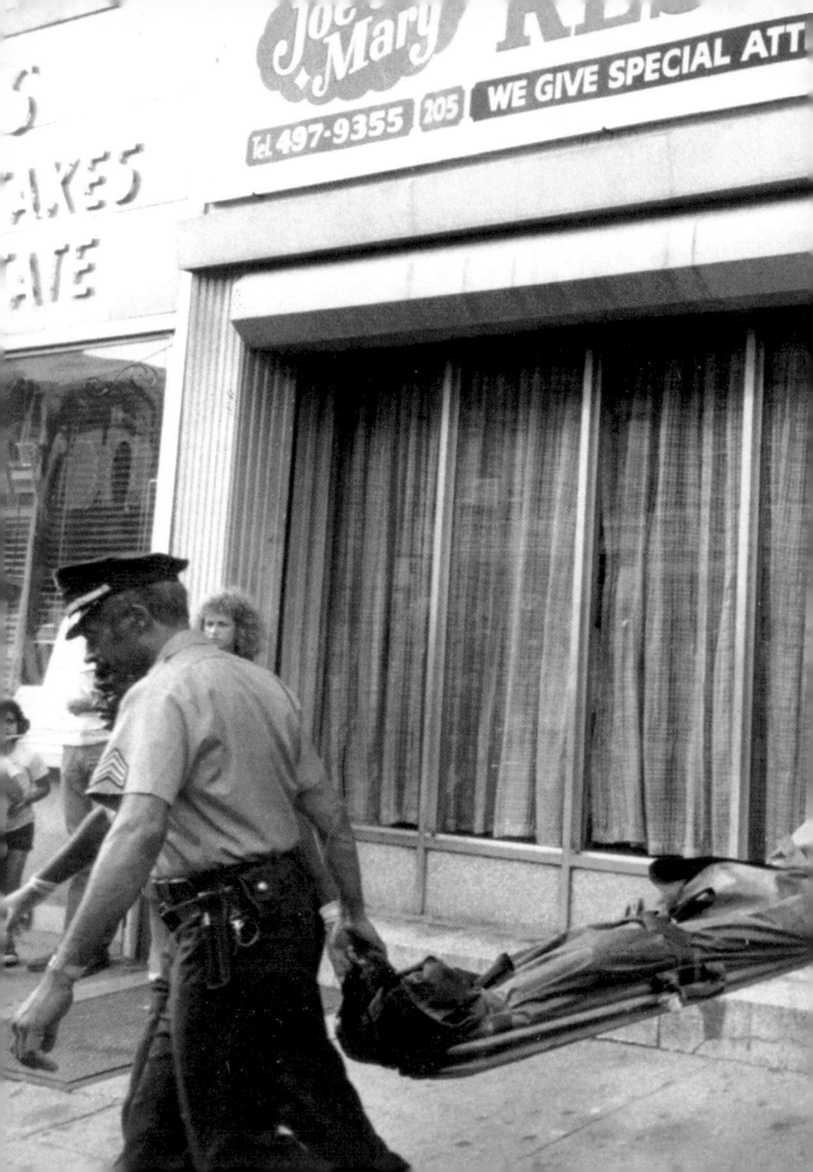
Mary
WE GIVE SPECIAL ATT
Tel. 497-9355
205
AKES
ATE

GANGSTERS AND ORGANISED CRIME

THE MAFIA (1880S–PRESENT)

Giuseppe Esposito was the first known Sicilian Mafia member to emigrate to the United States. Together with six other Sicilians, he fled to New York after murdering 11 wealthy landowners. He was arrested in New Orleans in 1881 and extradited back to Italy.

The US Mafia was dominated by the Black Hand Gangs around 1900 and then the Five Points Gang in New York until Al Capone's syndicate, based in Chicago, took over in the 1920s. By the end of this decade, two factions had emerged, sparking off a turf war in New York. The murder of Joseph Masseria, one of the faction leaders, united the Mafia and it became La Cosa Nostra (LCN).

Salvatore Maranzano, the first leader, was murdered within six months and Charles 'Lucky' Luciano became the new head. Maranzano had established the Cosa Nostra code of conduct, set up the family divisions and structure, and established procedures for resolving disputes. Luciano continued his work by setting up the Commission, which controlled all La Cosa Nostra activities, run by bosses from six or seven families.

Today the LCN is involved in corruption, drug trafficking, extortion, gambling, labour racketeering, loan sharking, murder, prostitution, pornography, stock manipulation schemes and tax fraud.

See Salvatore Maranzano p. 113

CAPONE, AL (1910S-1930S)

Al Capone was born in Brooklyn in 1899. He became involved with the Mafia at an early age, working for Johnny Torrio. He earned his nickname of 'Scarface' in 1917, after being slashed with a knife by Frank Galluccio,

▶ RIGHT: *Notorious Mafia boss Al Capone smoking a cigar.*

whose sister Capone had insulted. After a waterfront war with other gangs in 1918, Torrio decided to send Capone to Chicago. He arrived in 1920 and joined the Colosimo mob, which was mainly involved in illegal alcohol and similar rackets. Capone eventually killed Torrio's uncle, Colosimo, and took over the Chicago Mafia.

Capone led Torrio's men against O'Banion's gang when the latter refused to accept Torrio as their boss. Torrio was nearly killed in the war and decided to retire and leave the business to Capone. By 1925, Capone could deploy 1000 gunmen and although he was a racketeer, murderer and bootlegger, his popularity was enormous. Rival gangs were extinguished – the most famous instance being the St Valentine's Day Massacre in 1929.

The US authorities had difficulty in finding any hard evidence against Capone for any of his illegal activities, but in 1931 they managed to take him to court on charges of tax evasion. He was given a huge fine and a prison sentence. He was released in 1939, but he died of a stroke and pneumonia on 25 January 1947.

See St Valentine's Day Massacre p. 114

TORRIO, JOHNNY (1910S–50S)

Torrio was born in Italy in 1882, but was raised in the ghettoes of New York. By 1912, he was involved in brothels, hijacking and extortion, and was working with a young Al Capone. Torrio had been working in Chicago for his uncle Big Jim Colosimo, dealing with anyone who tried to muscle in on the family business. Torrio eventually took over from Colosimo and united the Chicago gangs. Dion O'Banion, a Chicago gang leader, refused to be controlled by Torrio and was murdered. O'Banion's gang was taken over by Hymie Weiss and Bugs Moran, who vowed revenge.

On 24 January 1925, Weiss and Moran ambushed Torrio and badly wounded him; from then on Torrio had 30 guards day and night. Torrio passed the business on to Capone, retiring as a millionaire to Brooklyn. Torrio died at the age of 75 in 1957.

See Al Capone p. 104

COSTELLO, FRANK (1916–57)

Frank Costello was born in Italy in 1891 and emigrated with his family to the United States as a child. As he grew up, he turned to petty crime and spent his teen years in and out of prison.

In 1916, Costello teamed up with gang leader Lucky Luciano and ran his bootlegging and gambling operations. He also nurtured his connections with politicians. His networking and contacts earned him the nickname the 'Prime Minister'. When Luciano was imprisoned in 1936, he chose Costello to run the business, with Vito Genovese as his second-in-command. By 1951, however, Genovese had planned to oust Costello and take over leadership of the gang himself.

Costello avoided death at this time as he was sentenced to 14 months in prison for contempt of court; he was released in October 1953. He received another prison term in 1956, spending a further year inside. In 1957, Costello survived a murder attempt by Vincent Gigante and was slightly wounded. Genovese appointed himself boss all the same. Costello was a practical man – he saw that Genovese had

▶ *RIGHT: Frank Costello puffs on a cigarette as he leaves court following his testimony.*

effective control of the mob and that he was always going to be target for murder.

Costello agreed to retire; he gave up all his interests and promised never to be involved in the business again. He was true to his word and passed away peacefully in a Manhattan hospital in 1975.

See Lucky Luciano p. 111

MORAN, GEORGE (1920S-40S)

George 'Bugs' Moran was born in 1893 and grew up in Chicago. He had served three prison terms by the time he was 21. He joined O'Banion's gang as a youth and took over leadership of the group in 1927 after his bosses had been killed. As leader, he was involved in the turf war with Johnny Torrio and Al Capone and attempted to kill them; indeed he had a pathological hatred of the man known as 'Scarface'. Moran was nearly killed at the St Valentine's Day Massacre, but was saved by arriving late at the meeting point. His gang was destroyed by Capone's attack, however, and he moved to Ohio where was arrested in 1946 for robbing a bank messenger. He was given 10 years, but died of cancer in 1957 at the beginning of a second 10-year sentence for an earlier robbery. He was given a pauper's burial outside Leavenworth prison.

See St Valentine's Day Massacre p. 114

SIEGEL, BUGSY (1920S–47)

Bugsy Siegel was born in Brooklyn in 1906. He teamed up with Meyer Lansky and became involved in bootlegging. By the late-1920s, he had joined the gang led by Joe Masseria. In 1937, Siegel went to the California to develop gambling ships, operating outside the jurisdiction of the authorities.

▸ RIGHT: *George 'Bugs' Moran, the Chicago gangster, appears in court with his wife.*

Siegel's partners in New York suspected that he was hiding some of the profits and on 20 June 1947 he was murdered in his Beverly Hills home.
See Joe Masseria p. 111

GAMBINO, CARLO (1920S–50S)

Carlo Gambino was born in Sicily in 1902 into a gangster family. He worked as a hit-man during his teens, and in the early 1920s he went to the United States to join forces with his cousins, the Castellanos.

During the period of Prohibition, he worked as a gun-man, driver and bootlegger, and became an associate of mob leader Lucky Luciano. He also married Paul Castellano's sister.

By the 1950s, Albert Anastasia had become the head of the family, but he was murdered (probably on Gambino's orders) in 1957. Gambino took

over and controlled the Mafia's New York operations, becoming a close associate of John Gotti. Gambino became ill in 1976 and appointed Paul Castellano as his successor, to ensure that there was no street battle for control of the family when he died.

See John Gotti p. 125

See John Gotti p. 125

YAKUZA (1920S-PRESENT)

The name Yakuza originates from the Japanese game of Oicho-Kabu, the goal of which is to reach 19. 'Ya' means eight, 'Ku' means nine, and 'Za' means three, which adds up to 20, a worthless score, and therefore Yakuza means 'outsiders'.

The Yakuza are organised crime gangs of outcasts who came to prominence in the 1920s. During the 1930s, several political leaders were assassinated by the Yakuza as a show of strength. Between 1958 and 1963, Yakuza membership increased to 184,000 members. It has been estimated that there are more than 5,000 different Yakuza gangs in operation. Today, they are involved in most areas of criminal activity and are always at war with one another over territory and control of legitimate business.

There are, effectively, two different types of Yakuza. The freelance Yakuza are petty criminals sometimes used by the Yakuza clans, but are also often preyed on by them. The clan Yakuza is similar to a Mafia family, with a head called an Oyabun ('father'). Ordinary members of the clan are called Wakashu ('children') or Kyodai ('brothers'); they all owe allegiance to the Oyabun and must obey his orders without question. The Yakuza are active in most of Asia and increasingly in Europe and America.

See The Mafia p. 104

MASSERIA, JOE (1920–31)

From 1920 to 1931 Giuseppe Masseria was the top Mafia don in New York, but in 1927 Salvatore Maranzano attempted to move in on his patch. Another gang leader, Lucky Luciano, decided to kill them both and on 15 April 1931, he invited Masseria to dine at his favourite restaurant in Coney Island. After they had eaten, four gun-men burst in and opened fire on Masseria. He was hit six times and finally killed by Albert Anastasia with a final shot to the head.

See Lucky Luciano p. 111

LUCKY LUCIANO (1920–36)

Luciano was born in Sicily in 1896. His family moved to America in 1906, settling in New York. He was arrested in 1915 for heroin dealing and given a prison term. In 1920, he joined Joe Masseria's gang and had risen to under-boss by 1925. Luciano was nearly killed in the war that broke out between Masseria and Salvatore Maranzano, earning him the nickname 'Lucky'.

In April 1931, Luciano was involved in the murders of Masseria and Maranzano, which made him the undisputed boss of New York. He was

◄ *LEFT: Carlo Gambino, 'The Godfather', is escorted by FBI agents in 1970.*

instrumental in the formation of Murder, Incorporated to enforce mob law.

In 1936, he was sentenced to 30 years, but was released in 1946 for his assistance during the war and deported to Italy. He died in Naples on 26 January 1962.

See Joe Masseria p. 111

LANSKY, MEYER (1920–83)

In 1920, Lansky Meyer met Bugsy Siegel and Lucky Luciano and became part of their gang. In 1931, Lansky was part of the conspiracy to kill enemy mob leader Joe Masseria. In 1936 he established gambling operations and ordered the death of his partner Siegel in June 1947, having found out that Siegel had been swindling him. In 1970 he fled to Israel to avoid charges of tax evasion, but was acquitted in 1973. He died in Miami Beach on 15 May 1983.

See Bugsy Siegel p. 108

DILLINGER, JOHN (1924–34)

John Dillinger was born in Indianapolis in 1902. Even as a child he was rebellious, joining the US navy in 1923 but deserting a few months later. He committed his first robbery in September 1924, and was caught and imprisoned.

While still on parole after his release in 1933, he began robbing banks in Indiana and Ohio. Dillinger

▶ *RIGHT: Lucky Luciano celebrates after being cleared of complicity in an international dope ring.*

was re-arrested, but his two partners, John Hamilton and Harry Pierpont, broke into the prison and released him. Between October 1933 and January 1934, the gang robbed a series of banks, netting over $100,000. They were arrested in Arizona, but Dillinger escaped in March and teamed up with Baby Face Nelson to commit more bank robberies. Dillinger was finally killed in a police ambush in Chicago on 22 July 1934.

See Baby Face Nelson p. 117

MARANZANO, SALVATORE (1927–31)

Salvatore Maranzano came to America in 1927. He had been sent by the original Boss of Bosses in Sicily, Vito Cascio Ferro, who wanted him to bring the New York underworld under the control of the Sicilian mob.

Back in Italy, however, Ferro had been imprisoned by Mussolini's fascist government and this left Maranzano pretty much to his own devices so he began to seek power for himself. Between 1928 and 1931, New York City and other crime capitals across the United States suffered the effects of the Castellemmarese War, in which Maranzano fought with the mobsters under the leadership of New York Mafia leader Joe 'The Boss' Masseria.

▶ *RIGHT: John Dillinger travels under heavy escort to Indiana, charged with murdering a policeman.*

While the two factions fought, a younger and more power-hungry group arose under the command of Charlie 'Lucky' Luciano. On 10 September 1931, Luciano sent four of his own hand-picked hit-men, posing as IRS agents, to Maranzano's office. There they stabbed and shot him to death. Along with Maranzano, 40 other associated figures in the crime world were murdered across the country. Luciano had been prompted to act when he learned that Maranzano had called in Vincent 'Mad Dog' Coll to kill him.

See Lucky Luciano p. 111

THE MURDER OF ARNOLD ROTHSTEIN (1928)

Arnold Rothstein was a big-time gambler who, in one game in September 1928, played against Nate Raymond, Alvin 'Titanic' Thompson and Joe Bernstein. By the end of the marathon game, he owed Raymond $219,000, Bernstein $73,000 and Thompson $30,000.

On 4 November, he was shot in the stomach at a hotel in New York. Rothstein signed a will and talked with several friends. When questioned by police as to who shot him, he replied, 'I'll take care of it myself'.

He died without naming his killer on 6 November 1928. It was Election Day and Rothstein had bet heavily on the election that year. Had he lived, he would have collected $570,000.

See Murder, Incorporated p. 120

ST VALENTINE'S DAY MASSACRE (1929)

On 14 February 1929, Al Capone orchestrated one of the most famous Mafia hits of all time. Chicago North Side gang leader, Bugs Moran, refused to cooperate with Capone's image of a new Mafia order and

▸ RIGHT: *The aftermath of the St Valentine's Day Massacre of 1929.*

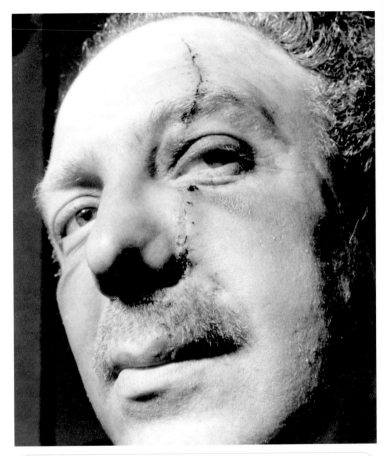

▲ *ABOVE: Jack Comer shows his scars after an ambush in which he was beaten and slashed with razors.*

Capone's plan was to put him permanently out of the picture. Capone's assassination squad got into police uniforms and drove in a stolen police car over to the garage used by Moran's men. The bootleggers thought they had been caught in the act and lined up against a wall; the assassins then opened fire with two machine guns, a shotgun and a .45. The four assassins then left in the same car.

Unfortunately, Moran was not one of the victims; he was late for the rendezvous with his gang. Capone had been popular with the public up to this point, but the massacre turn opinion against him, it also focused the attention of the law on Capone. He, as usual, had a cast-iron alibi; he was talking to a District Attorney at the time!

See Al Capone p. 104

NELSON, BABY FACE (1929–34)

Baby Face Nelson was born Lester Gillis in Chicago in 1908. He was a petty criminal, but in 1929 he began working for the notorious gang leader Al Capone. His youthful good looks earned him his nickname, which belied his willingness to carry out vicious killings.

In 1934 he joined up with the John Dillinger gang, taking part in several bank robberies. He was killed in a shoot-out with the police and FBI on 27 November 1934.

See John Dillinger p.112

SPOT, JACK AND BILLY HILL (1930S–55)

Jack Spot's career covered the Sabinis to the Krays, and he and his arch-rival Billy Hill were the undisputed kings of London's underworld. The Jewish Spot led a Whitechapel gang who attacked fascist leader Oswald Mosley's black-shirts in the battle of Cable Street on 4 October 1936. His career ended when he was stabbed on 12 August 1955.

Billy Hill formed a gang specialising in smash-and-grab raids; during the 1940s he was making £3,000 a week. Having served 15 years imprisonment, in 1954 he serialised his memoirs. After a period of peace with Spot, they fell out again; it was Hill who ordered an attack on Spot, forcing him into retirement. Spot emigrated to Ireland and Hill, assuming a lower profile, lived in Spain on the proceeds of his crimes.
See Mad Frankie Fraser p. 118

THE SABINI GANG (1930S–60S)

In the 1930s, in most of Britain's cities, there were warring gangs fighting for their territory. The London region of Clerkenwell, known as 'Little Italy', was controlled by the Sabini gang, which concentrated on racecourse protection. The fighting reached a peak in the 1960s, when the repeal of the death penalty replaced razor-blade attacks with regular contract killings.
See The Kray Twins p. 122

FRASER, MAD FRANKIE (1930S–90S)

Fraser was born in 1923 and his criminal career spanned the period of the Sabini gang and the Kray twins in London. Fraser won his nickname after a violent attack on Jack Spot in Praed Street, Paddington, on 2 May 1956. From 1936, Fraser spent 32 of the next 40 years in prison for a variety of criminal offences; indeed he spent a total of 40 years at Her Majesty's pleasure. He had a reputation as one of the Richardson gang's torturers and allegedly pulled out teeth with pliers. Fraser was shot in the head outside a nightclub in Farringdon in August 1991, but he survived and has written books on his exploits; he also conducts gangland tours around London. Two home secretaries labelled Fraser 'the most dangerous man in Britain'.

See Charlie and Eddie Richardson p. 123

HOFFA, JIMMY (1933–75)

Jimmy Hoffa was born in 1913 and rose to become a major American labour leader with Mafia connections. Hoffa's union activities began in 1933 and he proved to be a natural leader. He rapidly rose in the ranks of the Teamsters Union (truck drivers), taking over from the jailed Dave Beck in the 1950s. He cooperated with the Mafia to control entire industries in America and allowed the theft of money from the Teamsters Union pension funds to be used by the Mafia.

In 1967, he was convicted of attempted bribery of a jury and given 15 years. His associates funded Richard Nixon's presidential campaign and Hoffa was released in 1971. Hoffa mysteriously disappeared on 31 July 1975. His body was never found and he was pronounced dead in 1981.

See The Mafia p. 104

GIULIANI, HAROLD (1934)

On 2 April 1934, Harold Giuliani and an accomplice robbed milkman Harold Hall at gunpoint in the stairwell of a Manhattan building. As the attack was taking place, a police officer burst in through the front door of the building. Giuliani's accomplice, who was holding the gun and the money, fled down the stairs to the basement and escaped, but Giuliani was arrested.

Giuliani had friends with influence, however, and three days after he was

◄ LEFT: *Jimmy Hoffa, president of the Teamsters Union, at a 1959 press conference.*

arrested, a man named Valentine Spielman put up the $5000 bail. On 19 April, a week after the indictment was filed, Hall changed his statement and Giuliani spent just 18 months in prison.

Giuliani's story would have become just another mobster's tale if it had not been for the fact that he became the father of the future Mayor of New York, Rudolph William Louis Giuliani.

See The Mafia p. 104

FLEGENHEIMER, ARTHUR (1935)

Arthur Flegenheimer, also known as 'Dutch Schultz', is said to have been responsible for around 135 murders. He was the major New York City bootlegger of his time, and his fiercest rival was Vincent Coll. After years of fighting, the Dutchman's cronies shot Coll in a telephone booth.

In October 1935, Charles 'The Bug' Workman shot Schultz and he died the following day. Although Schultz came from an Orthodox Jewish family, he requested baptism on his deathbed.

See Murder, Incorporated p. 120

MURDER, INCORPORATED (1935)

Murder, Incorporated was a contract killing gang run by Louis 'Lepke' Buchalter and Albert Anastasia. They limited their targets to those in the mob, such as Bugsy Siegel, Dutch Schultz and the New York district attorney Thomas E. Dewey. In October 1935, Mendy Weiss and Charles 'The Bug' Workman, two of Murder, Inc.'s most notorious killers, walked into the Palace Chop House and Tavern in Newark, New Jersey and shot three of Schultz's men and then Schultz himself in the stomach. It has been estimated that over a period of 10 years, Murder, Inc. was responsible for between 500 and 700 murders from California to Connecticut.

See Bugsy Siegel p. 108

GALANTE, CARMINE (1940S–79)

Carmine Galante was born in 1910 and, after the death of Carlo Gambino in 1976, he made a play for the leadership of the Mafia. He had a rich pedigree in these circles, which began in the 1940s, and in 1978 had no less than eight major Mafia leaders killed to clear the road to succession. This, in addition to his major drug-trafficking activities, did not endear himself to the other mob families, and on 12 July 1979, they had him killed.

See Carlo Gambino p. 109

▸ *RIGHT: Carmine Galante is carried from a Brooklyn restaurant after being shot in the eye.*

JONES, BETTY (1944)

In October 1944, Betty Jones, an 18-year-old stripper, hooked up with a US Army deserter, Karl Hulten, who was masquerading as 2nd Lieutenant Richard Allen in the 501st Parachute Regiment. To Jones, he was a stereo-typical Chicago mobster and Hulten was keen to cultivate this image. After a series of amateurish robberies, they murdered George Heath, but were picked up while driving Heath's stolen car. Jones made a full confession, received an execution reprieve and instead spent 10 years in prison.

See Karl Gustav Hulten p. 196

GRAHAM, BARBARA (1950S)

Barbara Graham was born in 1923 in Oakland, California. She was a troublesome teenager and spent time in a reformatory. After this, she tried to mend her ways. She married in 1939, but when this fell apart within two years Graham drifted into prostitution, eventually marrying mobster Henry Graham, who introduced her to Jack Santo, a gang leader.

Graham and her husband, along with Santo, Emmett Perkins and John True, robbed an old lady, smothering her with a pillow when she resisted. True testified against them at the trial and Barbara tried to bribe a policeman to obtain an alibi. She was executed on 3 June 1955. When told she might get a stay of execution, she replied: 'I never got a break in my whole goddamned life and you think I'm going to get one now?'

See The Mafia p. 104

THE KRAY TWINS (1950S–69)

Twins Ronnie and Reggie Kray had been in trouble with the law since their mid-teens, when they were charged with gangland violence in Hackney, London. By the 1950s they had set up protection rackets and in

1960 opened a gambling club in the West End. In the mid-to-late-1960s they began to hit the headlines. Ronnie shot George Cornell in the Blind Beggar pub in the East End on 9 March 1966, after Cornell had called him 'a fat poof'; Cornell was a principle member of the gang led by Charlie and Eddie Richardson. In November Reggie stabbed Jack 'The Hat' McVitie to death in a flat in Stoke Newington; later they would also be linked with the murder of Frank 'Mad Axeman' Mitchell in December.

In 1969 the twins were sentenced to 30 years, along with their elder brother, Charlie, who was given seven years. They became the longest-serving prisoners in recent British history – Ronnie died in prison in 1995. In 1998 Reggie's parole application was refused; he also died in prison in 2000, after serving 31 years. Their brother Charlie also died in 2000, whilst serving a prison sentence for having masterminded a £69 million cocaine-smuggling plot.

See Charlie and Eddie Richardson p. 123

▸ RIGHT: *London gangland boss Charlie Richardson at the funeral of the infamous gangster Lenny Maclean.*

RICHARDSON, CHARLIE AND EDDIE (1960S)

The infamous Kray twins, Ronnie and Reggie, shared control of London with the Richardson gang, which was based in South London. The gang consisted of brothers Charlie and Eddie Richardson, Mad Frankie Fraser and George Cornell. Their primary business was fraud, but in the 1960s they began supplying West End clubs

◂ LEFT: *Ronald and Reginald Kray at 18 years of age.*

with gambling machines. By 1965 the gang had effectively been put out of business by the police and the brothers were briefly imprisoned. In March 1966 they were involved in a gun battle with the Krays, during which Fraser and Eddie were both shot. Later that year, Cornell was murdered by the Krays and the Richardson brothers began a 25-year prison sentence for fraud-related crimes.

See Mad Frankie Fraser p. 118

BONNANO, JOSEPH (1960S)

Joseph Bonnano took control of his gang at the age of 26 – the youngest of all the crime-family dons. Under Bonnano's control, the family businesses prospered, and included interests in clothing and cheese factories, as well as funeral homes.

When Joseph Profaci, head of the Profaci family gang, died in 1962, Bonnano approached the new boss of the Profaci gang, Joe Maglicco, with a plan to kill Carlo Gambino, Thomas Luchese and Sam Giancana and take over their rackets. Maglicco passed the order to hit-man Joe Colombo, but Colombo betrayed the plot.

The Cosa Nostra controlled the mafia families and settled disputes using the Commission, and so ordered Bonnano and Maglicco to appear before them and explain their actions. Bonnano refused and went into hiding. In 1964, Bonnano was kidnapped by his own

◀ LEFT: *Joseph Bonnano (Joe Bananas) arrives at the Federal Courthouse in New York, 1966.*

▶ RIGHT: *Attorney Bruce Cutler (left) during the trial of his client, crime boss John Gotti (right).*

enforcer Mike Zaffarano, and held for 19 months by his own cousin, Steven Magaddino. Bonnano agreed to retire and give up his family assets to the other members of the Cosa Nostra; he also agreed to live in exile in Haiti.

Bonnano was eventually allowed to return to America provided he stay out of Mafia business. He lived in peace in Arizona with his family and some of his rackets that existed there. In 1983, he released his autobiography, which created a furore. When brought before a grand jury to answer questions regarding his book, he refused to respond. Bonnano died on 12 May 2002, at the age of 97.

See The Banana War p. 129

GOTTI, JOHN (1960S–90S)

Gotti, born in 1940, was the head of the Gambino family of New York. Gotti had worked his way up in the family and in 1985 he arranged the shooting of his boss, Paul Castellano, in order to gain control. He became known as the 'Dapper Don' or the 'Teflon Don' because of his immaculate appearance and the fact that no charges against him ever seemed to stick.

Gotti faced numerous charges over the years, but used informants and intimidation to stay one step ahead of the law. Eventually, Gotti was convicted of 14 counts of murder, loan-sharking, racketeering, tax evasion, obstruction of justice (jury bribes and intimidation) and other crimes in April 1992, for which he was sentenced to life. He died in prison on 10 June 2002.

See Paul Castellano p. 131

GIGANTE, VINCENT (1960S–90S)

Vincent Gigante ran the Genovese mob family and was known as the 'Oddfather' because he would walk through Greenwich Village in a bathrobe and slippers.

In 1969, Gigante avoided bribery charges when several psychiatrists testified that he suffered from schizophrenia, dementia and psychosis. In 1997 he was convicted of racketeering and conspiracy and in 2003 he admitted that his insanity was an act. He was given an extra three years and is due for release in 2010.

See John Gotti p. 125

BULGER, JAMES J. (1960S-PRESENT)

James 'Whitey' Bulger has been described by the FBI as a major figure in the world of organised crime in the Boston area. He is currently one of the FBI's Ten Most Wanted and is being sought for extortion and racketeering influenced and corruption organisation (RICO) charges.

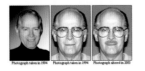

Over the years, Bulger has funded his activities through illegitimate criminal operations in Boston. His business interests include gambling, loan-sharking and drugs. Bulger is well travelled in Italy,

◀ *LEFT: An FBI Ten Most Wanted poster of James J Bulger.*

Ireland and Canada. The alleged don of the Winter Hill Gang in South Boston, Bulger is known to have a violent temper and usually carries a knife. He was indicted in October 2000 for his involvement in 19 murders in the Boston area. There is a reward of $1 million for information leading to his arrest.
See The Mafia p.104

▶ *RIGHT: Post office and railway workers unload the remaining bags following the Great Train Robbery.*

THE GREAT TRAIN ROBBERY (1963)

The Great Train Robbery took place on 8 August 1963 at Cheddington, Buckinghamshire, when a Royal Mail train was stopped near a bridge by a criminal gang who had tampered with the signals. The gang was led by Bruce Reynolds and included Ronnie Biggs, Buster Edwards, Brian Field, Gordon Goody, Charlie Wilson, Jimmy Hussey, John Wheater, Jimmy White, Tommy Wisbey and five others.

The only injury during the robbery was suffered by the train driver, Jack Mills, who was struck with an iron bar. He never fully recovered and died in 1970. Royal Mail staff put up no resistance and the gang got away with £2.6 million.

The police found their Oxfordshire hide-out covered in fingerprints, and managed to round up the culprits They were tried and sentenced to a total of 307 years. Edwards gave himself up after fleeing to Mexico for three years. After 15 months in prison, Biggs and Reynolds escaped; Biggs settled in Brazil. Reynolds was on the run for five years in Mexico and Canada after the 1963 robbery, until his £150,000 share ran out and he was eventually caught, penniless, in Torquay. Wilson escaped in 1964 and was on the run for four years, but was recaptured in 1968. The lost money has never been recovered. *See* Ronald Biggs p. 128

BIGGS, RONALD (1963)

Ronald Biggs, the public face of Britain's Great Train Robbery, actually played a fairly minor part in the crime. After being sentenced to 25 years, he spent just 15 months in Wandsworth Prison before escaping

and fleeing Britain. He had plastic surgery to change his appearance and moved to Spain, then Australia and finally Brazil. Biggs remained there for many years and made a good living from his fame. Illness finally forced him back to Britain in May 2001 and despite his age (71) and ill-health, he was sent back to prison to serve out his sentence. In July 2002, Biggs married his Brazilian lover, the mother of his two children.

See the Great Train Robbery p. 127

THE BANANA WAR (1964–69)

The Banana War was brought about in 1964 by an attempt on the life of Salvatore Bonnano, Joseph Bonnano's son. Bonnano ordered men who were still loyal to him to kill Paul Sciacca, the crime boss who had replaced him on the Commission, and who Bonnano believed was responsible for the hit. This caused a split within the family, some members siding with Bonnano and others siding with Sciacca. Bonnano proceeded to kill off capos for every man of his that was killed. He was winning the war and the Commission knew it. It was not until Bonnano suffered a major heart attack that the war ended in 1969, forcing Bonnano into real retirement.

See Joseph Bonanno p. 124

PISTONE, JOSEPH D. (1970S)

Joseph Pistone (alias Donnie Brasco) was an FBI agent who, in the 1970s, went undercover and managed to infiltrate Bonnano's Mafia family. Pistone's testimony led to more than 200 federal

◀ *LEFT: Great Train Robber Ronnie Biggs celebrates after being freed by the Supreme Court in 1981.*

indictments and over 100 convictions of mob figures. So thorough was Pistone's cover that the New York City Police Department actually listed him as a member of the Bonnano crime family. An open contract remains for his death. He later wrote books based on his exploits.

See Joseph Bonnano p. 124

DEMEO, ROY (1970S)

During the 1970s, Roy DeMeo was Paul Castellano's most trusted hit-man. He was a contract killer, possibly responsible for more than 200 deaths. In truth he was a serial killer – he would bleed his victims to death before dismembering their bodies. He and his associates became more erratic and violent, so Castellano ordered Nino Gaggi, Demeo's closest friend, to deal with the situation. DeMeo's body was found stuffed in the boot of his car.

See Paul Castellano p. 131

GRAVANO, SALVATORE (1970S–PRESENT)

Salvatore Gravano (Sammy 'The Bull') was under-boss to John Gotti, who was under-boss to the Gambino Mafia family. In 1990, Gravano turned against Gotti in an attempt to reduce the sentence he was likely to receive for his activities. He became the star witness against his old boss, receiving just five years, while Gotti was given life. Gravano then entered the Witness Protection Program.

Old habits die hard, and Gravano was later arrested in Arizona as the head of an ecstasy trafficking ring. Now back in the public eye and of great interest to prosecutors, in 2003 he was charged with his involvement in a murder in 1980. Gravano again faces the possibility of a life sentence.

See John Gotti p. 125

CASTELLANO, PAUL (1976–85)

Paul Castellano was born in Brooklyn in 1915. He was a member of the Gambino mobster family, and he married Carlo Gambino's sister. When Gambino died in 1976, he named Castellano his successor, with Aniello DelaCrosse as his second-in-command. Castellano ran the family like a regular business, even opening operations in Kuwait.

When DelaCrosse died of lung cancer in December 1985, the other crime bosses decided it was time to kill Castellano. On 16 December, Castellano and his driver were shot dead outside the Sparks Steak House in Manhattan.

According to the testimony of Sammy 'The Bull' Gravano, John Gotti's under-boss, Gotti had sanctioned the killing. This came to light in 1990, when Gravano was trying to negotiate a reduction in his sentence with the courts.

See Carlo Gambino p. 109

MURPHY, SANDY AND RICK TABISH (1998–PRESENT)

Murphy was convicted of the 1998 killing of a multi-millionaire gaming executive, Ted Binion. Binion was an associate of mobster Herbert 'Fat Herbie' Blitzstein, who was found shot dead in his Las Vegas home on 7 January 1997, the victim of an organised crime killing. Also convicted on a first-degree murder charge was Murphy's lover, Rick Tabish. Authorities said the pair either forced Binion to ingest a lethal amount of drugs or suffocated him; they were sentenced to life with a possibility of parole after 20 years.

On 14 July 2003, however, the US Supreme Court overturned the convictions, saying the pair's 2000 trial was flawed. Prosecutors have notified the Supreme Court that they intend to file a motion asking the justices to reconsider their decision.

See The Mafia p. 104

THE NEW MAFIA ORDER TODAY (2003)

The New Mafia Order, or the 'sistema', which has ruled Sicily for decades, has grown into a trans-national empire of crime and now has power across the world beyond its wildest dreams.

The Mafia's control now extends beyond the Cosa Nostra and the Neapolitan Camorra, and incorporates organisations based in Turkey and Russia. The scope of the sistema includes Colombian cocaine cartels and their operations in Spain, as well as triad gangs in Asia (active in London and Rotterdam) and organised gangs of Alabanians, Nigerians, Lebanese, Moroccans, Pakistanis and former Yugoslavs.

Back in the homeland, Palermo launders some $20 billion per year; the city is eightieth in Italy in terms of per capita income, but fifth in consumer spending, attesting to the fact that it is awash with Mafia money.

See The Mafia p. 104

THE TRIADS TODAY (2003)

Triad societies date back to the seventeenth century and have dominated the Chinese underworld for centuries. They base their organisations on secret rules and rituals, a sworn brotherhood built on kinship. They are actively involved in smuggling, drug trafficking, prostitution and other criminal activities, using fear and intimidation rather than violence. Triad societies occur wherever there is a Chinese community. Hong Kong was at the very centre of their operations for many years, but latterly they have turned their attention to China itself. They are active across the world to a greater or lesser extent, having established a presence in Chinese communities in a number of countries over the years.

The Triads have key connections in the United States, particularly California and New York, and in such European capitals as Amsterdam and London, but there is little prospect of the West being overrun by Triad gangs. Police estimate there are as many as 50 Triad societies in Hong Kong, the largest being the Wo Sing Wo and 14-K. Southern China and Hong Kong still represent their greatest sources of revenue.

Triads have become particularly active in Europe in recent years with their involvement in the trafficking of people, notably Chinese.

See Yakuza p. 110

YARDIES (2003)

The term 'Yardie' is used to refer to Jamaicans who have just arrived from their home country (referred to as the 'back yard'). A typical Yardie is a single male, age 18–35, usually but not exclusively of Jamaican origin, many of whom have false identities or are only known by their street names. Great Britain and lately the United States are attractive destinations for Yardies as they can more easily be assimilated into the West Indian populations.

Yardies are predominantly interested in drug trafficking and dealing and are renowned for their extreme violence. The US has made it increasingly difficult for Jamaican criminals to gain entry into the country, and consequently Britain has become a staging ground to illegally obtain passports, making international movement easier.

Yardies tend to deal in the production and distribution of cocaine and are usually well-armed. Jamaican crime groups have

▶ *RIGHT: Stephen Murray, part of a Yardie terror group jailed for assassinating a rival gang member.*

relatively small, flat organisations, making a rise to power easy if the individual has access to a drug supply and is prepared to protect his business. As a consequence, inter-Yardie warfare is commonplace and they are not adverse to using firearms to deal with trivial disputes. Yardie gangs frequently break up and reorganise, which causes temporary chaos and conflict.

See Yakuza p. 110

THE RED MAFIA TODAY (2003)

Russian organised crime is becoming a considerable concern, not only in Russia and the former Russian states, but in the rest of Europe and the US. The Red Mafia is actively involved in extortion, prostitution, fraud, car theft, counterfeiting, credit-card forgery, drug trafficking, money laundering and murder. An estimated 80 per cent of the private enterprises and commercial banks in Russia's major cities pay a tribute of 10–20 per cent of their profits to organised crime. During the 1970s and 1980s, it is believed that some 200,000 Russian citizens emigrated to the United States alone, a fair proportion of them unwanted Russian criminals.

It is estimated that some 5,000 Russian gangs operate in that country alone, with a membership of some 100,000. Each gang is run by a 'pakhan', who controls four cells through an intermediary called a 'brigadier'. The pakhan uses spies to ensure the brigadiers remain loyal. Regular members of the gang are unaware of the identity of their pakhan, but all strategy is decided by the pakhan and his closest associates.

The members are bound by 18 codes, by which they live or die – breaking one of the codes is punishable by death. The Russian Mafia is technically advanced and has counter-intelligence groups and access to the latest equipment and intelligence.

See Money Laundering p. 135

MONEY LAUNDERING (2003)

Money laundering is 'the conversion of the monetary proceeds of a criminal activity into funds with an apparently legal source'. All criminal activities, such as drugs trafficking, generate cash in the form of notes, making it difficult for the criminals to hide such large amounts of money by legitimate means.

The first step is to get the money into the commercial financial system, then to transfer the money to several different banks in different countries, hidden amongst normal and legitimate transfers of cash. The third step is to integrate the funds into legitimate business, making it impossible to trace the cash.

Typically, organised crime gangs would employ 'smurfs', or runners, who literally run from bank to bank depositing just less than the banks' reporting requirements to the Treasury or Inland Revenue.

See The Red Mafia Today p. 134

▲ ABOVE: *A West London bureau de change, used to change laundered money in a recent £50 million cocaine trafficking operation.*

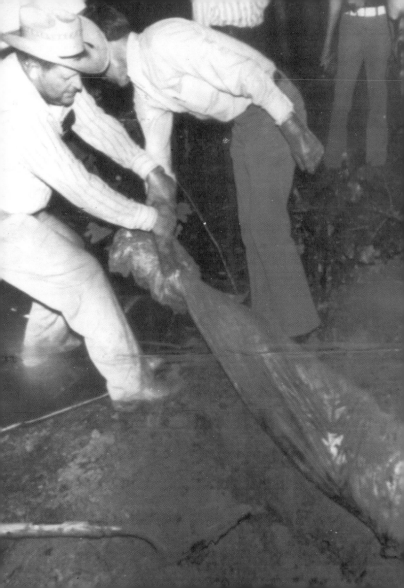

INTRIGUING CASES

BURKE, WILLIAM AND WILLIAM HARE (1828)

William Burke and William Hare were Irish labourers living in West Port, one of the slum areas of Edinburgh. When one of the lodgers in their rooms died owing rent, they hit upon the idea of selling her body to a Dr Knox, who was always interested in obtaining bodies for dissection. Amazed at the price they received, they set about providing corpses for the doctor by the simple expedient of murdering vagrants and beggars.

Over the next nine months they delivered 16 bodies to Knox.

The police eventually linked them to the disappearances and charged them. Hare testified against Burke and their accomplice, Nell MacDougal, received a 'not-proven' verdict. Burke was hanged at Edinburgh's Grass Market on 28 January 1829. His body was sent for dissection.

See Issei Sagawa p. 154

◄ *LEFT: William Burke, a murderer and body snatcher who was hanged for his crimes.*

THE IRELAND'S EYE MYSTERY (1852)

On Monday, 6 September 1852, William and Maria Kirwan spent the day alone together on a picturesque little island off the Irish coast called Ireland's Eye. When the boatman came back to collect them later that afternoon, William told him that he had not seen his wife for over an hour. In failing light, they searched the small, rocky island and found Maria's body washed up in an inlet. They took the body back to the mainland and Kirwan instructed a local woman to wash it.

The inquest returned a verdict of 'found drowned', but the authorities ordered Maria's body to be exhumed in October that year. In December

▸ *RIGHT: William Hare, William Burke's accomplice, whose evidence sent Burke to his execution.*

Kirwan faced a trial for murder. Despite the fact that there were no witnesses, and the cause of Maria's death could only be surmised, the jury returned a verdict of guilty. The information that Kirwan had kept a mistress was one of the most damning pieces of evidence against him and he was sentenced to death. However, experts believed that Maria had suffered an epileptic fit while in the water, and had drowned, so his sentence was commuted to life. Kirwan spent the next 25 years in Spike Island Prison.
See The Blind Killer p. 139

THE BLIND KILLER (1867)

On 26 December 1867 a blind man named Giles Clift visited the Coulston's Arms in Bristol, where he had discovered his estranged wife was living with his great-nephew, Thomas Farrant. Assisted by his friend Henry Lyons, Clift went upstairs to confront the couple and beat his wife with the leg of a bedstead. Shortly after he had left, the body of Farrant, a man half Clift's age, was found smashed on the cobbled streets below. The only way Farrant's body could have fallen was through a window just 17½ inches by 24 inches.

Clift was charged with murder on the basis that Farrant could not have accidentally have fallen out of such a small window. The jury disagreed and Clift was cleared. The truth may have been that Lyons had helped Clift push Farrant.
See The Joe Elwell Case p. 145

THE PROVIDENCE HOUSE MURDER (1901)

On the morning of 1 June 1901 the body of Rose Harsent was discovered by her father in the kitchen of Providence House in Peasenhall, Suffolk. Someone had tried, unsuccessfully, to burn the body. Her throat had been cut twice and there was a wound in her chest.

Suspicion immediately fell upon William Gardiner, who had been having an affair with Rose for several months. It was the gossip of the village that this Methodist elder, with a pregnant wife and children of his own, had been sleeping with Rose. When it was discovered at the inquest that Rose was heavily pregnant and that she and Gardiner had exchanged notes, it was inevitable that Gardiner would face a trial for her murder.

The evidence was circumstantial, but the trial took place at the beginning of November 1902. After considerable deliberation, the jury told the court that they were unable to agree a verdict. It was therefore decided that Gardiner should face trial once more. This began in January 1903; the same evidence was brought forward, laced with gossip, scandal and innuendo. Again the jury was unable to agree. Gardiner was cleared. It has been speculated that the real murderer was his wife, Georgina.

See Alice Crimmins p. 151

◀ LEFT: Newspaper report of Rose Harsent's murder in 1902.

THE HANSOM CAB MYSTERY (1904)

On 4 June 1904 a wealthy gambler called Francis Young was riding along Broadway, New York, in a hansom cab with his mistress Nan Patterson. A shot rang out and Patterson said 'Look at me Frank. Why did you do it?' When they arrived at the hospital, Young was dead. Ballistics suggested that Young could not have shot himself, yet three juries failed to convict Patterson of the murder and she walked free.

See The Blind Killer p. 139

THE RAILWAY MURDER (1905)

In September 1905 a railway inspector discovered the grisly remains of a woman who had been bound and gagged, then thrown out of a train into Merstham Tunnel in London. The body was identified by Robert Money, who confirmed it was his sister, Mary. Despite investigation, the police could not find the murderer and the case remained unsolved.

On 18 August 1911, police were called to a house in Eastbourne that had been gutted by fire. Inside they found the bodies of one Robert Murray, also known as Mackie, and the children of Florence, who had herself survived a gunshot and managed to get out of the house. It transpired that Murray and Money were the same person, and that whilst he was living with Florence as her husband, he had in fact married Florence's sister, Edith, in secret. His suicide note was found, so Florence had presumably discovered his bigamy and he had set fire to the house.

See The Camden Town Murder p. 141

THE CAMDEN TOWN MURDER (1907)

On 12 September 1907 the body of Camden Town prostitute Emily Dimmock was found by the man with whom she shared a home, Bertram Shaw. Meanwhile another prostitute, Ruby Young, had been asked by her artist lover, Robert Wood, to provide him with an alibi. She told a friend of Wood's request, who in turn contacted the police. Wood eventually faced trial, although the evidence was circumstantial, but he was found not guilty.

See The Murder of Bonny Lee Bakely p. 163

CRIPPEN, HARVEY HAWLEY (1910)

In 1900 Michigan-born Dr Hawley Harvey Crippen came to England. Crippen worked for a patent medicine company and moved into a home with his new wife, actress Cora Turner, whose stage name was Belle Elmore. Belle disappeared in 1910 and Crippen told everyone that she had returned to the US. However, Belle's friends noticed that Ethel le Neve, who soon moved in with Crippen, was wearing the missing woman's clothes. The police began an investigation but found nothing. Police interest obviously alarmed Crippen, though, and he fled to Antwerp with le Neve. There the couple boarded the SS Montrose, bound for Canada.

▶ *RIGHT: Artist Robert Wood, who was arrested and tried for the murder of a prostitute.*

Crippen's flight rekindled police interest and they went to his old house, where they found Belle's body in the cellar.

Le Neve had disguised herself as a boy for the voyage to Canada, but the ship's captain was suspicious of the fact that the couple were openly affectionate. He radioed London – the first time the wireless was used as part of a murder hunt. Chief Inspector Walter Dew boarded a faster ship and was awaiting Crippen when they docked. Crippen and le Neve were sent back to Britain; he was found guilty of murder and hanged on 23 November 1910.

See John George Haigh p. 149

▶ RIGHT: The Crippen case marked the first use of wireless telegraphy in the arrest of criminals.

KISS, BELA (1912)

Hungarian Bela Kiss murdered his wife and her lover in December 1912. He told the neighbours and the authorities that she had run away with her boyfriend. Prior to World War I, Kiss began collecting metal drums, reasoning that petrol would be scarce and he intended to stockpile it. It was around this time that women began disappearing in the Budapest area. In November 1914 Kiss was drafted into the Austro-Hungarian army, but 18 months later went missing, presumed dead. In June 1916 the authorities began looking for stockpiled petrol and when they investigated the drums collected by Kiss, they found the bodies of strangled corpses, preserved in alcohol. They also discovered correspondence from a man called Hoffmann, responding to a lonely heart's advertisement. The police discovered 23 female corpses and the body of Paul Bikari, Kiss's wife's lover.

Assuming Kiss had been killed in the war, the case was closed. In fact, Kiss had switched identity tags with a man named Hoffmann and after the war had joined the French Foreign Legion. The police tried to trace him, but again he disappeared and despite sightings, including a rumour in 1936 that Kiss, or Hoffmann, was working as a janitor in New York, he was never found.

See The Snowtown Murders p. 161

THE GREEN BICYCLE MURDER (1919)

On the morning of 5 July 1919 the body of Bella Wright was discovered beside her bicycle near Long Stretton in Leicestershire. She had been shot in the head. Bella had left her uncle's house and had been seen with a man riding a green bicycle. In February of the following year, a green bicycle was found in a nearby canal and its serial number linked it to a former police officer and teacher, Ronald Light. The police also retrieved a holster and ammunition similar to that used to kill Bella. Light denied any connection, but he was brought before the courts in June 1920. With no motive and Light's admission that he had been mistaken to dispose of the bicycle, his previous good character ensured his acquittal.

See The Providence House Murder p. 140

THE SACCO AND VANZETTI CASE (1920)

On 15 April 1920, in South Braintree, Massachusetts, a robbery led to a double murder. Quite by accident, two Italians, Sacco and Vanzetti, were questioned as they

◄ *LEFT: Crowds stage a demonstration to free Sacco and Vanzetti.*

had a similar vehicle to that used in the robbery. In a highly racist trial, the pair were found guilty of robbery and murder and sentenced to death; they were electrocuted on 23 August 1927. In 1977 their names were cleared by the governor of Massachusetts.

See The Lindbergh Case p. 146

THE JOE ELWELL CASE (1920)

On 11 June 1920, Joe Elwell's housekeeper found her employer slumped in a chair with a bullet wound in his forehead. There was no sign of theft or forced entry to the house and Elwell had last been seen alive six hours previously. He did not own a firearm and only he and his housekeeper had keys to the house. The police made extensive enquiries but no one was ever charged.

See The Hansom Cab Mystery p. 141

THE HALL AND MILLS MURDERS (1922)

On 16 September 1922 a young couple walking along Lover's Lane in New Brunswick, New Jersey, made a horrific discovery. Lying beneath a tree was the body of Reverend Edward Hall; he had been shot through the head. Alongside him was his lover, Eleanor Mills; she had been shot three times in the head and her throat had been cut. Strewn around them were their love letters.

Four years elapsed before a former maid in the Hall household told the police that the minister was intending to elope with Mills. As a result, Hall's wife and her two brothers were charged with the murder. Despite a rather dubious eye-witness coming forward and placing them at the scene, all three were acquitted and the case was never solved.

See The Providence House Murder p. 140

THE CASE OF THE SALMON SANDWICHES (1930)

On 18 October 1930, Sarah Ann Hearn accompanied her neighbours, William and Annie Thomas, on a trip to Bude in Cornwall. She made a supply of salmon sandwiches for the journey. On the way home Annie was taken ill and died a few days later; it transpired that the cause of death was arsenic poisoning. Hearn faked her own suicide, changed her name and moved to Torquay.

Meanwhile, the coroner had exhumed Hearn's sister's body and found that she, too, had died of arsenic poisoning. Hearn was eventually picked up and brought to trial in June 1931; she vehemently denied poisoning anyone and claimed she had not murdered Annie in order to marry William, which had been the suggested motive. The jury acquitted her.

See Christiana Edmunds p. 75

THE LINDBERGH CASE (1932)

On 1 March 1932 the baby son of pioneer aviator Charles Lindbergh was kidnapped from his home in Hopewell, New Jersey. Over the next few weeks, intricate arrangements were made to pay $50,000 in notes and $20,000 in gold bonds as a ransom. The police had no real clues to the kidnapper's identity; all they knew was that he had a German accent. The ransom was paid, but it turned out that the child had already been murdered.

The kidnapper laid low for three years, and in an effort to draw him out, police asked the banks to announce that gold bonds were about to be withdrawn and that they should be cashed immediately. Bruno Hauptmann was apprehended while attempting

◀ *LEFT: The clothes worn by Charles Lindbergh Jr at the time of his kidnapping are shown in court.*

to cash one of the bonds at a garage in New Jersey. He claimed from the outset that he was merely looking after the money for a friend who had recently died in Germany. The only other evidence linking Hauptmann to the crime was that the wood in his attic matched that which had been used to make a ladder to reach to the boy's bedroom. Hauptmann was sent to the electric chair in 1935, still protesting his innocence.

See Arthur and Nisamodeen Hosein p. 203

THE HOOP-LA MURDER (1933)

The trial of Jessie Costello for the murder of her husband – using potassium cyanide, a compound used to burnish kitchen boilers – was described as one of the most astonishing crime farces in American criminal history.

From the moment she was arrested on 17 March 1933, Costello became the darling of the press and the public for her undoubted sex appeal. There was never any chance that she would be found guilty and indeed she was acquitted. But for some time America could not forget her and she made a good living selling her story and posing for photographs. Nonetheless, just 12 months after her acquittal she had run out of money and lived the rest of her life on $65 a month from state aid.

See Adelaide Bartlett p. 287

BALL, JOE (1938)

Joe Ball ran a bar called the Sociable Inn, situated just outside Elmendorf, Texas. In his back yard he kept five alligators in a concrete pool. This was something of a local attraction and Joe always fed the alligators fresh meat. At least two of his wives disappeared, as did a number of barmaids and waitresses. The police followed up these missing persons and interrogated Ball. Ball committed suicide on 24 September 1938.

See Bela Kiss p. 143

THE BLACK DAHLIA (1947)

The naked body of Elizabeth Short was found on waste-ground near Los Angeles on 15 January 1947; her body had virtually been cut in half at the waist and the letters 'BD' had been carved into her thigh. Short, an aspiring film star, had been known as the Black Dahlia. Like many hopefuls, she had been disillusioned by Hollywood and had slipped into prostitution and alcoholism.

There were several false confessions, but no real leads, until a note arrived at a Los Angeles newspaper office, along with a package containing Short's birth certificate, address book and social-security card. The note promised that Short's clothes would be sent in another parcel. The FBI thoroughly checked the documents for fingerprints, but none matched any on their files. The most promising lead they had was an

unnamed army corporal, who told them 'When I get drunk, I get rough with women'. His background and movements were checked, but he was released as the police believed him to be mentally unbalanced. Theories and suspects abounded in the years following the murder, but the murderer of the Black Dahlia was never found.

See The Green Bicycle Murder p. 144

◀ *LEFT: Robert Manley is given a lie detector test over the murder of Elizabeth Short in 1947.*

▶ *RIGHT: 'Acid bath' murderer John George Haigh during his 1949 trial.*

HAIGH, JOHN GEORGE (1949)

In 1949 John George Haigh, who was known to be something of a charmer, became friendly with a wealthy widow named Olive Durand-Deacon. They talked about starting a business together. On 18 February 1949 he took her to Crawley in Sussex to visit his factory. Haigh had made preparations; he had bought an empty 40-gallon drum, rubber gloves and an apron and a considerable quantity of sulphuric acid. Once inside he shot the widow, took her valuables and then put her into the drum, which he then filled with sulphuric acid.

Shortly afterwards, he reported the widow's disappearance to the police. They checked their records and discovered that Haigh had a criminal record, so visited the Crawley factory. Fragments of the widow were found, along with a revolver and traces of blood. Haigh was arrested, but told the police that they could not prove anything without a body; he also admitted to eight other murders, believing that he had disposed of the evidence. Police found an acrylic denture belonging to the widow in the sludge at the bottom of the barrel and Haigh faced a murder trial in July 1949. He claimed that he was insane and that he had drunk his victims' blood. He was found guilty and executed on 10 August 1949.

See Harvey Hawley Crippen p. 142

ADAMS, JOHN BODKIN (1957)

In many respects, the case of Dr Adams is something of a prototype – albeit with a different outcome – for that of the Harold Shipman trial. Adams was brought to trial in Eastbourne in 1957, accused of killing elderly patients in order to benefit from their wills. Adams believed in euthanasia and circumstantially had poisoned scores of old ladies after they had altered their wills in his favour. At the end of a 17-day trial, the jury acquitted Adams. He sued the police and several newspapers, winning considerable damages.

When Adams died in 1983, a pensioner, Sybil Dreda-Owen, extracted £53,000 from his estate. She was later exposed as being an expert in defrauding elderly gentlemen by convincing them to change their wills shortly before their deaths.

See Harold Shipman p. 273

COOKE, ERIC EDGAR (1959–64)

Eric Cooke had served a three-year sentence for arson while he was still a teenager in Australia. In 1959 he stabbed a woman to death during a burglary and in 1963 went on a shooting spree, then broke into several homes and shot or strangled their occupants. He was eventually caught and hung in 1964. John Button was tried for one of the murders Cooke committed. In April 2003 he was formally acquitted and awarded $460,400 damages.

See Peter Dupas p. 211

HANRATTY, JAMES (1961)

On the evening of 22 August 1961, lovers Michael Gregsten and Valerie Storie were parked in a field near Slough, Buckinghamshire. They were approached by a man with a gun and told to drive to a lay-by on the A6. The gunman shot Gregsten and raped Storie, then shot her and

◀ *LEFT: The father of alleged A6 killer James Hanratty protests his son's innocence in 1970.*

made off in the car. Incredibly, Storie survived and, together with another witness who had seen Gregsten's car after the murder, two identikit pictures were created; none resembled Hanratty, but two cartridge cases were found at a London hotel in a room that he had occupied. Hanratty was arrested and claimed he had been in Rhyl on the day of the murder. The jury was unconvinced and found him guilty; he was hanged on 4 April 1962.

See The Murder of Bonny Lee Bakely p. 163

STANIAK, LUCIAN (1964–67)

Lucian Staniak, a Polish serial killer operating between July 1964 and January 1967, was known as the 'Red Spider' because he sent anonymous letters to either newspapers or the police, warning them that he was going to commit murder, written in spidery, red handwriting. His victims were young women who he either strangled or stabbed; after death he raped them, then mutilated their bodies. After investigation, Warsaw police realised the murderer was travelling to the scenes by train.

The arty writing and red paint used suggested an artist, which led the police to Staniak; they found knives and red art paint in his locker. Staniak confessed to 20 murders and was sentenced to death for the six known killings. His sentence was commuted to life and he was sent to an asylum.

See Nikolai Dzhumagaliev p. 236

CRIMMINS, ALICE (1965)

On 14 July 1965, Alice Marie and Eddie Crimmins' father reported his children missing. They were living in New York with their mother, Alice. Later that day Alice Marie's body was found and a few days later Eddie's body was also discovered; they had both been strangled. Nearly two years after the murders, Alice was charged with her daughter's killing and a witness testified at her May 1968 trial that she had been seen with a man carrying a bundle and holding her daughter in her arms. She was found guilty of manslaughter and sentenced to 20 years.

In March 1971 Alice was charged with the murder of her son; again she was found guilty and sentenced to life. The apparent motive was that she feared their father would win a custody battle.

See Susan Barber p. 95

▶ *RIGHT: Alice Crimmins, charged with murder, outside the New York courthouse in 1968.*

HENLEY, ELMER WAYNE AND DAVID BROOKS (1973)

In the period leading up to 8 August 1973, Elmer Wayne Henley and David Brooks lured 27 boys to the home of Dean Allen Corll, for which they were paid $200 per boy. At Corll's house the boys were drugged, subjected to

sexual assaults and mutilated until finally they were either strangled or shot. On 8 August Henley brought a girl to Corll, who turned on his suppliers. Henley drugged them all and tied them to a rack and told Corll that he wouldn't be killed if he raped then shot the girl. Corll didn't and so Henley shot him six times. He then

◀ *LEFT: Police recover a body from the rented boat shed where Elmer Henley led them.*

called the police and showed them where the 27 bodies had been hidden.

In July 1974 he and Brooks were sentenced to six consecutive 99-year jail terms for Corll's murder and their involvement in the killing of the boys.

See Rosemary and Fred West p. 230

CHASE, RICHARD TRENTON (1977)

Richard Trenton Chase, who became known as the 'Sacramento Vampire', began by killing animals and drinking their blood, eating birds alive and injecting himself with rabbit blood. His schizophrenia saw him in and out of mental institutions until 1976, but in January 1977 he went on a four-day murder spree, killing six people and drinking their blood. After the killings, he took various parts of their bodies with him to gnaw on later.

On 26 December 1980 Chase was found dead in his prison cell; he had committed suicide by hoarding three weeks' worth of medication and taking it all in one dose.

See Marc Sappington p. 163

CHANTLER, WANDA (1980)

Wanda Chantler lived with her husband Alan in the Welsh village of Pant Perthog. Although they loved their home, they decided to sell and move to Australia. It was a mistake and they were back in Wales by the late-1970s. The house was now owned by the Hartlands. Wanda wanted the house back and begged them to sell it to her; they told her it was out of the question. Wanda wrote several threatening letters to the Hartlands and on 16 June 1980 she knocked on the Hartlands' door and shot them both.

On 24 October she was committed to Broadmoor indefinitely. Wanda, a Russian by birth, had been held in a Nazi baby farm, and this experience may have resulted in her mental imbalance.

See Florence Iris Wouida Ransome p. 87

JONES, GENENE (1981)

Between May and December 1981, the paediatric department at the Bexar County Hospital in San Antonio, Texas, saw the death of 20 infants. A drug called heparin, a blood-thinning agent, was discovered in one of the victim's bodies. There was a number of internal enquiries and one nurse accused Genene Jones of having killed the children. Speculation linked her to as many as 42 deaths. Jones was sentenced to 99 years on specimen charges.

See Beverly Allitt p. 158

SAGAWA, ISSEI (1981)

In 1981 Issei Sagawa, Japanese by birth, was studying in Paris. Obsessed with tall, blonde women, he focused on one such, Renee Hartvelt, shooting her on 11 June 1981. He claimed he had always wished to show a

woman his love by eating her; this he did to Renee. Two days later he was arrested and confessed. After transfer to Japan he was freed in 1985 and has been featured on the front of a Japanese gourmet magazine.

See Hadden Clark p. 159

◀ *LEFT: Issei Sagawa arrives in Tokyo accused of murdering and consuming parts of a woman.*

THE SHERGAR KIDNAPPING (1983)

On 8 February 1983, at the Ballymany Stud in County Kildare, an armed gang kidnapped the Derby-winning horse Shergar. There were as many as eight kidnappers and Shergar was put into a box and driven away. The kidnappers had said they wanted £2 million for his return. The horse was valued at as much as £100 million and was owned by a syndicate that included the Aga Khan amongst its members. There was no further contact from the kidnappers, but in 1992 a former IRA man, Shaun O'Callaghan, claimed that he and Kevin Mallon, a racing expert, had planned the kidnapping. He explained that the horse had become out of control and they had killed it, digging a pit to bury it in the mountains near Ballinamore in County Leitrim.

See The Lindbergh Case p. 146

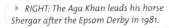
▶ *RIGHT: The Aga Khan leads his horse Shergar after the Epsom Derby in 1981.*

HARVEY, DONALD (1983–86)

Between April 1983 and September 1986 Donald Harvey, the self-professed 'Angel of Death', committed innumerable murders of patients at the Drake Memorial Hospital in Cincinnati, Ohio. On 11 August 1987, after extensive enquiries and a mountain of evidence, including poisons and a diary, Harvey admitted to 33 murders over the previous 17 years. Ultimately he confessed to 70. On 18 August he pleaded guilty to 24 counts of murder, four of attempted murder and one count of assault. He was given four life sentences. In Kentucky in September he was given a further eight life sentences for 12 murders and in February 1988, three life sentences for three murders and three attempted murders. Harvey's first scheduled parole hearing is in 2047, by which time he will be 95.

See Efren Saldivar p. 162

THE HILDA MURRELL CASE (1984)

On 24 March 1984 the half-naked body of Hilda Murrell was found in a copse near Shrewsbury. The probable cause of death was hypothermia. As the police investigated who was responsible for her death, they found evidence that linked Murrell with the nuclear-power industry and British intelligence. She had confided to friends that she thought she was under surveillance. It appears that MI5 had used freelance operatives to search Murrell's home, believing she was on the verge of exposing serious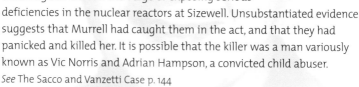
deficiencies in the nuclear reactors at Sizewell. Unsubstantiated evidence suggests that Murrell had caught them in the act, and that they had panicked and killed her. It is possible that the killer was a man variously known as Vic Norris and Adrian Hampson, a convicted child abuser.
See The Sacco and Vanzetti Case p. 144

THE SUZY LAMPLUGH CASE (1986)

Estate agent Suzy Lamplugh disappeared while meeting an unknown client called Mr Kipper in Fulham, south-west London in 1986. Her body has never been found. Police are currently studying claims that her remains may be buried at the former house of the mother of the man who is suspected of the murder – a convicted rapist and murderer called John Cannan who is serving life for the killing of Bristol woman Shirley Banks.

In December 2002, newspaper reports claimed that in letters written by Cannan he mentioned that he had blood stains on his coat when laying a patio at his mother's home in Solihull a year after Suzy went missing. In January 2003, Cannan went to the High Court to secure 'free and unimpeded' access to his legal advisors. He claimed the governor of

▶ RIGHT: *Missing estate agent Suzy Lamplugh, who vanished in July 1986.*

the maximum-security prison in Yorkshire where he is serving his sentence has violated his human rights, by preventing him from exchanging legal documents with his solicitors. His case was dismissed, but he may appeal.

At present, the Crown Prosecution Service has been advised there is insufficient evidence to bring charges against Cannan. His legal team insist he is being wrongly targeted by police.

See The Rachel Nickell Case p. 159

CONSTANZO, ADOLFO DE JESUS (1989)

Adolfo de Jesus Constanzo was a Cuban-American bisexual cult leader who managed a drug-smuggling ring in Matamoros, Mexico. He and his girlfriend, Sara Aldrete, disposed of their drug-smuggling rivals by murdering them in a sacrificial ritual and making magical necklaces from their bones. They drew attention to themselves when they sacrificed American Mark Kilroy, prompting the authorities to search their ranch, where innumerable corpses were discovered. Constanzo committed suicide on 6 May 1989, but his schizophrenic priestess is in an asylum.

See Nicolas Claux p. 161

SEDA, HERIBERTO (1990)

An uncaught serial killer terrorised the Bay Area in the 1960s and 1970s, but a bizarre and cryptic letter arrived at East New York's 17th Precinct on 17 November 1989, claiming to be from the Zodiac killer himself, predicting a new wave of murders.

In March 1990, the killings began; just as the letter had predicted and it soon became clear that the police were dealing with a copy-cat murderer. The killer was Heriberto 'Eddie' Seda and he revelled in the press coverage he was receiving. After a siege, he turned himself over to the police and in June 1998 he was sentenced to 236 years. His tally was three dead and eight attempted murders.

See The Zodiac Killer p. 302

ALLITT, BEVERLY (1991)

Allitt suffered from Munchausen's syndrome by proxy, a disorder that creates an uncontrollable urge to draw attention, and in Allitt's case by causing injury to babies in her care. A career as a nurse provided her with that very opportunity. She worked in the children's ward at the Grantham and Kesteven Hospital in Lincolnshire and over 58 days in 1991

she killed four children and injured a further nine. The bodies contained high potassium readings; rotas were checked and Allitt's name emerged. On 22 April 1991 she was formally charged, but did not stand trial until 15 February 1993. The jury found her guilty of murder and attempted murder on 11 May 1993 and she was sentenced to 13 life sentences.

See Efren Saldivar p. 162

◀ *LEFT: Child-killer Beverly Allitt arrives at court in 1991.*

THE RACHEL NICKELL CASE (1992)

On 13 July 1992 the body of Rachel Nickell was found on Wimbledon Common. She had been stabbed 49 times in just three minutes, in full sight of her two-year-old son. The police released a psychological profile of the man who may have perpetrated the crime, and were approached by a woman called Julie Pine, who had received letters from her pen-friend, a man called Colin Stagg. She and the police both thought there was a connection between Stagg and the killing. The police used an undercover agent calling herself Lizzie James and, over the course of five months, she attempted to obtain a confession from him. It was a classic example of entrapment; Stagg and Lizzie met a total of four times and they discussed Rachel's murder, which Stagg incorrectly described. Nonetheless, the police amassed 700 pages of transcripts and intended to take Stagg to court. A judge ruled that the evidence was inadmissible and that the undercover operation had proved nothing. However, Stagg's name has been forever linked to the Nickell murder and the police have never been able to establish who really carried out the killing on Wimbledon Common.

See The Suzy Lamplugh Case p. 156

CLARK, HADDEN (1992)

In 1992 Hadden Clark was arrested for the murder of 23-year-old Laurie Houghteling in Bethesda, Maryland. Clark was a transvestite and a cannibal, believing that by killing and eating women, he would become one himself. Clark would later admit to the murder of at least 12 women, including a six-year-old, Michele Dorr. His first trial in Maryland gained him 30 years imprisonment; a second, in 1999, a full life sentence. Clark continues to make prison confessions to a fellow inmate, whom he believes to be Jesus, and has often taken the police to try and find the shallow graves of his victims. Each time, he is dressed as a woman and is in his alter-ego of Kristen.

See Issei Sagawa p. 154

SIMPSON, O. J. (1994)

Orenthal James Simpson was one of the most famous running-backs in American football history. He retired from the game in 1979 and married Nicole Brown, his second wife, in 1985. It was a rocky marriage and Nicole filed for divorce in 1992. There had been incidents in the marriage that suggested that Simpson may have been a violent man.

On 12 June 1994 Nicole and a restaurant employee, Ronald Goldman, were found brutally murdered and five days later millions of television viewers watched a long, slow police chase that finally ended with the arrest of a suicidal Simpson. Although he claimed to be innocent, he was charged with the murder of Nicole and Goldman.

The year-long trial was televised, with the witnesses and court officials becoming household names in what was dubbed the 'Trial of the Century'.

On 4 October 1995, Simpson was acquitted, but in the following civil trial Simpson was found liable for the deaths of Brown and Goldman. In February 1997 the jury ordered Simpson to pay $33.5 million in compensatory and punitive damages. Evidence is slowly emerging about Goldman's ties to organised crime and a Colombian drug cartel.

See The Murder of Bonny Lee Bakely p. 163

BK 4013970 06-17-94
LOS ANGELES POLICE: JAIL DIV

◀ *LEFT: A Los Angeles Police Department photograph of O. J. Simpson from 1994.*

CLAUX, NICOLAS (1994)

On 15 November, 1994, the Parisian police arrested Nicolas Claux, a 22-year-old occultist, in connection with what appeared to be a series of homophobic shootings. When the police searched his apartment, they found skeletal remains, blood bags and jars filled with human ashes. Claux described his habit of eating strips of human flesh at the mortuary in which he worked. He admitted to drinking human blood, mixed with human ashes that he stole from the hospital. He also admitted to grave-robbing – the source of the bones and the ashes.

Based on his inability to see right from wrong, he was sentenced to just 12 years, but was released on 22 March 2002. He now makes his living as an artist, displaying his work in graveyards in Paris.
See Marc Sappington p. 163

THE SNOWTOWN MURDERS (1994–97)

The residents of the small South Australian town of Snowtown never suspected that in the old bank just across the road from the pub was a terrible secret – six barrels full of human remains. There were 10 victims allegedly killed for little more than their pension money. Police who broke into the locked bank vault found putrid human remains, handcuffs and an electric-shock machine. The victims had either been strangled or asphyxiated. Several of them were found with gags stuffed in their mouths, others had ropes around their necks; feet and limbs had been amputated and there were burns on some of the bodies. The killings were allegedly carried out as part of a macabre social-security fraud.

John Justin Bunting, Mark Ray Haydon, James Vlassakis and Robert Joe Wagner were charged with between four and 10 of the murders. Bunting, Haydon and Wagner were also charged with the murder of Thomas Trevilyan, whose body was found hanging from a tree in

Adelaide in 1997. In addition, Haydon and Bunting were also charged with the murder of Clinton Trezise, who was found in a shallow grave at Lower Light, north of Adelaide, in 1994. Committal proceedings continue. *See* Bela Kiss p. 143

SALDIVAR, EFREN (1997)

Efren Saldivar was a nurse at the Glendale Adventist Medical Center in Southern California. In 1997, a series of suspicious deaths broke out there and Salvidar came under scrutiny. When Saldivar was given a polygraph test, he admitted he had been injecting patients since he was 19 years old. He was asked about 500 patients and confessed to having killed between 40 and 50. Over 1,000 patients had died during Saldivar's shifts over the previous eight years. It was impossible to exhume the bodies and many had been cremated. In March 2002 he pleaded guilty to six counts of murder and on 17 April he was given six consecutive life sentences, with an additional 15 years.
See Donald Harvey p. 155

PANDY, ANDRAS (1997)

On 20 October 1997 Belgian authorities charged Andras Pandy with the murder of two of his ex-wives and four of his children. Large pieces of human flesh had been found in his fridges and he may have been responsible for as many as 14 killings.

Pandy, a Hungarian by birth, had moved to Belgium in 1957 and was a former Protestant pastor. In a joint operation between Belgian and Hungarian police, following child-abuse accusations against Pandy, his two homes were searched. A series of interconnecting cellars were found in the homes where Pandy and his daughter Agnes carried out the murders and the disposal of the corpses.

Belgian police believe that the Pandy in custody may actually be the younger brother of the real Andras Pandy, who may have died in 1956. Pandy is also believed to have adopted an unspecified number of Romanian orphans who are also missing. On 8 March 2002, a jury convicted Pandy of six counts of murder. He was also convicted of raping his daughters. Agnes Pandy was convicted of five counts of murder, and of the attempted murder of her stepsister Timea. Now 44, Agnes Pandy was sentenced to 21 years in prison.

See Rosemary and Fred West p. 230

SAPPINGTON, MARC (2001)

On 16 March 2001 Marc Sappington answered the voices in his head, which were telling him to harvest human flesh and blood. He killed four people – two in one day – and tried to suck their blood. This practice earned him the nickname the 'Kansas City Vampire'.

Sappington's mother discovered a body in their basement and called the police, who soon tracked down Sappington. He jumped into a car, however, and led police on a brief chase. Sappington will spend the rest of his life in an asylum.

See Nicolas Claux p. 161

THE MURDER OF BONNY LEE BAKLEY (2001)

On the evening of 4 May 2001, actor Robert Blake and Bonny, his wife of only a few months, ate at Vitello's Restaurant in Studio City, a suburb of Los Angeles. After the meal, they went back to the car, but Blake had forgotten something and returned to the restaurant. When he came back he found Bonny slumped over in the passenger seat, unconscious and bleeding profusely from a wound to her head. Blake faces charges of conspiracy to murder.

See O. J. Simpson p. 160

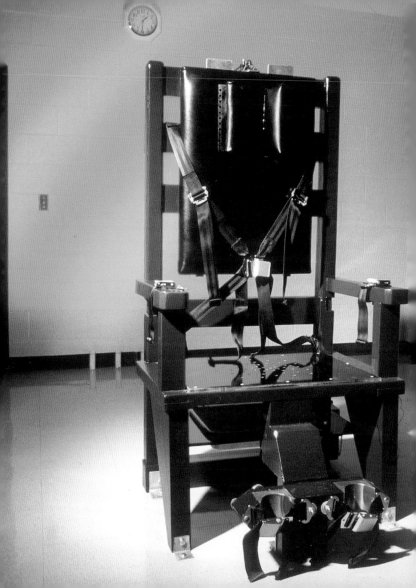

INVESTIGATIVE TECHNIQUES & PUNISHMENT

INVESTIGATIVE TECHNIQUES

1890's	First fingerprint investigations
1963	Firearms first used
1970's	Trace evidence analysis
1970's	Psychological profiling
1980's	DNA testing became acceptable
1990	Autopsy reports
2001	Sarah Payne Case – forensic analysis lead to conviction of Roy Whiting
2002	Jill Dando Case – firearms testing led to the conviction of Barry George

PUNISHMENT

16th C.	Burning used during witch trials
1541	First recorded use of a guillotine
1781	last instance of execution by drawing and quartering
1792	20,000 terrorists executed by guillotine
1820	Last beheading in Britain
1870	Drawing and quartering was officially abolished in Britain
1890	Electrocution was first used in US
1924	Gas was first used as an execution method in the US
1964	Last two cases of hangings in Britain
1972	US Supreme Court ruled to ban the death penalty
1976	US re-adopts the death penalty
1982	Lethal injection was first used in US
1996	Latest case of death by firing squad in US
1999	Latest case of death by gas in US
2003	Four thousand convicted offenders on death row in the US

THE CASE OF NORA TIERNEY (1949)

Nora Tierney was convicted of murder in October 1949 for the killing of three-year-old Marion Ward. Investigators discovered samples of Marion's garments under Nora's fingernails, and a plaster cast made of a foot imprint at the scene of the crime matched one of her shoes. These discoveries came after a police search involving hundreds of people, following the discovery of Marion's body near her home in St John's Wood.
See Fibre Analysis p. 174

LIE DETECTORS AND POLYGRAPHS

A suspect subjected to these tests has a strap around the abdomen and chest to record the breathing rate, another strap around the bicep to measure blood pressure and electrodes on the fingertips to measure perspiration. The subject is then asked baseline questions, to which the answers are already known, such as their age or gender. These measurements are then used to compare with the suspect's reactions to other, more penetrating questions regarding a particular crime.

The technique is not 100 per cent reliable, although the new computerised polygraphs are considerably more accurate. Accomplished liars, or those who can control their stress levels, are able to trick the test.

Under normal circumstances, the tests are only admissible if the judge agrees. New developments include using a voice analyser and a brainwave monitor to back up the test.
See Roland McDonald p. 45

◀ *LEFT: A lie detector operator performing a test on a suspect.*

▶ *RIGHT: A Scientist extracts DNA from crime scene samples at the Forensic Science Service, London.*

DNA TESTING

In 1985, British researcher Alec Jeffreys discovered that with the exception of identical twins, each human being has unique DNA. DNA profiling allows the scientist to separate an individual's unique fragments from those that are common in all. DNA is found in white blood cells, which can be taken from hair follicles, skin, blood, saliva and semen.

DNA tests were used in solving the Green River murders. Small amounts of DNA from the killer were found during the autopsies in the early 1980s and in 1987 a saliva sample was taken from Gary Ridgway. By 2001, advances in DNA technology allowed scientists to identify the source of semen taken from the autopsy and these were compared to the DNA in Ridgway's saliva. The DNA matched and, acknowledging the improbability of Ridgway having an identical twin, he was convicted of the rapes and murders.

As DNA technology has improved, researchers have been able to narrow down matches from several thousand people to an individual. DNA can be left at the murder scene accidentally by the perpetrator in the form of hair or flakes of skin. As long as the sample is immediately tested or deep frozen, even the smallest trace of skin cells can be used.

See Peter Dupas p. 211

BRAIN FINGERPRINTING

Brain-fingerprint testing has proved to be accurate in over 170 tests, which actually included criminal cases. It determines whether information is present or absent in the brain and is able to identify, by measuring brainwaves, the recognition or non-recognition of aspects of a crime. A suspect can be tested for knowledge that only the perpetrator would know. It can place someone at the crime scene, or prove that they were not there.

In pre-court tests, the subject can be asked questions about the crime without the danger of them having knowledge of it through court proceedings. The tests can also be used for convicted criminals, as even knowledge that they have picked up from the trial or press coverage can be distinguished from their own knowledge.

See Lie Detectors and Polygraphs p. 166

AUTOPSIES

In New York alone it has been estimated that there are around 8,000 autopsies, or post-mortems, each year. In the case of a suspicious death, a minute dissection and examination of the body is essential in the hunt for evidence. In effect, the first function of an autopsy is to establish the cause of death. Once this has been done, trace elements are collected from the body and then the surgeon begins to dissect the corpse itself, exposing all the internal organs. X-rays of injuries are taken in order to identify trajectory paths of bullets or knife wounds. Blood samples are taken. The organs, including the brain, are examined and weighed. By the end of the process the surgeon should be able to provide investigators with a precise cause and time of death, an indication of whether the body had been moved and, once various tests have been returned, the probable age, whether poisons or drugs were in the system and information that could lead to the identification of an unknown corpse.

The autopsy results should provide vital evidence for a future prosecution, perhaps linking a suspect to the corpse by a variety of means, such as gunshot residue, trace elements or sexual assault.

See Serology p. 169

SEROLOGY

Serology is the study of serums, derived from blood, sweat, saliva, semen or faeces. The minute traces of serum can be analysed, and scientists know how bodies and blood behave in certain circumstances. In the case of a wound that may or may not lead to a death, the blood will spray in particular directions and specific distances according to the atmospheric pressure, humidity or temperature. Within the blood itself, there are a number of standardised groups based on the red blood cells. Types A and O are the most common and AB is the most rare. An identification of the type of blood, particularly if it is not the blood of a victim, can be most telling and may narrow down the search for the perpetrator.

Blood typing now also includes the different types of enzymes and proteins. Again, in order to ensure that there is no cross-contamination between the investigators and the blood traces, extreme measures are taken to ensure that the evidence is not corrupted. In the event that attempts have been made to clean away blood traces at a scene, the use of Luminol can pinpoint where the blood traces can be found and then samples can be taken for further analysis.

See Luminol p. 170

▶ *RIGHT: A murder weapon is tested for the victim's blood group.*

LUMINOL

Luminol is a chemical that reacts with haemoglobin and can detect blood at one part per million. It glows greenish-blue when it comes into contact with blood. Scene-of-crime investigators spray the chemical over a wide area, in as close to near-darkness as possible. When a photograph is taken of the area, the camera's flash will pick up the glow.

Luminol does react to some metals, cleaning products and paints, but

the reaction is different and the glow fades quicker compared to blood. Once the blood has been identified it can then be tested to see whether it is human. The glowing areas can also show investigators whether a body had been dragged across a surface, or the direction in which the victim was shot, through blood spatters.

See Serology p. 169

TRACE-EVIDENCE ANALYSIS

Since the human body is constantly shedding hair, skin or fragments of fingernail, a suspect may inadvertently leave some of this trace evidence behind at the crime scene. Clearly, blood will provide the opportunity for DNA analysis and for blood-typing. Saliva, which can also be found on cigarettes, envelopes or glasses and cups, will yield DNA. Sperm again provides DNA and, since it remains alive for a short period of time, can also help indicate when the attack was carried out. Fingernails on each person have unique patterns and since the mid-1970s, individual matches have been made and used as evidence in court. Hair roots offer DNA and they can also show whether a struggle took place at the crime scene. Skin cells, perhaps left underneath the fingernails of a victim, can again be linked through DNA to the perpetrator.

Collectively, hair strands, dirt particles, glass fragments, fibres from clothing and paint smears are known as 'mute witnesses'. They are microscopic remnants of a person or an object that was present at the crime scene. Unless the perpetrator takes the ultimate step of wearing a full body suit, it is almost certain that something of them will be left behind.

See DNA Testing p. 167

◀ *LEFT: These cells, found on the clothing of a burglar, could help to convict him.*

HAIR AND DUST ANALYSIS

Human hair at a murder or crime scene can tell much about the victim or the perpetrator. Its presence suggests contact between the victim and a suspect. Analysis of the hair itself allows the scientist to identify racial differences, the presence of poison or dyes, and of course the roots may yield DNA.

Dust found at a crime scene can be almost as unique as DNA. Microscopic fragments of clothing fibres, pollen, house dust or building dust can suggest where a crime may have been committed, or can help indicate the normal surroundings of a suspect. The assortment of trace materials, such as hair, fibre, insect scales and pollen, make each building's dust unique. Dust related to work or a particular industry may also prove useful.

See Trace-Evidence Analysis p. 171

PSYCHOLOGICAL PROFILING

In the 1950s, psychologists began theorising that certain criminals had similar behavioural patterns and personalities. The FBI began using this kind of profiling extensively in the 1970s and profilers began to look for unique details that could indicate the perpetrator's background, experience or motivations. The profile can also suggest the age, lifestyle, habits and employment of the perpetrator, along with gender, race, physical size and marital status.

Profiling can be very specific and there is now a national computer database in the US that can be used to cross-reference and connect similar crimes across the country. The profiler can determine whether certain behaviours link crimes together. In the US there are around 30 professional criminal profilers, who concentrate on the study of the characteristics of some of the most violent and persistent criminals in the country. Although psychological profiling has its detractors, who suggest that more traditional forms of investigative techniques reap greater benefits, profiling helps to narrow the hunt.

In recent years, profilers have been used in many of the biggest cases, helping investigators to recognise patterns in the behaviour of a perpetrator and match these to potential suspects. In most major crimes, in both the US and UK, profilers are integral to the team.

See Kenneth Bianchi and Angelo Buono p. 267

TOXICOLOGY

Toxicology may be an integral part of an autopsy, as it is the series of chemical tests that aim to detect the substances that an individual has ingested prior to death. A toxicology test may be able to identify the precise type of poison used to kill a victim, identifying the differences in the condition of the body as a result of the poisoning and, perhaps, the discovery of minute traces of the poison itself. Every poison has a different series of chemical reactions with the body and affects particular organs in different ways. More common forms of toxicology tests include the presence of alcohol, prescription drugs, soft and hard illegal drugs and the presence of lead in the body or its organs.

See Autopsies p. 168

FORENSIC ENTOMOLOGY

A dead body will inevitably attract flies and maggots. Forensic entomology examines the presence of insects and in doing so the scientist can determine the victim's time of death or how long the body has been in a particular place. Integral to the investigation is assessment of how far into their lifecycle particular insects have developed. Blow flies, for example, lay eggs within 48 hours of death; these eggs becoming larvae between 16 and 25 hours. The larvae become pupae within six to 12 days; this all, of course, depends on the ambient temperature. 'Foreign' insects to a particular area indicate that the body has been moved. The presence of beetles that eat bones will again indicate how long the body has been in situ.

See Autopsies p. 168

FIBRE ANALYSIS

Minute fibre analysis can link a suspect to a particular crime scene, either where they have left traceable fibres, or when they have carried fibres away from the scene. In 1982 Kristen Harrison was found raped and strangled in Ohio; there were orange fibres in her hair. Scientists surmised they were carpet fibres. Sometime later another woman was abducted and held prisoner; she was tortured but escaped and she had the same orange fibres in her hair. They were traced to a manufacturer and only 74 yards had been sold in the Ohio area, allowing the police to arrest rapist and murderer Robert Buel.

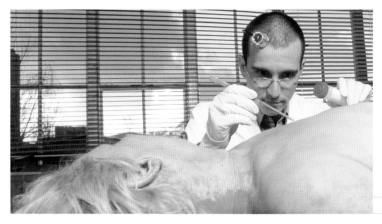

▶ *RIGHT: Detectives study fingerprints displayed on a Live Scan fingerprint system.*

Fibres can be examined to see if they are natural or manufactured and matched to see if they come from carpets, furniture, blankets, clothing or even wigs.
See The Sarah Payne Case p. 178

FINGERPRINTS AND OTHER IMPRESSIONS

The multiple murderer Richard Ramirez was finally betrayed by his fingerprints. This area of investigation began to develop in Britain in the late-1890s. One of the first times it was used was in the case of a murder in Deptford in 1905. The Stratton brothers left just one thumbprint at the scene, condemning them to be hanged.

Each fingerprint is unique, with its own mixture of arches or ridges, oval formations and loops. A perpetrator could leave visible prints, perhaps in ink or blood, latent prints, which can later be recovered, or prints left on soft surfaces. Experienced fingerprint specialists can retrieve fingerprints and then compare them to automated fingerprint identification systems housed on computers. The process may take days.

Other prints may be left at a scene, as in the case of the murder of Juana Gillette, who according to her husband had died suddenly. Investigators found a plastic bag and by turning it inside out, there was a discernable impression of the dead woman's face. In this case her husband, who had suffocated her, was undone by a nose print. Ear prints are now also used, as are footprint impressions.
See Richard Cottingham p. 268

◀ *LEFT: German forensic entomologist Mark Benecke at work.*

FIREARMS TESTING

The science of firearms testing or interpretation allows the scientist to compare bullets and match them to a specific firearm. It can also estimate how far the bullet travelled before it hit its target. Above all, it can detect gunpowder residue around the wounds of a victim and on the person who used the gun. By using an electron microscope, tiny particles of the gunshot residue can be traced to clothing and to skin, even if the clothing has been washed or a considerable time has elapsed since the event.

In the case of the assassination of President Kennedy, it was possible to show that the shots had come from behind by tracing the trajectory of the bullets. In modern analysis, a computerised simulation can now show the trajectory of bullets and map precisely from where the weapon was fired.

Each bullet fired from a specific gun has unique grooves and marks made on it whilst it travels down the rifled barrel. By firing a test shot with the weapon, analysts are able to positively state whether a particular bullet was fired by a particular gun.

See The Jill Dando Case p. 178

FORENSIC HANDWRITING

Specialists who examine handwriting fall into two main categories. Forensic document examiners compare handwriting samples and make an assessment as to whether they were written by the same person. Graphologists look at particular aspects of the handwriting and relate these to particular personality traits, enabling the investigators to build up a profile of the suspect.

One of the most famous cases cracked by handwriting analysis was the Lindbergh kidnapping. Hauptmann had distinctive handwriting and formation of letters. His ransom demands were carefully examined and compared to samples of his writing after his arrest and the two matched.

Handwriting analysis can also identify the speed of the writing by examining the beginning and end of each word.

See David Berkowitz p.263

PRINT-LIFTING

The first 'super-glue' was introduced in the 1970s as a fast-bonding adhesive. Since then, it has been used by doctors instead of stitches to close wounds.

A further, unintended use of the glue has been discovered to lift 'impossible' prints on plastic bags, car windows and on bodies. The glue contains a chemical called cyanoacrylate, which is attracted to amino acids, fats or proteins that can be left on surfaces by human touch. The glue is heated in a metal container and the vapour produced attaches itself to the human residue and forms a hard coating.

The coated prints can then be removed, dyed to make them visible and then compared to known prints on a database. The technique can be used for small objects such as bullet casings, as well as bodies, telephones and other surfaces that are not ideal for conventional print identification.

See Fingerprints and Other Impressions p. 175

CRIME-SCENE INVESTIGATION

Under normal circumstances, the first police to arrive at a crime scene are the uniformed officers. A decision will quickly be made as to whether specialists need to be called in. Whatever the crime, there will be evidence to collect from the scene, which may require the services of specialists. Once the crime scene has been secured, a minute search begins to see whether the perpetrator has left any traces. There are

◁ *LEFT: A police van undergoes investigation following an attempted hijack.*

various crime-scene kits that are used to collect latent fingerprints or trace evidence. Fingerprinting kits may be required, as may casting kits, in the case of footprints or vehicle tyre prints.

At the scene of crime, laser pointers are often used to track the trajectory of a bullet that may be lodged in furniture or the victim. With the use of angle-finders, the precise location where the shot was fired can be discovered. The evidence collected at the scene of the crime is correctly labelled and then despatched to a laboratory for processing. One of the major hazards in investigating a crime scene is the danger of the police themselves contaminating the scene inadvertently; protective clothing, therefore, is always worn.

See Luminol p. 170

THE JILL DANDO CASE (1999)

On 26 April 1999, Jill Dando, a 37-year-old TV presenter, was shot dead on the doorstep of her home in Fulham, London. Forensic science discovered a particle of gunpowder only 11 microns in size. The tiny particle was found on a coat belonging to the suspect. In the trial, an expert explained that when a gun is fired, minute traces of the discharge residue are found on the body or clothes of the shooter. The particle could have been produced by the type of cartridge used in the murder; the particle was discovered over a year after the coat came into police hands. One of the objections was the possibility of cross-contamination, in other words, could the particle have found its way onto the coat by being in proximity to other evidence? The experts described the extreme operating conditions to eliminate this situation.

▶ *RIGHT: CCTV footage shows TV presenter Jill Dando in a shop, 40 minutes before her death.*

The minute particle helped to convict Barry George; in December 2002 his appeal request was turned down.

See Firearms Testing p. 176

THE SARAH PAYNE CASE (2000)

On 1 July 2000, eight-year-old Sarah Payne went missing in Kingston Gorse, Sussex. A local man on the sex offenders' register soon became the prime suspect. Over 500 items were submitted for forensic analysis; more than 20 experts in the fields of entomology, pathology, geology, archaeology, and environmental profiling were deployed after Sarah's body was found on 17 July.

The first breakthrough was a link between Sarah's shoe and the suspect's sweatshirt; then fibres from his van were found in her hair and her DNA was found on his clothing. The police had seized the suspect's van, where they found the sweatshirt, a pair of socks, a shirt, a pair of curtains and a petrol receipt that placed the suspect near where Sarah's body had been found. Sarah's shoe had trapped 350 fibres on the Velcro fastener and some of these matched the sweatshirt. On the sweatshirt one of the 40 hairs matched Sarah's DNA profile. A single multi-coloured cotton fibre on the shoe was found to match the curtains.

In December 2001 Roy Whiting was found guilty and

◀ *LEFT: Eight-year-old Sarah Payne, who was murdered in 2000.*

sentenced to life imprisonment, despite objections to some of the forensic evidence. The trial judge, Richard Curtis, recommended that the life term should mean life.

See Fibre Analysis p. 174

GUILLOTINE

Although this method of decapitation is named after the Frenchman Dr Joseph Ignace Guillotin and is usually associated with French capital punishment, it was invented and used in Halifax, Yorkshire, between 1286 and 1650. The first recorded use of the guillotine-like device was the execution of Richard Bentley on 20 March 1541.

The French version of the machine was originally called the Louisette, designed to quickly and efficiently despatch the growing number of aristocrats who had been rounded up and denounced during the French Revolution. The condemned individual would lie on a bench with their head secured between two sliding wooden planks and at the signal, the immense blade would travel down grooves and severe the head. The head would fall into what was ghoulishly named a 'family picnic basket'. The first victim of the French contraption was Nicholas-Jacque Pelletier; it was a complete success. Later, it would be variously called the 'People's Avenger' or the 'National Razor'.

After the storming of the Tuilleries Palace on 10 August 1792, which heralded the start of the Reign of Terror in France, over 20,000 'enemies of the state'

◀ LEFT: *The guillotine – named after Dr Guillotin, who suggested it be used for public executions.*

▶ RIGHT: *This 1684 design for a playing card shows 'Hanging Protestants in ye West'.*

Hanging Protestants in ye West.

would meet their end from the Yorkshire invention. Officially, it remains France's method of execution.

See Beheading p. 187

HANGING

For centuries the sight of a criminal dangling at the end of a rope, dying from slow strangulation, was popular entertainment in many countries around the world. It was a cheap means of execution: a tree with a convenient bough, a wooden beam protruding from a dwelling or a purpose-built scaffold all afforded the means by which the criminal could be despatched. When John Smith was hanged at Tyburn on 12 December 1702, he was granted a reprieve and cut down, but only after he had been left hanging for a full seven minutes.

The last two men to be hanged in Britain were murderers Peter Allen and Gwynne Evans, on 13 August 1964; the last woman was Ruth Ellis on 13 July 1955; by this time such executions were carried out within prison walls and were no longer public entertainment.

In the US there have only been three hangings since 1977, as the method of execution has largely been replaced by electrocution. Three states retain the hanging option: Delaware, New Hampshire and Washington. As in the latter years in Britain, the 'drop' is based on the condemned person's weight, enough to deliver sufficient force to break the neck. Death is achieved by the dislocation of the third and fourth cervical vertebrae.

See Ruth Ellis p. 90

FIRING SQUAD

The firing squad was a fate usually reserved for military deserters or spies, with the firing squad itself made up of trained marksmen. In the US, three states officially authorise the use of the firing squad: Idaho, Oklahoma and Utah. The most recent examples of death by this method include Gary Gilmore (1977) and John Albert Taylor (1996).

A five-person firing squad (police officers) are selected and armed with rifles, positioned some 6 m (20 ft) away from the condemned person, who has been strapped into a specially designed chair. A Velcro circle is placed over their heart. The firing squad takes up position behind a wall and fires a volley on order through ports (holes) in the wall. One of the squad has been given a blank cartridge, so that each man can take comfort that he may not have fired the fatal shot. If the condemned is not despatched by the volley, then the officer in charge delivers a pistol shot to the head.

Alternatives to the firing squad – such as the method used in China – is a single executioner who fires at very short range into the back of the condemned man's head. Other firing-squad numbers may vary from three to six shooters.

See Gary Gilmore p. 233

DRAWING AND QUARTERING

While the rope or the axe was reserved for lesser mortals, the ultimate execution method was only meted out on those who had committed high treason. Those who had plotted against the king or the country could expect no mercy in a punishment that amounted to public butchery – drawing and quartering.

> ▶ RIGHT: *The unfortunate regicides, executed in 1660, were hung, drawn and quartered.*

In effect, this meant the criminal would be partially hung, taken down, then disembowelled (with the intestines being burned before the miscreant) and then decapitated by a blow with an axe. After this, the body would then be quartered – parts of the body were sent to the four corners of the kingdom as a stark warning of the fate for others who considered high treason.

In Britain, the height of this method of dealing with treasonable characters came after the failure of the Monmouth Rebellion (1685), when over 330 rebels in the West Country were dispatched in this manner. One of the last instances of this form of execution took place in 1781, when Francis Henry de la Monte was found guilty of passing British shipping orders to the French. It was officially abolished in 1870.

See Hanging p.181

LETHAL INJECTION

Lethal injection was first considered in the US in 1888, but it was not until 1977 that the first state, Oklahoma, adopted the method. The first use of the lethal injection took place in Texas in 1982, with the execution of Charlie Brooks.

Lethal injection actually involves three different drugs. The first is sodium thiopental (or sodium pentothal), which renders the condemned person unconscious. The second is then delivered, pancuronium bromide, a muscle relaxant that effectively paralyses the diaphragm and lungs. Finally, potassium chloride is used, which induces cardiac arrest. Before the intravenous lines are inserted, a sedative may well be given to the condemned. Two intravenous lines are usually put in; the second as a back up should there be a blockage in the first line.

Currently, 18 US states and the federal government can authorise the use of lethal injection as the sole means of execution. Some 19 other states use lethal injection as an execution alternative. Since 1976, 81 per cent of US executions have been carried out by lethal injection. Recently, questions have been raised about its efficiency.

See John Wayne Gacy Jr p. 269

GAS

Nevada was the first US state to adopt and use gas as an execution method, in 1924. The most recent execution in this way occurred in Arizona in 1999.

◄ *LEFT: Jack Sullivan, a 23 year old murderer cheerfully awaits death in a lethal gas chamber.*

An airtight chamber is used, in which a chair with restraints is placed. The condemned person is strapped into the chair (chest, arms, waist and ankles) and a hood is placed over the head. Three keys are required to trigger the mechanism, which causes cyanide pellets to be released from a container under the chair; this falls into a second container with a sulphuric acid solution. A lethal gas is created by the chemical reaction. Death usually takes place within 6–18 minutes of the release of the gas. A heart monitor attached to the condemned indicates the time of death.

Ammonia is then pumped into the chamber to neutralise the gas and then exhaust fans remove the fumes from the chamber, a process which takes around 30 minutes. Normally the condemned loses consciousness within seconds, but if the victim holds their breath, then they suffer an agonising death during which they suffer convulsions. As a result of this, the method has been rarely used by US standards – only 11 times since 1976.
See Electrocution p. 185

ELECTROCUTION

In 1888, New York became the first US state to adopt electrocution, first used in the execution of William Kemmler in 1890. By 1949, the majority of US states had adopted the method and between 1930 and 1980 it was the most popular method. Presently, only Nebraska uses electrocution as its sole method of execution.

The condemned person is strapped to an oak chair placed on a rubber net. A leg-piece is fixed to the right calf, to which an electrode is attached. A metal headpiece is then put on, with a leather

▶ RIGHT: *The electric chair at Riverbend, a maximum security institution in Nashville, Tennessee.*

hood to cover the face. Another electrode is fixed to this contraption. At the appointed time, the safety switch is closed and a current of 2,300 volts is passed through the body for eight seconds; this is followed by a 22-second burst of 1,000 volts and finally another 2,300 volts for another eight seconds. If the condemned is not dead, the process is repeated.

The most common problem with electrocution is the failure to cause instant death and therefore the necessity to repeat the process several times. Equally, the body suffers burning at the point of contact with the electrodes. As a result, electrocution has largely been replaced with lethal injection.

See Albert Fish p 252

BURNING

Burning at the stake was undoubtedly the most popular means of dealing with religious heretics and those believed to be witches in England during the sixteenth century. It was considered an appropriate method of execution, as the flames were thought to cleanse the soul.

During the witch trials of the sixteenth and seventeenth centuries in England – and indeed across Europe and the Colonial states in America – hundreds, perhaps thousands of women, and some men, met their fate in this agonising way.

Theoretically, the smoke should render the victim unconscious or asphyxiated before the flames began to course their bodies. In practice, however, this was not always the case and the victim would, quite literally, be burned to death. In some cases, a rope was attached to the condemned's neck and as a favour this would be

◀ *LEFT: Catherine Hayes is burned at the stake for the murder of her husband in 1725.*

stretched to either strangle or render the victim unconscious before the fire consumed their bodies.

At Smithfield in London, a further mercy or privilege was often accorded to the condemned in the shape of a small bag of gunpowder attached to the neck. As the flames licked up around the torso, the head would literally be blown off. For some years burning remained the alternative to hanging, which was reserved for common criminals.

See Hanging p. 181

THE WHEEL

The wheel, or the Catherine Wheel, was used in legend as a means to execute St Catherine. She was strapped to a large vertical wheel with spikes and propelled around, to be impaled on spikes set in the ground. The wheel broke and she was beheaded.

The French used the wheel for a different purpose; the condemned was strapped, spread-eagled to the device and the executioner would then smash each limb with an iron bar, breaking the limbs in two places. The ninth blow would be on the chest.

By the sixteenth century, a further period of agony was added, with the executioner nipping the condemned with red-hot tongs before delivering the blows. On some occasions it would take over 30 blows to dispatch the victim.

See Drawing and Quartering p. 182

BEHEADING

In the UK, the last time a criminal was beheaded was in 1820; for some time it had been reserved for those who had committed high treason. The last unfortunate victims were the men behind the infamous Cato Street Conspiracy, who had plotted to slaughter the whole of the British

Cabinet. They then planned to seize the Mansion House, the Bank of England and the Tower of London. The plan was doomed as one of the conspirators was an undercover agent; they met their end on 1 May 1820.

Death by decapitation was the usual method of execution reserved for members of the nobility in many countries. Compared to hanging, it was considered a more honourable way to die, reflecting a noble death on the battlefield by an edged weapon.

The axe needed to be accurate and an accomplished 'headsman' could

decapitate with a single blow. Typically, the condemned would be required to place their head on a solid block of oak designed to facilitate the executioner's task. It was in this way that Lady Jane Grey, Anne Boleyn, Catherine Howard and Charles I were dispatched.

See Guillotine p. 180

◄ *LEFT: The beheading of a leader of the 1358 French insurrection, under the king's orders.*

STOCKS AND PILLORY

Minor miscreants were often confined to the stocks, particularly in the UK, and this form of punishment was used as late as 1872, when Mark Tuck of Newbury was found drunk and disorderly in a parish church; he was confined to the stocks for four hours.

The stocks secured the offenders' ankles, where they would sit for up to three or four days, victim to rotten vegetables and jibes from a crowd. Beggars, vagrants, prostitutes, drunks and gamblers were commonly sent to the stocks.

The pillory, or the 'stretch neck', held the offender in a standing position, with their hands and head secured. Liars, swindlers and scolding women would be prime candidates. Again, the offender was powerless to prevent rotten eggs, dead rats and a variety of other missiles being thrown at them. They would also have to endure the wrath of those they had wronged, by receiving blows to the face or spitting in the eyes. The pillory could also be used to deliver a whipping, ear-cutting or branding.

On 30 April 1731, Mother Needham, a habitual criminal, died from her injuries in the pillory from a mob in St James's Street, London. Peter James Bossy was the last to be pilloried in 1832, at Tower Hill.

See Hanging p. 181

IMPRISONMENT

In the past, a prison sentence was considered a punitive punishment imposed on a convicted criminal for the crimes committed. There was no notion of re-education, re-adjustment, counselling or training to ensure that the offender did not re-offend. It was a question of society exacting the punishment and removing that individual for a period of time. In recent years, programmes have been introduced to make the offender less likely to commit crimes on their release, but opinions differ as to whether these are effective.

'Life' often meant just that; hard labour also meant that the offender would work long and hard during their sentence. More recently, 'life' can mean anything

▶ *RIGHT: Two men sit in the stocks, a common punishment for minor offences.*

from 15 to 30 years, with the opportunity for parole at roughly the half-way stage of the sentence. A judge can recommend that the convicted criminal is not considered for parole before a precise term of the sentence has elapsed. Assuming good behaviour, life may mean as little as eight to 12 years. Some criminals, such as the Moors Murderers and the Kray twins are, or were, never likely to be released, despite that fact they may have served 30 years. They are considered too dangerous or recidivist.

See Death Row p. 190

◀ LEFT: *An upholstery workshop in HM Prison Manchester (formerly Strangeways).*

DEATH ROW

The term 'death row' refers to convicted criminals who have had the sentence of death passed on them after a trial and are awaiting a date to be sent for the execution. It has been estimated that the number of convicted offenders on death row in the US is currently around 4,000. Under most circumstances, the US appeals process – during which the convicted person can request that the death penalty be reconsidered and commuted to life imprisonment – takes an average of 10 years.

During the stay on death row, the death sentence can be upheld and a date set for the execution of the prisoner. At present the population of America's death row is 98 per cent male. The large numbers of people on

▶ RIGHT: *A death row prisoner is escorted to the shower.*

death row are a result of the US Supreme Court ruling to ban the death penalty between 1972 and 1976; there is still a 'back-log' of executions to be carried out. On average, the death-row population is reduced by 60 to 75 per cent each year due to executions. The southern states account for 80 per cent of those on death row; 12 states now have no death penalty. Following the 1972–76 moratorium, Gary Gilmore was the first to leave death row for his execution in Utah in 1977.

See Gary Gilmore p. 233

MALE KILLERS

DEEMING, FREDERICK BAILEY (1891–92)

Liverpool-born Frederick Bailing Deeming was a bigamist, swindler, thief and murderer, using aliases to perpetrate a number of crimes in Australia, England and South Africa. In 1891, using the name Williams, he posed as an agent for a baron in the Liverpool area, obtaining a rent-free villa. Although married with four children, he began courting Emily Mather, the villa owner's daughter. He murdered and buried his wife Maria and all their children, and married Emily. The newlyweds arrived in Melbourne, Australia, in December 1891; by the end of the first month Emily had also been killed. The Australian police caught Deeming in March 1892, by which time he was posing as Baron Swanton and had become engaged to Katie Rounsefell. Deeming was hanged for his crimes on 23 May 1892.

See Hanging p. 180

HOCH, JOHANN (1895–1906)

German-born Johann Schmidt adopted the name Hoch around 1895, the name being the maiden name of his first wife and his first victim. Hoch travelled around the United States, meeting women through lonely hearts advertisements, after which he bigamously married them. He is believed to have murdered at least 15 of them.

Hoch's chosen method of murder was arsenic poisoning; the poison was found in his fountain pen when he was finally arrested. He was hanged on 23 February 1906. In 1955 a pile of bones found hidden in the walls of a Chicago house were linked to Hoch. It is believed that he married at least 55 women and that such was his desire to obtain money from them that on one occasion he even removed gold false teeth from a glass of water beside his wife's bed.

See Henri Desire Landru p. 195

DUNHAM, JAMES C. (1896)

One of the most infamous murders in nineteenth-century America was that committed by university student James C. Dunham. When relations with his wife, Hattie Wells, soured, she moved back to live with her mother and step-father, a Civil War veteran Colonel McGlincey, in the Santa Clara Valley in San Francisco. In 1896, when his attempts at reconciliation with Hattie failed, Dunham strangled her, killed her mother and a maid with an axe and shot the Colonel, another family member and a ranch hand. Dunham subsequently disappeared; he was never caught.

See Scott Stuart Douglas p. 213

▶ *RIGHT: France's infamous war widow killer, Henri Desire Landru.*

LANDRU, HENRI DESIRE (1915–19)

In a five-year killing spree, Frenchman Henri Desire Landru murdered 11 women – although there were allegations that the figure may have been as high as 300. World War I had left many women widows; Landru plundered their assets, either using confidence tricks to control their life savings or acquiring them on the deaths of the women. He disposed of the majority of bodies in the kitchen stove. Landru was executed by guillotine on 25 February 1922.

See Johann Hoch p. 194

WILSON, OTTO STEVEN (1944)

On 15 November 1944 the strangled and mutilated body of Virginian Lee Griffin was found in a Los Angeles hotel. Hours later a second prostitute, Lillian Johnson, was discovered similarly killed. Wilson was arrested that night, and confessed to both killings. The 'LA Ripper', as he had become known, had been taking a third woman to a hotel when he was arrested. The jury believed he was sane and Wilson died in the gas chamber on 20 September 1946.
See Gas p. 184

HULTEN, KARL GUSTAV (1945)

A wartime American deserter abroad in Britain – and suffering delusions of being a high-rolling gangster – Karl Gustav Hulten assumed the rank and name of 2nd Lieutenant Richard Allen. He teamed up with a young

stripper, Betty Jones, and the pair embarked on a spree of Bonnie-and-Clyde-style petty robberies. Their careers ended abruptly when they were arrested for the cold-blooded murder of George Heath. Hulten waived his right to be tried by a US court and was executed in Britain on 8 March 1945.

See Betty Jones p. 128

HEIRENS, WILLIAM (1945–46)

William Heirens was a Chicago-based burglar and arsonist who turned to murder in 1945. For him, crime was an outlet for his suppressed sexuality; he claimed to feel physically sick when he touched a woman. This aversion did not prevent him from mutilating and killing Josephine Ross, Frances Brown and six-year-old Suzanne Degnan. The first murder probably took place as a result of being discovered whilst burgling Ross's apartment.

When he was arrested in 1946, handwriting tests linked him with a note left at the scene of the Brown murder, which read 'for heaven's sake catch me before I kill more. I cannot control myself.'

Heirens claimed he was controlled by a malignant alter-ego he called George Murman, but this did not prevent him from being sentenced to three life terms in prison.

See Forensic Handwriting p. 176

▲ ABOVE: *The 17-year-old William Heirens, who was sentenced to 71 years imprisonment in 1946.*

◀ LEFT: *The scene outside Holloway Prison gates on the morning of Karl Gustav Hulten's execution.*

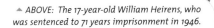

CAMB, JAMES (1947)

On board the *Durban Castle* ocean liner in October 1947, James Camb raped and murdered the actress Gay Gibson in her cabin. Camb, a ship's steward, disposed of the body through a porthole; he carelessly left evidence at the scene of the crime, though, suggesting that he had strangled Gibson. Blood-flecked saliva on a pillow and scratches on his arms secured a conviction. Camb did not hang, as executions were temporarily suspended in 1948, whilst the issue of abolition was being debated.

See Crime Scene Investigation p. 177

GRIFFITHS, PETER (1948)

The abduction of three-year-old June Anne Devaney from Queen's Park Hospital, Blackburn, and her subsequent murder, saw the first mass fingerprinting exercise in the UK. The young girl was snatched from a children's ward in the early hours of 15 May 1948. Her body was found before dawn; she had been molested and had died from terrible head injuries.

The police found 642 sets of fingerprints on the ward, tracing and eliminating all those who had a legitimate reason to enter the hospital over the past two years. One set of prints was left unaccounted for. Between June and July the police collected in excess of 50,000 prints, cross-referencing the electoral register and rationing cards. In this way they followed a trail to Peter Griffiths who, damned by the evidence, was hanged on 19 November 1948.

See Fingerprinting p. 174

INGENITO, ERNEST (1950)

By the time Ernest Ingenito was 15, he already had a criminal record for burglary and his war service was spent in a military prison after he assaulted an officer. In 1947 he married Theresa Mazzoli, with whom he had two children. The couple lived with her parents in New Jersey, but Ingenito's drunkenness and womanising eventually led Theresa's parents to throw him out of their home. Faced with the prospect of rarely seeing his children, he decided to take matters into his own hands.

On 17 November 1950 he returned to the Mazzoli's home, heavily armed. There he gunned down Theresa's parents, grandmother, two brothers, a sister-in-law and a nine-year-old girl. He then set off to kill Theresa's father's parents, Frank and Hilda. The only family member to survive his killing spree would be Theresa herself, who had been badly wounded in the first attack. Ingenito was given five life sentences.

See Mohammed Abequa p. 215

CARIGNAN, HARVEY (1950–75)

Harvey Carignan was a drifter, a rapist and killer who committed his first murder in 1950. He was sentenced to death in Alaska for killing Laura Schowaller, but was released on appeal in 1959. In 1975, he was sentenced to 150 years for the double killings of Eileen Henly and Kathy Schultz in Minnesota. Carignan has also been linked to the 1973 murder of Kathy Miller in Seattle and other rapes and crimes in North Dakota and Canada.

See Arohn Kee p. 217

MILLS, HERBERT LEONARD (1951)

Herbert Leonard Mills met his victim at a Nottingham cinema on 2 August 1951. Mabel Tatters Law was a 48-year-old mother of two. The day after they met Mabel – flattered by the attentions of the 19-year-old Mills – consented to go with him into a local woodland area. There he beat and strangled her

▲ ABOVE: The outcome of the Mills murder trial is reported in the Daily Express in November 1951.

to death. The case then took a bizarre twist as Mills called the *News of the World* and offered them an exclusive on the murder, claiming that he had just discovered the body. The police were informed and Mills was interviewed. During this period Mills gave increasingly lurid descriptions of his 'discovery' to the press in return for money. The statements culminated in a confession to the *New of the World* on 14 August, after which he was charged with the murder and hanged in December of the same year. It seems his motive had simply been to commit the perfect murder.

See Arthur and Nazimodeen Hosein p. 203

DOMINICI, GASTON (1952)

On 5 August 1952, French police received a call from a man named Gustave Dominici. He said he had discovered the bodies of the British bio-chemist Sir Jack Drummond, his wife Ann and their 11-year-old daughter, Elizabeth. The family had been shot whilst on a camping holiday near Marseille.

Gustave and his brother, Clouis, worked for their father, Gaston, on the family's farm, Grand Terre, just 150 m (500 ft) from the murder scene. For some weeks the police found no leads on the killer, although they had their suspicions about the Domini family, and relentlessly pursued them, hoping one would crack. The brothers finally pointed the fingers at their father. Gaston admitted to having been discovered by Sir Jack watching his wife undress; in the ensuing struggle he had shot the Englishman, then killed Ann and Elizabeth. At 75 years of age, Gaston was spared the guillotine and released from prison in 1960.

See Guillotine p. 180

> ▶ RIGHT: Gaston Dominici, who was found guilty of killing Sir Jack Drummond and family in 1954.

CRAIG, CHRISTOPHER AND DEREK BENTLEY (1952)

Christopher Craig and Derek Bentley were cornered on the roof of a wholesale confectioner they were attempting to rob in Croydon on the night of 2 November 1952. Bentley, armed with a knife and a knuckle-duster, was grappled and captured by the police. As Craig stood at bay, armed with a pistol, Bentley yelled at him 'Let him have it, Chris!'. Craig shot and wounded one of the police officers but had Bentley meant for him to hand the weapon over to the police? As further officers arrived, more shots were fired and PC Miles was killed as he emerged on to the roof; it was key to the trial that at the time the murder was committed, Bentley was being escorted downstairs in police custody. When his gun was empty, Craig threw himself off the roof, breaking several bones.

Both Craig and Bentley were charged with the murder of PC Miles and stood trial at the Old Bailey in December 1952. Although a verdict of 'Guilty' was returned for both defendants, the jury recommended mercy for Bentley, who was not present at the time of the killing. Craig was just 16 and so was spared from execution but Bentley, at 20, was sentenced to death. His ambiguous words to Craig had condemned him and he was hanged on 28 January 28, in one of Britain's most notorious miscarriages of justice. *See* Hanging p. 180

SHEPPARD, SAM (1954)

In 1954, neurosurgeon Sam Sheppard claimed that his wife had been killed by an intruder to their home in Cleveland, Ohio. He also claimed to have been knocked unconscious twice by the same intruder.

▶ *RIGHT: Following an appeal 12 years on, Sam Sheppard is cleared of murder and leads his second wife from court.*

Circumstantial evidence led to the conviction of the doctor, despite his pleas of innocence. Twelve years later, in 1966, an appeal was lodged and Sheppard walked free. The 'bushy haired intruder' has never been traced, although many still believe Sheppard murdered his own wife.

See Michael Fletcher p. 216

MERRETT, JOHN DONALD (1954)

New Zealander John Merrett moved to Edinburgh with his mother in 1925. After forging several cheques in her name, he murdered her, but set up the scene so it looked like an accidental shooting. He was cleared of the murder charge, serving only eight months for fraud.

Adopting the name John Ronald Chesney, he married Vera Bonner in 1929, who had inherited £50,000. They separated in 1953 and Merrett moved to Germany. However, his wife had £8,400 in trust and this would become Merrett's on her death. On 10 February 1954, Merrett returned to the UK under an assumed name. He rendered his wife unconscious through drink and drowned her in a bath, then battered her mother to death. Fibre traces on his clothing confirmed his guilt, but Merrett chose suicide rather than facing the hangman; he died by his own hand in Germany six days later.

See Fibre Analysis p. 174

HICKOCK, RICHARD AND PERRY SMITH (1959)

On the night of 14 November 1959 Richard Hickock and Perry Smith broke into the home of the Clutter family in Holcomb, Kansas. Unable to find much of value, they stole $50,

◀ *LEFT: The four members of the Clutter family who were found dead in their Kansas home in 1959.*

a radio and a pair of binoculars – and murdered Herbert Clutter, his wife Bonnie and their children Nancy and Kenyon. The killers set off for Mexico, where they tried to sell the stolen radio; the move turned out to be their downfall as this helped police pick up their trail and they were arrested in Las Vegas in January 1960. They confessed to the burglary and murders. Hickock and Smith were sentenced to death on 29 March 1960 and the sentences were duly carried out by hanging on 14 April 1965.
See Ronald DeFeo p. 206

NELSON, DALE (1970)

Dale Nelson went on a killing spree in September 1970, after a serious drinking binge created in him an uncontrollable rage. He first visited his distant relative, Shirley Wasyk's house in British Columbia, Canada, killing her and one of her children and raping another. Nelson then drove to the Phipps' family home, killing Ray and Isabelle and three of their four children, then abducted their eight-year-old daughter Cathy; the following day her body was found horribly mutilated. Nelson was caught sleeping off the effects of the alcohol. He was found guilty of all eight murders and was sentenced to life imprisonment in April 1971. The sheer violence, particularly in the Wasyk's house, shocked the Canadian community near the US border. It was said that after killing Tracy Wasyk, Nelson cut her stomach open and ate the contents.
See Ernest Ingenito p.198

HOSEIN, ARTHUR AND NIZAMODEEN (1970)

By all accounts Trinidad-born Arthur Hosein was an accomplished tailor, yet he had chosen to live beyond his means when he bought Rooks Farm in Stocking Pelham, Hertfordshire. In a desperate attempt to raise money, he and his brother Nizamodeen planned to kidnap the wife of media millionaire Rupert Murdoch. Instead they kidnapped Muriel McKay, the wife of the Deputy Chairman of the *News of the World*. She was taken from her home on 29 December 1970. Undeterred by the error, the brothers made a series of telephone calls and sent notes and letters to the newspaper's editor, demanding a ransom of £1 million. They made bodged attempts to collect the ransom money and were possibly frightened off by a large, undercover police presence at the pickup point. The brothers' car was spotted in the area and they were linked by fingerprints and handwriting to the ransom notes. Although the brothers were positively linked to the kidnapping, they never admitted killing McKay and her body was never found. It is strongly believed, however that the body was fed to the pigs on Rooks Farm. The brothers were sentenced to life for murder and given concurrent sentences for kidnapping and blackmail.

See Handwriting p. 176

▶ *RIGHT: Nizamodeen Hosein who, along with his brother, kidnapped and murdered Muriel McKay.*

LASHLEY, DAVID (1970–89)

Jamie Shepherd disappeared on the night of 4 February 1977; her grave in Hertfordshire was not discovered until 18 April. She had been bound, raped and strangled. During the investigation, police became suspicious of David Lashley, who had raped five women in 1970 and had also been convicted of a vicious attack in which the victim miraculously survived in July 1976. Lashley was charged with this attack and sentenced to 15 years. He was

released on 7 February 1989 but was rearrested after just 30 seconds and charged with the Shepherd murder. New DNA evidence from 13-year-old semen samples and testimony from inmates to whom Lashley had confided in prison proved damning, and he was sentenced to life imprisonment. After 13 years, DNA profiling had positively linked Lashley to the scene.
See DNA Testing p. 167

LIST, JOHN (1971)

Following a television reconstruction in 1989, respectable accountant John Hardy was positively identified as John List, who had disappeared 17 years earlier, in 1971, after the entire List family – mother Alma, wife Helen, daughter Patricia and sons John Jr and Frederick – had all been slaughtered in their large Victorian home in New Jersey. List's car had been discovered at the airport, but he could not be traced.

List, a strict Lutheran, claimed that he had killed his family to save them from a godless world. The police had retained fingerprint evidence, ballistics and autopsy reports, all of which damned List. He claimed that he could not kill himself because he would be sent to hell. He was found guilty of all five murders on 12 April 1990 and given five life sentences.
See Autopsies p.168; Fingerprinting p. 174

JACKSON, CALVIN (1973–74)

In 1973 Calvin Jackson began a series of burglaries and murders in New York, primarily targeting older, solitary women in a poorer part of the city. Jackson worked at the Park Plaza Hotel, which became the epicentre of the murders. He killed Theresa Jordan in April 1973 and murdered Kate Lewisohn shortly after this. In April the following year he murdered Mabel Hartmeyer and Yeria Vishnefsky. In June 1974 he killed Winifred Miller and Blanche Vincent, in July Martha Carpenter, and finally, in

August, Eleanor Platt and Pauline Spanierman. All the victims had been strangled and raped, both before and after death. Jackson was linked to the murders when Spanierman's television was found in his room. He confessed to the killings and was sentenced to 18 consecutive life terms.
See John Glover p. 212

KNOWLES, PAUL JOHN (1974)

Paul John Knowles was already on parole for burglary when he was picked up by police in Jacksonville, Florida in July 1974, on suspicion of murder. He escaped from his police cell, however, and that same evening he robbed and murdered Alice Curtis. During the next four months he drove all over America, killing at least 17 others. His method was to approach a house and threaten the occupants with a gun, then rape, rob and kill his victims, two of whom were young children. Knowles was eventually caught whilst trying to drive through a police roadblock, but on 18 November he was shot dead by an FBI agent when he tried to seize a sheriff's pistol during an escape attempt. It may never be known how many people fell victim to Knowles' attacks.
See Lawrence Bittaker and Roy Norris p. 208

DEFEO, RONALD (1974)

On the evening of 13 November 1974, the Amityville Police Department received information from a bar owner that a young man had reported the shooting of his mother and father. The man, Ronald 'Butch' DeFeo Jr, claimed his father had found himself on the wrong side of the mafia and that two weeks previously they had been behind an armed robbery at his father's business. Inside the DeFeo home, High Hopes, the police found the bodies of wealthy car dealer Ronald Sr, his wife Louise, daughters Dawn and Allison, and young sons Mark and John.

The police found that the murder weapon was Butch's own rifle and his claim of mafia involvement could not be substantiated; he was charged and put on trial for the murders. Butch's defence claimed insanity and also stated that he killed his family before they could kill him. The court took the view that he was a sociopath and had slaughtered his family as he felt little for them. Butch was sentenced to six concurrent life sentences. The case would have been all but forgotten except for the experience of the family who bought High Hopes; after a year they were driven out of their home by evil spirits, providing the inspiration for the Amityville Horror movies.

See Lyle and Erik Menendez p. 212

▶ *RIGHT: Ronald DeFeo who killed his entire family in their Amityville home in New York.*

DAVIS, T. CULLEN (1976)

T. Cullen Davis was one of the richest men in the United States, and the inspiration for the Dallas character, J. R. Ewing. In August 1976, at the home of Davis's estranged wife in Mockingbird Lane, Fort Worth, Texas, a black-clad assassin shot and killed Andrea Wilborn and Stan Farr, and grievously wounded Priscilla Davis, the supposed intended target, as well as Gus Gavrel, Jr. Priscilla positively identified her estranged husband, T. Cullen Davis, as the murderer. Cullen was charged but he had access to the best legal representation money could buy and claimed to have been in bed with his girlfriend at the time.

The defence suggested that Farr had been the real target with Priscilla behind the intended assassination. Cullen was ultimately acquitted, but in August 1978 an FBI informant, David McCrory, came forward to say that Cullen had given him a list of a dozen people to kill. The FBI faked a photograph of one of the targets, Judge Eidson, who was handling the Davis divorce and taped an incriminating conversation between Cullen and McCrory. Despite this, Cullen was again acquitted. Legal costs had crippled Davis and the murders remain unsolved.

See Robert Durst p. 210

HANCE, WILLIAM (1978)

In March 1978 a Georgia newspaper received a letter signed by 'the forces of evil', threatening to kill a black woman every 30 days. The first victim was discovered within days; Brenda Faison had been beaten to death and buried near the army base of Fort Benning. Two more black women had also been reported missing. The body of Irene Thirkield was found near a rifle range and Karen Hickman's body was discovered in a ditch. The prime suspect, William Hance, had been seen drinking with the first victim shortly before she disappeared; he was interrogated and confessed to the three murders. Hance was convicted and sentenced to death by a civil court for the murder of Faison and given two life sentences by an army court for the other two murders.

See Otto Steven Wilson p. 196

BITTAKER, LAWRENCE AND ROY NORRIS (1979)

Lawrence Bittaker and Roy Norris met in prison. After their release they planned a series of rapes and murders in the Los Angeles area. Cindy Schaeffer's body was found in June 1979 and in July they abducted, raped and murdered Andrea Joy Hall. This was followed in September by the

LEFT: Roy Norris (right) is charged with murder, rape and burglary.

murders of Jackie Gilliam and Leah Lamp. Shirley Ledford fell victim on Halloween. Between the double murder and the Halloween killing, Bittaker and Norris had raped another woman but had released her – a fatal mistake, as she was able to give the police enough information to catch the two men.

Norris confessed to the murders and showed the police where the bodies had been hidden. He claimed Bittaker had taken the leading role but both were charged with five rapes, robberies, kidnappings and murders. Norris testified against Bittaker to avoid the death sentence and was given 45 years. Bittaker remains on death row.

See Death Row p. 190

DUFFY, JOHN FRANCIS AND DAVID MULCAHY (1982–86)

Between 1982 and 1986 railway carpenter John Duffy committed at least 26 rapes in the London area. Duffy attempted to remove all evidence by scrupulously cleaning the women after the attacks. Rape turned to murder with the killings of Anne Lock, Alison Day and Maartje Tamboezer. Ultimately Duffy would be convicted of the Day and Tamboezer murders and of five rapes. He was positively linked to the Tamboezer murder when traces of his semen were found on her

RIGHT: John Duffy (left) and David Mulcahy

body and fibres of his clothing were discovered on Day's jacket. Lock's body was so decomposed there was insufficient scientific evidence to link Duffy with her murder. Another damning piece of evidence was the British Rail string used to tie the victims. On 26 February 1988 he was sentenced to 30 years. Ten years into this sentence he implicated his childhood friend, David Mulcahy as his accomplice. Mulcahy was sentenced to life imprisonment in 1999.

See DNA Testing p. 167; Fibre Analysis p. 175

DURST, ROBERT (1982–2002)

Despite having over $500 in his pocket, millionaire Robert Durst chose to steal a sandwich and a newspaper from a supermarket in Pennsylvania. He was caught and handed over to the police, who discovered to their amazement that the heavily disguised man was wanted for murders in Texas, Los Angeles and New York. Durst's wife, Kathleen, had disappeared in New York January 1982. On Christmas Eve 2000, Susan Berman – a long-time friend of Durst – was found shot in her home in Los Angeles. This was believed to have been a contract killing. In September 2001 a human torso was discovered in Galveston, Texas. The body was later identified as Morris Black. Durst was picked up nine days later and linked to the murder, but was given a $300,000 bail and promptly disappeared, until he was picked up once more in Pennsylvania. Durst was sent back to Texas in January 2002; he would claim that he killed Black in self defence. Legal arguments continue, with all three US states eager to convict Durst of the three killings, despite the lack of conclusive evidence to place him at the scenes of the murders.

See T. Cullen Davis p. 207

▶ *RIGHT: Gary Heidnik, the psychotic sex killer who kidnapped women and took them to his 'cellar of death'.*

DUPAS, PETER (1983–99)

Between 1974 and 1994 Australian Peter Dupas was convicted several times for sexual offences, including rape, and his offences were becoming increasingly violent. In March 1999 he murdered Nicole Patterson in Melbourne, stabbing her 30 times. Dupas was caught and given life imprisonment; from this time he became the focus of several unsolved murders in the Melbourne area. It is believed that his first victim was Helen McMahon, who was raped and killed in February 1983 at the exact location where Dupas had raped another woman a few weeks before. He was also linked with the murder of Mersina Halvagis, who was stabbed to death in a Melbourne cemetery. In February 2002, DNA evidence linked Dupas with the murder of Margaret Maher, who had been stabbed and killed in October 1997.

See DNA Testing p. 167

HEIDNIK, GARY (1986)

In 1978 Gary Heidnik was jailed for four years for kidnap and rape. After his release he began to assemble a harem of sex slaves by kidnapping women in the New Jersey area. By 1986 some five women were imprisoned in Heidnik's basement, where they were tortured, raped and where two were eventually murdered. One of the women managed to escape and Heidnik was convicted and sentenced to death, a sentence carried out by lethal injection on 6 July 1999.

See Lethal Injection p. 183

MENENDEZ, LYLE AND ERIK (1989)

On the night of 20 August 1989, Erik and Lyle
Menendez claimed they had returned home to their
parents' luxury house in Beverley Hills to discover
that their father, José, had been shot eight times and
their mother, Kitty, five times. Both were dead. José
was a successful Cuban-American businessman and
the boys claimed he had subjected them to years of
child abuse. When the brothers were charged with

their parents' murder in March 1990, the motive seemed to be the
enormous inheritance they would receive. Indeed they had gone on a
huge spending spree in the months after the death of their parents.

In a complex and lengthy court case, with much contradictory
evidence, the brothers were found guilty on 20 March 1996 and
sentenced to two consecutive life prison sentences.
See Ronald DeFeo p. 206

GLOVER, JOHN WAYNE (1989–91)

John Wayne Glover was nicknamed 'The Granny Killer' – his victims were
six elderly women in Sydney, Australia, and Glover murdered them all in
just over a year. He claimed his first victim in March 1989, forcing
Gwendolin Mitchelhill into a side street, where he hit her on the head
with a hammer, raped her and then strangled her. This was the same
technique he would use on the next four women whose lives he claimed.
He also carried out a series of rapes at nursing homes in the Sydney area.
It was only when he murdered Joan Sinclair, a woman known to him,
that he was finally arrested and charged with a total of six murders. He
stood trial in November 1991 and was sentenced to life imprisonment.
See Calvin Jackson p. 205

◀ *LEFT: Tammy Saccoman on the day of her marriage to convicted parent-killer Eric Menendez, with whom she fell in love with while watching television coverage of his trial.*

BRANDO, CHRISTIAN (1990)

Without the family connection to Marlon Brando, this case would have been a simple matter of a drink-induced shooting. Marlon Brandon's son had shot Dag Drollet, his sister Cheyenne's boyfriend, on the night of 16 May 1990 on the Brando estate. The media circus surrounding Brando's witness statements, the closing of the family's ranks and the deployment of the best lawyers available, secured Christian a reduced sentence of 10 years

See also: Dale Nelson p. 203

TANNER, JOHN (1991)

Five years after the Suzy Lamplugh case, the disappearance of a 19-year-old Oxford student, Rachel McLean, hit the headlines. Her boyfriend, John Tanner, claimed to have last seen her at Oxford railway station on the evening of 15 April 1991. Despite assisting police with their investigations, Tanner fell under suspicion, and when Rachel's strangled body was found beneath the floorboards of her home, Tanner was arrested, charged and sentenced to life imprisonment.

See Suzy Lamplugh Case p. 157

DOUGLAS, SCOTT STUART (1991)

The marriage of Scott Stuart and Ann Scripps had broken down by 1991. Ann, a rich heiress, had married the younger Scott, who favoured the high life. Whilst she was petitioning a court in New York to have Scott removed from the house, he bludgeoned Ann to death, leaving his car at a bridge. The family believed he had faked suicide, but in 1994 his body was found on the banks of the Hudson River.

See Michael Fletcher p. 216

HIGHTOWER, CHRISTOPHER (1991)

To all intents and purposes, Christopher Hightower was a pillar of the community and devoted family man. But on 20 September 1991 he murdered his neighbour at his Rhode Island home with a crossbow. He shot Ernest Brendel five times with the bow, then drugged and strangled his wife Alice and buried their daughter alive. Hightower was sentenced to three life terms but continues to protest his innocence, claiming the murders were committed by drug dealers.

See Gaston Dominici p. 200

BARONE, CESAR (1991–92)

Cesar Barone, formerly Adolph James Rode, was suspected of murder in Florida in the 1970s. In April 1991 he murdered Margaret Schmidt, raping her and then strangling her to death. In October 1992 he shot, wounded and assaulted Martha Bryant, despatching her with another shot after his attack. In December he assaulted and shot Chantee Woodman and in January 1993 Betty Williams, who died of a heart attack during the assault. Barone was sentenced to death.

See Harvey Carignan p.199

GINGERICH, EDWARD (1993)

Edward Gingerich murdered his wife Katie in Crawford County, Pennsylvania in 1993. He has the distinction of being the only Amish man to have been convicted of murder. He killed and disembowelled his wife in a schizophrenic frenzy that was witnessed by his two children. He was found guilty of involuntary manslaughter.

◀ *LEFT: An Amish farmer in Pennsylvania. Edward Gingerich remains the only Amish man to have been convicted of murder.*

At the time, he had stopped taking medication for paranoid schizophrenia for nine months. Gingerich was released from prison in March 1998.

See John List p. 205

DENYER, PAUL CHARLES (1993)

A blow to the head as a child was the apparent reason that Paul Charles Denyer turned to murder later in life. As a child he had cut a kitten's throat leaving it hanging on a tree, and had attacked school friends. In 1993 he became known as the Frankston Serial Killer, claiming the lives of three women – chosen at random – all of whom were slashed and stabbed to death. His blood had been found on one of the victims, and with such overwhelming evidence Denver confessed to the murders. He said 'I've always wanted to kill, waiting for the right time, waiting for that silent alarm to trigger me off'. In December 1993, before a Melbourne court, he pleaded guilty and was sentenced to 30 years with no possibility of parole.

See Serology p. 169

ABEQUA, MOHAMMED (1994)

Jordanian-born Mohammed Abequa married Nina Gussal in January 1986. The couple lived in New Jersey and had two children, Sami and Lisa. The previously happy marriage fell apart in 1989 and they began a custody battle for their children. In July 1994 Abequa strangled his wife, then fled to Jordan with the children. It took the intercession of King Hussein of Jordan to secure the return of the children to their family in America. In 1994 Abequa was tried in a Jordanian court and sentenced to 15 years imprisonment; he was released in 2000. Nina's US-based family still live in constant fear that Abequa will return to retrieve his children. The children live with their mother's sister, Nesime Dokur.

See Ernest Ingenito p. 198

EVONITZ, RICHARD (1996–2002)

It took forensic examinations of fibres found in Richard Evonitz's apartment to positively link him with at least three abductions, rapes and murders in Virginia. Sofia Silva disappeared on 9 September 1996 whilst doing homework on her own front doorstep. Her body was discovered six weeks later. On 1 May 1997, sisters Kristin and Kati Lisk disappeared after getting off their school bus in Fredericksburg. The two were found dead five days later. All three victims had been strangled or suffocated and then dumped in water. Evonitz made his fatal mistake in June 2002 in South Carolina. He had abducted a girl, raped her and then fallen asleep, allowing her to escape. Police finally caught up with him in Florida, but he killed himself before he could be arrested.

See Fibre Analysis p. 174

FLETCHER, MICHAEL (1999)

In 1999 the pregnant Leann Fletcher was shot and killed in Macon County, Michigan. Her husband Michael had called the police from the crime scene, claiming that she had committed suicide. Investigators were suspicious, however, and Fletcher soon became the prime suspect.

It took jurors only 15 minutes to rule out the possibility of suicide or accidental shooting. They took four days to agree that it had been a premeditated murder, based on the fact that the couple had separated on several occasions and were known to be at loggerheads. The judge found Fletcher guilty of the murder of Leann and her unborn child. He will remain in prison until at least 2017.

See Mohammed Abequa p. 215

> ▶ *RIGHT: DNA samples are loaded into a DNA sequencer. A DNA sample taken from a cup used by Arohn Kee while he was being questioned over a theft charge linked him to many rapes and murders.*

KEE, AROHN (2000)

In December 2000 Arohn Kee was found guilty of 22 crimes, including murder, rape and robbery, and was sentenced to life imprisonment in January 2001. He had murdered three young girls in the Harlem area: Johalis Castro, Rasheda Taylor and Paola Illera. It was also established that he had raped at least another four women. Kee had been under surveillance and when he was arrested on a theft charge, a DNA sample was taken from a cup he had used whilst being questioned. This linked him to the rapes and murders. Kee fled to Miami, Florida, but was picked up in the company of a 17-year-old girl who police believed would have been his next victim. Kee was sentenced to a total of 400 years for his crimes.

See DNA Testing p. 167

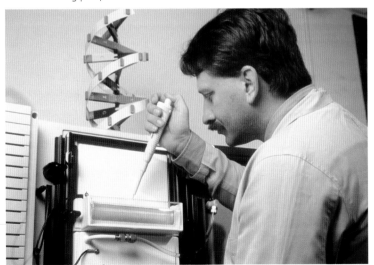

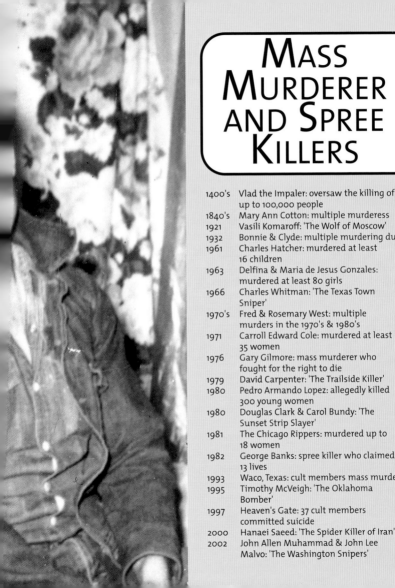

MASS MURDERER AND SPREE KILLERS

VLAD THE IMPALER (1400S)

Vlad the Impaler, or Vlad Tepes, was a fifteenth-century Wallachian ruler who, over 400 years later, was immortalised as *Dracula ('son of the devil')* by the author Bram Stoker.

During his various dynastic struggles and wars against the Turks and Hungarians, Vlad had tens of thousands of victims impaled on stakes. In 1461 Vlad ordered the massacre of all Turks at Giurgiu; nearly 24,000 perished. When he was captured by the Hungarians in the late-1460s, Vlad spent his time in prison impaling small animals. Vlad would relish having banquets surrounded by impaled victims in agonising pain; unfaithful women would be skinned alive and other victims would be literally worked to death.

Vlad's end came in January 1477 when his small army was attacked by Turks near Bucharest; his head was conveyed to the Turkish sultan in triumph.

See Ivan the Terrible p. 220

◀ *LEFT: Vlad the Impaler, the fearsome ruler who provided the basis for Bram Stoker's* Dracula.

IVAN THE TERRIBLE (1530–84)

Ivan the Terrible was a sixteenth-century Russian tyrant who used unparalleled savagery to create an empire. As a child, Ivan liked to throw dogs from a castle tower. At 13 he set hunting dogs on a key rival and at 17, during his honeymoon, he set fire to men who interrupted his celebrations. He created a secret police to kill for him and in 1570 he virtually eliminated Novgorod, murdering over 60,000 people. Ivan's life of murder, torture and rape ended in 1584.

See Vlad the Impaler p. 220

THE SAWNEY BEAN FAMILY (1600S)

The Sawney Bean family lived in Ayrshire in Scotland perhaps as far back as the seventeenth century. They lived in a cave complex and were robbers and cannibals. The family were certainly active over two decades, interbreeding until they had created a small army. A 400-strong force, with tracker dogs and supported by local volunteers, were sent to root out the cannibals. They found the cave, with human meat hung up like a butcher's shop. The family was overpowered and taken back to Edinburgh. The 27 Sawney Bean men had their limbs cut off and were bled to death in front of the women, after which the 21 women were burned alive on pyres.

See Burning p. 186

COTTON, MARY ANN (1840S–72)

Mary Ann Cotton murdered her first husband and five children in the 1840s; she then married George Ward, who met a similar fate. She married again, to a man named John Robinson, who also fell victim to Cotton, along with his children. Cotton moved on again and remarried; her new husband's sister was first to go, then her husband Frederick in 1871, followed by two of their children and a lodger. The last child of the marriage succumbed in 1872.

All the victims over the years had apparently died from gastric fever, but in fact the cause of death was arsenic poisoning, a fact discovered in 1872 when the latest batch of corpses was exhumed. Cotton was tried for the last four murders, the jury taking only an hour to find her guilty. She was executed by hanging at Durham on 24 March 1873.

See George Banks p. 238

▸ RIGHT: *Ivan the Terrible was a cruel tyrant and even killed his own son.*

GOHL, BILLY (1903–12)

Gohl was a trade-union official who worked in the office of the Sailors' Union of the Pacific in Aberdeen, Washington. He checked that the seamen visiting the port did not have any relatives there, then asked whether they wished to lodge their cash and valuables with him. Between 1903 and 1912 he murdered at least 41 men, dropping their corpses into the Wishkah River, which ran into the sea, via a chute from the union building. He was only convicted of two of the murders and the state had suspended the death penalty at the time. Gohl's case directly led to the reinstatement of the death penalty soon after, but the mass murderer escaped this fate and died in prison in 1928.

See Amelia Dyer p. 79

DOSS, NANNIE (1920–64)

Nannie Doss, of Tulsa, Oklahoma, killed at least 11 people, including five husbands, her own mother, two of her sisters and two of her children.

Doss murdered her two children by poisoning them, an event that caused her first husband to flee in fear of his own life. She remarried and poisoned her second husband, and a third in 1952. Two more husbands succumbed to Doss's stewed prunes laced with arsenic; during this time her sisters and mother faced the same fate.

On the death of her last husband, the doctor demanded an autopsy and contacted the police. The post-mortem clearly showed he had died from arsenic poisoning. Doss confessed to the string of murders and in 1964 she was sentenced to life imprisonment. She died the following year from leukaemia.

See Belle Gunness p. 81

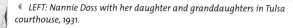

◀ *LEFT: Nannie Doss with her daughter and granddaughters in Tulsa courthouse, 1931.*

KOMAROFF, VASILI (1921–23)

Komaroff seemed to be the most unlikely killer: he was a contented family man and a Moscow horse trader. Only his closest friends knew he had once tried to kill his own son. Between 1921 and 1923 some 33 male bodies were found in sacks close to the Moscow horse market. Police made systematic searches of the area and when they visited Komaroff's home found his latest victim in the trademark sack. Robbery was the probable motive and all the victims had either been killed with a hammer or strangled. The 'Wolf of Moscow' had finally been discovered; he showed the police the resting place of his last five victims, though most of the bodies had been thrown into the river and were never recovered. Komaroff and his wife – who was implicated in the crimes – were shot by firing squad on 18 June 1923.

See Billy Gohl p. 222

DENKE, KARL (1924)

Denke ran a ramshackle lodging house in Munsterberg, Silesia, now part of Poland. He was a cannibal and preyed on solitary travellers until he was caught in the act of murder in 1924. Police found over 30 different sets of body parts, the rest of which he had eaten himself or fed to other guests. Denke, a religious man, hanged himself with his braces in prison before he could be brought to trial.

See The Sawney Bean Family p. 221

DRENTH, HERMAN (1932)

Drenth passed his time by answering lonely heart's advertisements and then murdering those who replied, in his purpose-built concrete gas chamber. Drenth killed more than 50 women at his hideaway, Quiet Dell, in West Virginia. He used a number of false names, including Harry Powers and Cornelius O. Pierson, but the names all had one thing in common – the same post-office box number. Drenth was eventually identified and police found five bodies; the rest of his victims were never found. He was hanged on 18 March 1932.

See Belle Gunness p. 81

BONNIE AND CLYDE (1932–34)

Clyde Barrow was 21 when he met the 19-year-old Bonnie Parker; he already had a criminal record for theft and she had been deserted by her robber husband. The day after they met, Clyde was arrested and sentenced to two years in prison; Bonnie helped him escape but he was recaptured and sentenced to 14 years. In order to gain freedom, he cut off two of his toes with an axe and was paroled.

Bonnie and Clyde's first murder took place in April 1932; later that year they raided a petrol station in Texas. Bonnie shot and killed a storekeeper in the same state, then they killed a man to steal his car on Christmas Day 1932.

In March 1933 in Missouri they shot and killed two policemen in a gun battle; a few weeks later they had to

shoot their way out of trouble again, during which Clyde's brother, Buck, was killed. On 23 May 1934 their luck finally ran out when their car was ambushed by six police officers. Over 160 shots were fired into the car and the lives of Bonnie and Clyde came to an end, although their legend lives on.

See Karl Hulten p. 196

◀ *LEFT: A 1933 photograph of Bonnie and Clyde, taken by Clyde's brother Buck.*

PETIOT, DR MARCEL (1944)

Dr Marcel Petiot had attracted the attention of the police before World War II for drug trafficking activities, but was still a practising physician in Paris during the war. He posed as a member of the Resistance and offered help to Jews wishing to escape from occupied Europe. Once he had them in his power, he gave them lethal injections and stole their money and treasured possessions. His diabolical scheme was brought to an end when the chimney of his Paris surgery caught fire during a corpse-burning session in 1944.

When arrested, the remains of 27 people were found, part-burned or ready for incineration. Petiot claimed they were German collaborators, admitting to having killed at least 63 individuals. He was found guilty of murder and executed on 26 May 1946.

See Harold Shipman p. 273

HEATH, NEVILLE (1946)

Heath's preoccupation was sado-masochism, in the pursuit of which he murdered Margery Gardner and Doreen Marshall. It was a bizarre case in which Heath acted as witness, describing a fictitious man as the perpetrator of the crimes. Clear evidence linked him to the murders and experts concluded that he was not insane. Heath made no appeal against the death sentence, neither did he make a confession. He was executed on 16 October 1946 at Pentonville Prison in London.

See Rosemary and Fred West p. 230

▶ *RIGHT: Sadistic killer Neville Heath is driven away from court in July 1946.*

LEY, THOMAS (1946)

Thomas Ley was the former minister of justice for New South Wales, but in November 1946, with the aid of Lawrence Smith, he murdered a love rival, John McMain Mudie. Mudie's body was found in a chalk pit near Woldingham in Surrey. Ley was undone by Smith's testimony and that of a third man, Buckingham, who had provided the car to dispose of the body. Ley died in prison on 24 July 1947 and Smith served a life sentence.

See Martin Bryant p. 245

FERNANDEZ, RAYMOND (1948)

Fernandez was the charmer in the Lonely Heart's Killers duo with Martha Beck. He appears to have led a fairly normal life before suffering brain damage in an accident, after which he came to believe he had supernatural powers, along with the ability to hypnotise and compel women to fall in love with him. He used this to great effect, deceiving several Lonely Hearts, but turned to murder in 1948, killing at least three and possibly as many as 17 women. Fernandez's career ended in the electric chair in 1951.

See Martha Beck p. 88

STARKWEATHER, CHARLES (1958)

On 21 January 1958, Charles Starkweather murdered the family of his 14-year-old girlfriend, Caril Ann Fugate – her mother, father and younger sister. The couple then fled and for the next week over 1,200 National Guardsmen and police combed Nebraska and Wyoming in search of them. Before he was finally cornered, Starkweather shot or stabbed a further seven people. He claimed that the killings had begun when Caril Ann's parents had made fun of him. Initially, Starkweather claimed Caril Ann was a hostage, but he later changed his story. She was sentenced to

life and was released in 1977. Aged 19 Stark-weather had a one-way trip to the electric chair in Nebraska on 25 June 1959. He had modelled himself on James Dean and in at least one respect he was correct: they both died young .

See Bonnie and Clyde p. 224

◄ *LEFT: Charles Starkweather and Caril Ann Fugate embarked on a killing spree across Nebraska.*

HATCHER, CHARLES (1961–81)

Hatcher was already serving a sentence for abducting a newspaper boy when he committed his first recorded murder in prison in 1961; lack of evidence saved him from prosecution. He was released in 1969 and in August he abducted and strangled a 12-year-old boy. By Hatcher's own later admission, this was his sixth or seventh murder. Later in the month, he was arrested for raping a five-year-old in San Francisco. Hatcher was released on license in 1977. In May 1978 he murdered a four-year-old child, and was arrested the following year for attempted murder; he was confined in a secure hospital for a year. In June 1981 he stabbed a man to death in Illinois and then murdered an 11-year-old girl in July 1982. Hatcher was again arrested and confessed to three murders.

He pleaded guilty to one of the murders in court in October 1982 and was found guilty of another in September 1984. Hatcher committed suicide in prison on 7 December 1984. Over the period 1961 to 1982, Hatcher had committed at least 16 sex-related murders.

See The Station Strangler p. 240

GONZALES, DELFINA AND MARIA DE JESUS (1963–64)

Over a 10-year period, these Mexican sisters claimed the lives of over 80 girls. Delfina and Maria ran a brothel at their Rancho El Angel, staffed by abducted girls forced into drug dependency. If the girls caused problems or lost their appeal, the sisters killed them.

In 1964 a woman named Josefina Guttierez was picked up by the Mexican police. She told them of her procurement of girls for the Gonzales sisters and their brothel near San Francisco del Rincon. The police mounted a raid – they found dormitories full of prostitutes and in the grounds the graves of over 80 women. The police also discovered innumerable aborted foetuses, the product of crude operations carried out by the Gonzales sisters. The police found other corpses, too; those of some of the clients, migrant workers returning from the United States with significant cash.

Inexplicably, for the abduction, enslavement, appalling treatment and eventual murder of the 80 or more victims of their business, the Gonzales sisters were sentenced to just 40 years. However, the mystery of the disappearance of 80 young girls in the Guadalajar region had finally been explained.
See Rosemary and Fred West p. 230

SPECK, RICHARD (1966)

On the night of 14 July 1966, an intoxicated Richard Speck broke into a Chicago nurses' residence

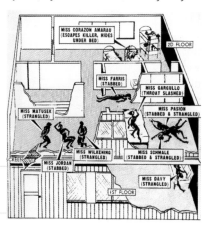

▶ *RIGHT: A cutaway drawing of the Speck murder scene from the* Chicago Tribune.

and slaughtered eight nurses, either stabbing or strangling them. One nurse, Corazon Amurao, managed to hide and subsequently provided an accurate description of Speck. He was picked up two days later and on 6 June 1967 sentenced to death; he was later re-sentenced to 400 years, after making a full confession in 1978.

See Robert Diaz p. 236

▲ ABOVE: *The eight student nurses who became Richard Speck's unfortunate victims.*

WHITMAN, CHARLES (1966)

On 31 July 1966 Charles Whitman stabbed and shot his mother, then killed his wife. The following morning he continued his killing spree with the murder of a receptionist, after which he headed for an observation tower on the Austin campus of the University of Texas, shooting two more people en route. In just 96 minutes, Whitman killed 16 people and wounded 30 others before the tower was stormed by police. Whitman died in the ensuing gun battle. His attack had been well-planned: he had taken with him several guns, plenty of ammunition, food, a radio and even toilet paper. An autopsy of his body discovered a brain tumour, which may have been the cause of his murderous outburst.

See Washington Snipers p. 249

▶ RIGHT: *The University of Texas tower, from which Charles Whitman shot his victims.*

WEST, ROSEMARY AND FRED (1970S–90S)

On 13 December 1994 Fred West was charged with 12 murders; his wife, Rosemary, would later be found guilty of 10 murders and sentenced to 10 life sentences. The Wests lived at 25 Cromwell Street, Gloucester, which had literally, over a period of many years, become a house of horrors. Fred's murderous tendencies pre-dated even meeting Rosemary.

The Wests lived a bizarre life of extreme sex, prostitution, rape, imprisonment and murder. Their cellar was a torture chamber, where Rose would entertain clients and Fred would murder women. A succession of young women and unfortunate family members were raped, strangled, suffocated and then buried within the grounds of the house; several unwanted children were also despatched.

It was only the tenacity of Detective Constable Hazel Savage, who was investigating the rape of a young girl, that linked the Wests with a series of disappearances. When the police finally searched the house, on 24 February 1994, no fewer than nine different sets of bones were found in the cellar alone. The forensic evidence was overwhelming and, rather than face trial, Fred West committed suicide at Winston Green Prison, Birmingham on New Year's Day 1995.

See Delfina Gonzales and Maria de Jesus p. 228

EVANS, DONALD LEROY (1970)

When Evans left the US Marines in 1970 he went on a killing spree, slaughtering anyone who crossed his path. After his arrest in Gulfport, Mississippi, for the rape and murder of a 10-year-old, Beatrice Routh, Evans confessed to over 60 killings. In 1993 he was tried,

▶ *RIGHT: The Cromwell Street killers, Fred and Rosemary West.*

convicted and sentenced to death for the Routh murder, then the Florida courts sentenced him to life in 1995 for the strangling of Ira Jean Smith.

Police authorities found it difficult to amass any clear evidence to link Evans with many of the murders he claimed to have committed, but circumstantially he was probably responsible for a large percentage of these unsolved murders. Evans was stabbed to death by fellow Mississippi inmate, Jimmy Mack, in January 1999.

See Timothy McVeigh p. 244

COLE, CARROLL EDWARD (1971–81)

Between 1971 and 1981 Cole murdered 35 women. His victims were what he described as 'loose women'; his motive being that they reminded him of his mother.

In San Diego in 1971, he strangled Essie Louie Buck; in Las Vegas in 1977 he strangled Kathlyn Blum. He dodged between San Diego, Las Vegas and Dallas from 1979 to 1980, strangling Marnie Cushman, Bonnie O'Neil, Dorothy King and Wanda Faye Roberts. In most of the cases, Cole had sexually abused the bodies after death.

In November 1980 he strangled Sally Thompson, but neighbours called the police to investigate the noise. Incredibly, Cole was released before being rearrested and subsequently confessing to the murders. A Texas court tried him on three counts of homicide in April 1981; he confessed to having killed in Oklahoma, Texas, Nevada, California and Wyoming. He pleaded insanity on the basis that he had cannibalised one of his victims. The court was unconvinced and sentenced him to three life terms. Cole then faced trial in Nevada for two murders; again he pleaded guilty and asked for the death sentence to be imposed; they duly obliged and Cole was executed by lethal injection on 6 December 1985.

See The Chicago Rippers p. 237

GRETZLER, DOUGLAS AND WILLIAM STEELMAN (1973)

Douglas Gretzler and William Steelman were spree killers who terrorised the south-west of America during the 1970s. Essentially, they were armed robbers, but they never missed an opportunity to commit murder. They met in Denver, Colorado in the early 1970s and murdered nine people in Arizona. They then held up a store in Victor, California, during which nine more people were killed, four of them children.

The murderous duo were finally cornered at a hotel in Sacramento, California in 1973. Gretzler gave himself up, but Steelman had to be tear-gassed out. The Californian courts gave them life, but the courts in Arizona sentenced them to death. Steelman died on death row, but Gretzler was executed on 3 June 1998. Police suspect they had actually killed 30 people in total.

See George Banks p. 238

GASKINS, DONALD (1975)

The disappearance of a 13-year-old girl in South Carolina in 1975 took police on a sickening journey into the world of mass murderer Donald Gaskins. While investigating the disappearance, police found two graveyards, one containing six corpses, the other two. With the assistance of one-time associate, Walter Neely, the police identified Gaskins as the contract killer in all cases. Known as 'Pee Wee', Gaskins had strong connections with the underworld.

Using a truth serum, Gaskins admitted to 13 killings and was sentenced to eight life terms. Unrepentant, Gaskins accepted another contract while in prison, this time to kill Rudolph Tyner. He rigged up an intercom packed with dynamite and blew off the side of Tyner's head. For this Gaskins was finally sent to the electric chair.

See Electrocution p. 185

GRAY, MARVIN (1975)

Marvin Gray described himself as 'a natural-born murderer' and said 'all I think about is killing people'. On 5 June 2001 Gray was convicted of the 1975 shooting of a bank worker in Denver, Colorado. During the trial he was forced to represent himself, having made threats to his own legal counsel. He was repeatedly removed from the court and was restrained with leg irons on his wrists. Police had used polygraphs to confirm Gray's assertions that he had committed over 40 murders; the lie detectors confirmed at least 20 of the statements. Gray was subsequently given three life sentences, but police are still piecing together his evidence and trying to link him with other cases. Authorities believe he may kill again in prison in order to achieve his desire to be executed.

See Lie Detectors and Polygraphs p.166

GILMORE, GARY (1976)

Gilmore was sentenced to death for the murder of a motel clerk in Provo, Utah on 20 July 1976. He also faced charges – but was never brought to trial – for another killing in Crem, Utah, the previous day. What is particularly significant about Gilmore is not the scope of his killings, but his desire to die; indeed he fought the US legal system for years to gain the right to be executed. He was an incorrigible criminal who had spent 18 years of the last 20 of his life in prison. He had twice attempted suicide and on three occasions his execution had been delayed at the

◂ *LEFT: Gary Gilmore, who insisted that his death penalty be carried out immediately.*

last moment. The US Supreme Court had suspended the death penalty between 1972 and 1976 and Gilmore became the first convicted murderer to be executed after this period. He was shot by firing squad on 17 January 1977; his last words as a hood was placed over his head were 'let's do it'. Gilmore's body was donated to the Utah Medical Center for medical research.

See Firing Squad p. 181

LEWINGDON, GARY AND CHARLES (1977–78)

The same murder weapon was used in the killings of two girls in 1977 as five others in Columbus, Ohio in 1978. The gun was used again on 4 December when Joseph Annick was murdered. Lewingdon was arrested when trying to use Annick's credit card; under questioning he implicated his brother, Charles. Charles faced nine murder charges for which he received nine life sentences. Gary received eight life terms.

See the Chicago Rippers p. 237

CARPENTER, DAVID (1979–81)

David Carpenter, also known as the 'Trailside Killer', had a history of sex crimes and was a major suspect in the investigation into the Zodiac killings. Between 1979 and 1980 Carpenter murdered four women in the Mount Tamalpais Park area near San Francisco. Between October and November 1980 Carpenter killed another four women, three of them in the space of just

◄ *LEFT: Sunset Strip in Los Angeles, where Douglas Clark laid siege in the summer of 1980.*

one weekend. His spree continued in March 1981; this time the girl's boyfriend survived and gave police a good description of their attacker. Carpenter struck again on 1 May. When an ex-girlfriend of his, Heather Scaggs, went missing, police followed the trail to Carpenter and finally arrested him. He was sentenced to death in 1984.

See The Zodiac Killer p. 302

LOPEZ, PEDRO ARMANDO (1980)

Pedro Lopez was the seventh son of a Columbian prostitute. At the age of 18 he had been raped while in prison serving a sentence for car theft. Within days, he had murdered three of the rapists. On his release, Lopez travelled widely throughout Columbia, Ecuador and Peru, largely without companions. He claimed the lives of 100 young girls. He nearly met his end in northern Peru when an Indian tribe caught him trying to make off with a nine-year-old girl. They tortured him and began to bury him alive, but the timely arrival of an American missionary saved him.

In April 1980, a river swollen by rain revealed the bodies of four of his victims near Ambato, Peru. Lopez had recently abducted, raped and murdered another local girl and this time the police had a description. Lopez confessed to the abduction, rape and strangulation of at least 300 young girls over a considerable period of time. He was ultimately tried for multiple murders in Ecuador, where he was sentenced to life. The reign of terror of the 'Monster of the Andes' was finally over.

See Vladimir Bratislav p. 246

CLARK, DOUGLAS AND CAROL BUNDY (1980)

Douglas Clark used his cohort Carol Bundy to convince girls to get into their car. Clark was a necrophile and whilst raping the girls, he would shoot them in the head. He also kept the heads as trophies and for further abuse. Clark killed Gina Marano, Cynthia Chandler, Exxie Wilson and Karen Jones in June 1980. Clark became known as the Sunset Strip Killer, as all his murders took place around the Hollywood area. The last victim was a friend of Bundy's, John Murray, in whom she had confided. Bundy finally turned Clark over to the police; she was sentenced to two life sentences and Clark was sent to the gas chamber.

See Ian Brady and Myra Hindley p. 257

DZHUMAGALIEV, NIKOLAI (1980–89)

Despite his strange, metal false teeth, Nikolai Dzhhumagaliev was a hit with women; they never suspected his evil desires to rape them and hack them to pieces with an axe. Dzhumagaliev had already served a prison sentence for manslaughter in Kazakastan in 1980, but now he was loose in Moscow.

Dzhumagaliev was a cannibal and it is this habit that brought about his downfall. When two friends were invited for a meal they discovered the severed head of a woman. They contacted the police and Dzhumagaliev was arrested. He was convicted of seven murders and confined to a mental institution.

See Vladimir Bratislav p. 246

DIAZ, ROBERT (1981)

Diaz was a death-dealing nurse who killed 19 people over a 12-day period in April 1981 at the Perris Community Hospital in California. Police received an anonymous tip-off and found vital medical records missing. Diaz (see opposite, left) was arrested in November, but his trial did not begin until March 1984. In the preceding months, exhumations had confirmed that Diaz had used Lidocaine and morphine to despatch the patients. On 29 March he received the death sentence.

See Beverley Allitt p.158

THE CHICAGO RIPPERS (1981–82)

The Chicago Rippers terrorised the city between May 1981 and October 1982 and may have claimed as many as 18 lives. The rippers were four men: Robin Gecht, Ed Spreitzer and Andrew and Tommy Kokoraleis. The gang abducted women, raped them, strangled them to death then mutilated and cannibalised parts of their bodies. On 6 October 1982 Beverly Washington, a 20-year-old prostitute, fell victim to the Rippers, but survived and was found barely alive by the police. She had been raped and slashed and her left breast had been removed – one of the gang's signatures. She was able to give the police a good description of the men and while following this lead they found Gecht's trophy case, which housed the amputated breasts of his victims, parts of which had been eaten.

Gecht was given 120 years; Thomas Kokoraleis was given 70 years, whilst his brother Andrew and Spreitzer were condemned to death. Andrew Kokoraleis was the first to be executed on 17 March 1999, but in January 2003 Spreitzer's death sentence was reduced to life without the possibility of parole. Thomas Kokoraleis had been a key witness in damning the rest of the men and as a result had received the lowest of all the sentences.

See Jack the Ripper p. 288

BANKS, GEORGE (1982)

George Banks, from Wilkes-Barre, Pennsylvania, awoke early on 25 September 1982 and proceeded to slaughter his whole family. His three girlfriends, Regina Clemens, Susan Yuhas and Dorothy Lyons were shot, followed by his four-year-old son, Bowendy, his one-year-old daughter, Mauitania, then his other daughter, Montanzima. He then shot 11-year-old Nancy Lyons and her half-brother, Forarounde Banks, before shooting two neighbours, Jimmy Olsen and Ray Hall. Banks then drove to a former girlfriend's home and killed her, her mother, the son they had together,

her brothers and a nephew who happened to be staying with them. After a brief siege, Banks surrendered and was subsequently sentenced to death. His sentence has not been carried out as appeals continue; his latest appeal was heard in 2001.

See Lyle and Erik Menendez p.212

COLEMAN, ALTON AND DEBRA BROWN (1984)

Reminiscent of the Moors Murderers, Alton Coleman used Debra Brown to allay the fears of the young girls he intended to rape and murder. The mass murders began in the summer of 1984 with the death of Vernita Wheat, aged nine, who they abducted from Waukegan in Illinois. The couple then abducted two girls from Gary, Illinois, but one survived and gave a description of Coleman. This was followed by the discovery of the body of Donna Williams on 11 July and shortly after that of Virginia Temple in Detroit. The couple then murdered Tonnie Storey, Harry and Marlene Waters and Eugene Scott in Ohio. They were recognised and

picked up in Chicago; Ohio gave them two death sentences, as did Illinois and Indiana. Coleman was executed by lethal injection in Ohio on 26 April 2002.

See Ian Brady and Myra Hindley p. 257

▶ *RIGHT: A lethal injection table, such as the one used in the execution of Alton Coleman in 2002.*

CODE, NATHANIEL JR (1984–87)

Nathaniel Code Jr was released from prison in 1984 after serving two years for rape. He married, and seemed a reformed man. This was not the case, however. On 31 August 1984 he murdered Debra Ford, and the following year he slaughtered a whole family just a short distance from his home in Shreveport, Louisiana. On 5 August 1987 he killed his own grandfather, William, and the two young grandsons of a friend. Code was known to hate his grandfather and was questioned by police in the wake of the killing; fingerprints from the scene matched the other family slaughter in 1985 and he was charged, tried and convicted of multiple murders.

Code is still in the process of appealing against the death sentence, but will never be freed, so violent and atrocious were his crimes.

See George Banks p.238

THE STATION STRANGLER (1986–94)

Between 1986 and 1994, 21 mixed-race boys and young men were raped, strangled and buried in shallow graves in the Cape Town area of South Africa. The alleged killer is Norman Afzal Simons, who was given a 25-year sentence in 1994 for the murder of a 10-year-old boy, whom he had abducted from Cape Town's Strand Station; the body was found 10 days later.

Although Simons has never admitted to the sex killings, he related the reason for killing the child to when he was raped by his own brother as a young boy. He claimed that when his brother was murdered in 1991 his spirit entered him and ordered him to rape and kill. Serial killer profilers are convinced that Simons is the Station Strangler.

See Vladimir Bratislav p. 246

▶ *RIGHT: Harrison Graham smiles and gestures as he leaves court after being found guilty.*

GRAHAM, HARRISON (1987)

Harrison Graham was a rather slow-witted man from Philadelphia, but he appears to have been fairly well-liked. Eventually, however, neighbours complained to the landlord about the rank smells emanating from his apartment. Graham argued with the landlord, which resulted in his eviction; he made sure he had nailed the bedroom door shut before leaving, claiming his valuables were inside.

On 9 August 1987 the landlord called the police to break down the door; inside were the decomposing corpses of seven women. Graham claimed they had been there when he moved in, but forensics showed they had been strangled then abused after death by Graham. He was found guilty on all counts and sentenced to life and six electrocutions – after serving his full sentence he will be electrocuted.

See Forensics p. 173

FELTNER, JEFFREY LYNN (1988)

In 1988 the police received a telephone call from a man claiming to have committed a series of murders at a nursing home in Melrose, Florida. Investigation showed there had been only one sudden death at the nursing home, on 10 February 1988. As a result, Jeffrey Feltner, who had made the call, received four months imprisonment for making false statements. Whilst incarcerated he discovered he had contracted AIDS. On his release, Feltner again began making nuisance calls to the police, but he was linked to the murder of a pensioner at Daytona Beach. He told police he was indeed guilty of the sudden death, as well as four other murders at the Melrose nursing home, plus another at a medical centre. In January 1989 Feltner was given a life sentence without parole for 25 years.

See Robert Diaz p. 236

LUNDGREN, JEFFREY (1989)

Jeffrey Lundgren led a small group of around 12 people who broke away from the large establishment, the Reorganised Church of Jesus Christ of Latter Day Saints, in 1987. Officially he claimed that the group was too liberal, but there were suggestions that he had been embezzling money. Lundgren set up his new church at Kirtland, Utah, where he enjoyed exclusive rule and gave his followers paramilitary training; there were also rumours of strange sexual rituals. One family, the Averys, opposed Lundgren and he had them thrown into a pit, where he executed them and then buried them. Working from a tip-off, police raided the cult's headquarters and Lundgren was sentenced to death for the murders whilst his wife and son were given long prison sentences.

See Waco, Texas p. 243

WACO, TEXAS (1993)

While David Koresh, born Vernon Wayne Howell, believed he was an angel and an agent of God, US authorities saw him as a gun-toting criminal who had physically and sexually abused his own children and those of members of his cult. Koresh led a group called the Branch Davidians in an impressive stronghold near Waco, Texas. He had gained control of the cult through force, in a shootout in which the former leader, George Roden had been wounded.

Koresh believed that the end of the world would come when the US Army attacked their Mount Carmel compound; he began stockpiling

▶ *ABOVE: Branch Davidian survivors leave Federal Court in Waco, Texas.*

food, weapons and ammunition. The authorities did indeed come on 28 February 1993 to arrest him for illegally holding firearms and explosives. The siege, which began in a volley of shots from the cultists, claimed four US agents, with a further 16 wounded. The siege continued with a war of words until 19 April, when the FBI began organising a dawn attack. By noon, the compound was engulfed in flames and Koresh and his 76 remaining followers perished. The debate still rages as to who set the fires, although it seems clear that the wooden buildings were doused in petrol.

See Heaven's Gate p. 247

MCVEIGH, TIMOTHY (1995)

Timothy McVeigh is one of a rare breed: a domestic, home-born American terrorist. McVeigh was a former US Army veteran, who had served during the first Gulf War and had been decorated for his services. After his military career, however, he became violently disillusioned with the American government and was further outraged by the way in which the Waco siege had been handled in 1993.

Deciding to make a stand against the government, he hired a truck and parked it outside the Alfred P. Murrah Federal Building in Oklahoma City. It was packed with a 7,000 lb explosive device, a mixture of ammonium nitrate fertiliser and fuel oil. This was detonated on 19 April 1995, shattering the building and killing 168 people. McVeigh faced federal charges for the murder of eight of their employees; the other deaths came under the jurisdiction of the state of Oklahoma. McVeigh's cohort, Michael Fortier, confessed to his involvement and was the prosecution's star witness; he was sentenced to just 12 years in prison. McVeigh became the first person in over 38 years to be executed by the US federal government when he was given a lethal injection in the federal prison at Terre Haute, Indiana, on 11 June 2001.

See The Weathermen p. 27

▶ RIGHT: Timothy McVeigh is placed under arrest, two days after the Oklahoma bombing.

BRYANT, MARTIN (1996)

Tourists were wandering around the former penal colony at Port Arthur, Tasmania, in April 1996 when a gunman opened fire. Thirty-five people were slaughtered and 18 seriously wounded. Police eventually identified Martin Bryant, a man with no criminal record but with a history of psychological problems, as the assailant. Bryant pleaded guilty to 72 charges of murder, attempted murder, grievous bodily harm, aggravated assault, wounding and arson. The Tasmanian Supreme Court issued 35 life sentences.

See Charles Whitman p. 229

FRANCOIS, KENDALL (1996–98)

Between October 1996 and the early months of the following year, three New York prostitutes disappeared without a trace. In March 1997 another was reported missing, then a fifth. Mary Giaccone failed to attend her mother's funeral in the November. All the women closely resembled one another – they were all short, petite and with brown hair and blue eyes. Sandra Dean French's car was discovered just a short distance from Francois' home in June 1998,

▶ RIGHT: Martin Bryant, who went on a shooting spree in Port Arthur, Tasmania in 1996.

then in August Catina Newmaster similarly disappeared. On 1 September Francois was picked up for assaulting a woman. Under interrogation he admitted to being responsible for the disappearances. When the police searched his home they found eight putrefying corpses. Francois pleaded guilty in court and was sentenced to life. He had contracted AIDS from one of his victims.

See Saeed Hanaei p. 248

◀ LEFT: *The front door of the house where Kendall Francois lived and stored his victims' corpses.*

BRATISLAV, VLADIMIR (1997)

Vladimar Bratislav received the nickname the 'Beast of Lysva' for the rape, mutilation and murder of 30 women. He thought all women were prostitutes and preyed upon local women from March 1997. All the victims had their eyes removed before being raped and most were strangled. Chosen at random, the women were lured to their death when Bratislav invited them to walk with him after meeting and entertaining them at a nightclub.

On 10 June 1998 Bratislav attacked Natalya Mezentseva in a park but only robbed her; she recognised him and called the police. They put the park under surveillance and Natalya pointed out Bratislav two days later. He was convicted of 10 murders and six attempted murders, although he claimed his total number of victims was around 30. He was sentenced to life imprisonment.

See Francois Kendall p. 245

▶ *RIGHT: Andrew Cunanan, who murdered fashion designer Gianni Versace in 1997.*

CUNANAN, ANDREW (1997)

On 29 April 1997 Andrew Cunanan, a member of San Diego's gay community, bludgeoned Jeffrey Trail to death in the apartment of David Madson, a former lover living in Minneapolis. Cunanan killed Madson himself four days later; his body was found with multiple gunshot wounds. In May he stabbed Lee Miglin to death in Chicago and shot William Rees in New Jersey. On the morning of 15 July he shot the fashion guru Gianni Versace outside his Miami Beach mansion. There followed a nationwide manhunt that ended when Cunanan's body was found in a house boat near the Versace murder scene.

See The Station Strangler p. 240

HEAVEN'S GATE (1997)

The Heaven's Gate doomsday cult was centred in California and was led by Marshall Herff Applewhite and Bonnie Lu Trusdale Nettles. They believed that a UFO would come to Earth and 'recycle' the population. They also believed that if the group committed suicide they would be resurrected, as Jesus had been in the Bible and others in the book of Revelations. They thought the body was only a temporary container for the soul and that extra-terrestrials would bring humanity to a higher level. Over three days in 1997, 39 members of the cult committed suicide. Nettles had already died of cancer in 1985. Applewhite was one of those who committed suicide in preparation for the UFO, which they believed was following the Hale-Bopp comet; at Easter 1997 it was at its closest point to the Earth, undoubtedly signalling the suicides.

See Waco, Texas p. 243

HANAEI, SAEED (2000–01)

Hanaei turned to murder after a man propositioned his wife, believing her to be a prostitute. Hanaei embarked on his own personal crusade to clean up the streets of the Iranian city of Mashhad; he was to become known as the 'Spider Killer'. Between 2000 and his capture in July 2001, Hanaei strangled 16 women with their own headscarves and dumped their bodies. He posed as a customer, sexually assaulted the women, then killed them. He admitted to the murders and was hanged before his relatives on 16 April 2002. Three other similar murders in the city, at first attributed to Hanaei, were later proved to have been committed by copy-cat killers. At the time, Hanaei was hailed as an Islamic hero as he 'did not spill the blood of innocents'.

See François Kendall p. 245

IQBAL, JAVED (2001)

Iqbal kept a meticulous diary detailing his slaughter of 100 young boys. He strangled each of the victims and dissolved their bodies in vats of acid, which he then poured into the drains. The police in Lahore, Pakistan, had been investigating the disappearance of the children when Iqbal wrote a letter to the police, confessing to sexually abusing the boys and then murdering them. Iqbal's surrender came after two accomplices were arrested when trying to cash travellers' cheques belonging to him. His motive, he alleged, was the treatment he had received at the hands of the police when he had been questioned in the early 1990s for raping small boys. The court in January 2000 sentenced him to be strangled and his body to be dissolved in acid.

See The Station Strangler p. 240

▸ *RIGHT: John Allen Muhammad, who was arrested over the DC area sniper attacks in 2002.*

MUHAMMAD, JOHN ALLEN AND JOHN LEE MALVO (2002)

Between 2–22 October 2002 the Washington DC, Maryland and Virginia areas of the US were subjected to a series of indiscriminate sniper incidents that sent fear to the heart of those who lived in the region. The snipers used a standard family saloon, which they had converted to allow them to shoot through a hole in the boot with a telescopic rifle. After many false leads, John Allen Muhammad and his 17-year-old stepson, John Lee Malvo, were found sleeping in their car and arrested. The two men, who became known as the Washington Snipers, had targeted civilians and had left a tarot card at the scene of one of the shootings, which stated 'Dear Mr Policeman, I am God'. In a letter left at another scene the snipers stated 'Your children are not safe anywhere or any time'. They had demanded $10 million. At present the three states are still vying for who will be first to place the men on trial.

See Charles Whitman p. 229

John Allen
Muhammad
aka
John Allen
Williams

CNN

CONNIE CHUNG
TONIGHT

A SHOOTINGS, AUTHORITIES SAY *POP STORIES* 2 MEN IN CUST

SERIAL KILLERS

HOLMES, DR HARRY HOWARD (1890–95)

New Hampshire-born bigamist Harry Holmes, also known as Herman Webster Mudgett, acquired the nickname 'The Torture Doctor' due to his sinister activities. In 1890 Holmes's drugstore boss, Mrs Holden, disappeared and he subsequently inherited the business. This thrived sufficiently for him to build a 100-room hotel opposite the shop and it was here that he developed his death house. When an insurance fraud led the police to search Holmes's hotel, they found a basement containing vats of acid, windowless torture rooms and a number of female bones and skeletons. He was brought to trial in 1895, where he

represented himself. Found guilty of murder, he was hanged in May 1896. Before his death he confessed his crimes to a newspaper, for which he was paid $7,500 – he had apparently committed a total of 27 murders.

See Harold Shipman p.273

◀ LEFT: *Harry Holmes designed his 'castle' for murdering, torturing and disposing of his victims.*

FISH, ALBERT (1917–34)

A murderer, necrophile and cannibal operating in the US between 1917 and 1934, Fish's capture came four years after he had murdered and eaten a 12-year-old girl from New York, Grace Budd. Fish wrote a letter to Grace's mother, detailing his murder and cannibalism of her daughter. The police found traces of a partially

▶ RIGHT: *Albert Fish, thought to have inspired Hannibal Lecter in Thomas Harris's novels.*

erased address on the envelope. Fish was apprehended and confessed to 12 murders and 100 assaults; he was electrocuted on 16 January 1936.

See Electrocution p. 185

CHRISTIE, JOHN REGINALD HALLIDAY (1940–53)

Between 1940 and 1953, 'Reg' Christie murdered eight women. During World War II Christie was a special reserve constable and had a reputation for his authoritarian and officious attitude. His first two victims, Ruth Fuerst and Muriel Eady were raped and strangled, then buried in Christie's back garden whilst his wife, Ethel, was away from the house on holiday or visiting relatives. Beryl Evans, a neighbour, turned to Christie for an abortion in 1949; he battered and strangled then raped her, before killing her baby daughter, Geraldine. Surprisingly, Beryl's husband Timothy confessed to the murders and was hanged in 1950, but he received a posthumous pardon when the evidence against Christie came to light.

In January 1950, prostitutes Rita Nelson and Kathleen Maloney fell victim to Christie, who hid their bodies in a cupboard. By March of the same year, the cupboard also contained the body of Hectorina McLennan. After Christie's sister-in-law informed the police that she had not heard from Ethel, his home at 10 Rillington Place was searched and her body was found buried in the back garden. Christie was charged with her murder and later confessed to the seven other killings. He was hanged on 15 July 1953.

See Hanging p. 180

GEIN, EDDIE (1954)

When his mother died in December 1945, the lonely, eccentric bachelor Eddie Gein's found it impossible to bear. He skinned her body and tanned the flesh, wearing it and her clothes in an attempt to reincarnate her. He then began robbing graves and taking the bodies home to preserve them, before finally turning to murder. Mary Hogan was Gein's first known victim in 1954, followed by Bernice Worden. When Worden's son found a receipt from their hardware store in Bernice's handwriting made out to Gein, the killer was charged with and confessed to the two murders, but insufficient evidence linked him with the skin and body parts of a further 15 women that were found around his home. Gein was deemed to be insane and committed to an institution, where he died in 1984.

See Jeffrey Dahmer p. 272

GLATMAN, HARVEY
(1957–59)

Harvey Glatman had been an odd child and as he grew older his sexual activity took to extremes that bordered on hanging himself. In 1945, armed with a cap-gun, he attempted to make a girl undress, for which he was caught and arrested. Breaking bail, he fled to New York, but

▶ RIGHT: *Eddie Gein, the model for numerous cinematic psychos including Leatherface and Norman Bates.*

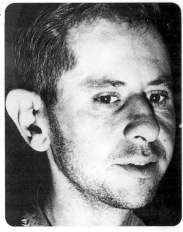

▶ *RIGHT: Harvey Glatman, a serial strangler.*

was arrested again and imprisoned for robbery. After his release in 1951 he moved to Los Angeles, living a life of a near-recluse. In 1957 he began recruiting women to accept nude-modelling photographic assignments. His first victim, Judy Dull, was repeatedly raped then strangled and buried. In March 1958 he claimed a second victim, Shirley Bridgeford, whose body was abandoned in a desert near San Diego. In July he murdered Ruth Mercado. His downfall came after a desperate struggle with intended victim Lorraine Vigil; a policeman intervened and arrested Glatman. He confessed and was executed in the gas chamber at San Quentin in August 1959.

See Ian Brady and Myra Hindley p. 257

MCDONALD, WILLIAM (1961–62)

William McDonald became known as the 'Sydney Mutilator', claiming the lives of four vagrants between June 1961 and November 1962. McDonald had been indecently assaulted whilst in the army and sought revenge through the sexual mutilation of other men. After he was found guilty of the murders in September 1963, he nearly killed again in prison and was transferred to a mental institution. It is almost certain that McDonald was a schizophrenic.

See Vaughn Orrin Greenwood p. 258

DE SALVO, ALBERT (1962–64)

De Salvo stalked the streets of Boston between June 1962 and January 1964, claiming least 13 victims – all women who he raped or sexually assaulted then either strangled, bludgeoned or stabbed. He became known as the 'Boston Strangler'. In December 1962, a psychological profile described him as being of Spanish or Italian origin, of average height, a schizophrenic and probably a mother-hater. Many of his early victims were mature or elderly women, but four of them were either in their late teens or early twenties. He gained entry to women's homes by posing as a workman or policeman.

On 27 October 1964 De Salvo sexually assaulted a woman whom he may have intended as his fourteenth murder victim. Inexplicably, he left her alive. Her description of him prompted other women to identify De Salvo as their attacker. While he was being held on a rape charge in 1965, he confessed that he was the Boston Strangler. With no physical evidence to link him to the killings, he never stood trial for any of the crimes but was imprisoned for life for robberies and rapes. He was found murdered in his cell on 26 November 1973.

See Kenneth Bianchi and Angelo Buono p. 267

BRADY, IAN AND MYRA HINDLEY (1963–64)

Manchester lovers Brady and Hindley became known as the 'Moors Murderers'. Brady was a sadist, Nazi and pornography-lover when he met Hindley and the couple soon began a cruel campaign of child-abduction, using Hindley's grandmother's home in Wardle Brook Avenue, Hattersley as their base. Amongst their victims were John Kilbride, who had disappeared in Ashton-under-Lyne in November 1963, and Lesley Ann Downey, who disappeared on Boxing Day 1964. Hindley's brother-in-law, who Brady had been grooming as an accomplice, witnessed Brady's brutal murder of Edward Evans on the night of October 6 1965. The next day he reported it to the police and Brady and Hindley were arrested. On 16 October 1965 Lesley Ann's body was discovered in a shallow grave on the moors; the investigating team had managed to locate her grave from photographic evidence showing Hindley crouching in the exact spot. Although police were unconvinced that John and Lesley Ann were the couple's only victims, Brady and Hindley were sent to trial at Chester Assizes in 1966. Brady was found guilty of three murders, and Hindley of two; both were sentenced to life.

In 1987 Hindley confessed to the additional murders of Pauline Reade (12 July 1963) and Keith Bennett (16 June 1964), and Brady confirmed her confession. Despite numerous appeals for release, Hindley died in prison in 2003 and Brady remains in Ashworth Special Hospital in Merseyside.

See Charles Manson p. 259

▲ *ABOVE: Ian Brady and Myra Hindley, who were imprisoned for life in 1966.*

◀ *LEFT: Albert de Salvo is recaptured by police after escaping from a mental hospital.*

257

MOSELEY, WINSTON (1964)

Winston Moseley was arrested in March 1964; he had no criminal record but he had committed innumerable burglaries, dozens of rapes and at least three murders. In 1964 he had been picked up literally in the act of murdering Kitty Genovese in New York, and immediately made a confession. In 1968, having been found guilty and sentenced to death – later commuted to life imprisonment – he escaped from the hospital where he was being held and took five people hostage, during which time he committed a rape. He was returned to prison after surrendering. In recent years he has attempted to secure his release after nearly four decades in prison. He is eligible for parole in 2004. Undoubtedly, Moseley was a psychopath and whether he has truly been rehabilitated is uncertain.

See Tommy Searl p. 260

GREENWOOD, VAUGHN ORRIN (1964–75)

Vaughn Greenwood became known as the 'Skid Row Slasher', preying on vagrants in the Los Angeles area. He began his murderous career in 1964, but the 11 killings, which included nine slasher murders, were not connected until 1975. In a bizarre ritual, Greenwood cut his victims' throats, then scattered salt around the body, removed the shoes and placed them pointing towards the victim's feet. Greenwood had been arrested on 3 February 1975 in connection with the attempted murder of two men in Hollywood. The following month police linked him to the slasher murders, and formally charged him in January 1976. In January 1977 Greenwood was found guilty of nine murders and sentenced to life imprisonment. He was charged separately for the two early murders in 1964, but these were declared to have been a mistrial.

See Dennis Nilson p. 270

MANSON, CHARLES (1969)

Charles Manson was an ex-convict and a drop-out, but he had a magnetic personality that apparently made him irresistible to women. He assembled around him 'the family', a group of disciples who began occupation of a disused ranch in California in the summer of 1969. Manson was something of an early survivalist, believing that the end of civilisation was nigh and that he and his 'family' would inherit the Earth. Their first murder took place on 25 July 1969 when they killed Gary Hinman in an attempt to seize his inheritance. On 9 August the same year, they broke into the home of film director Roman Polanski and his wife, Sharon Tate. In an orgy of violence the family slaughtered five people in this Beverley Hills massacre. But they were not content with this. Two days later they murdered the LaBianca family. One of Manson's followers, Susan Atkins, was imprisoned for prostitution shortly afterwards and, through a confession to a fellow inmate, the authorities learned of the family's involvement in the two slaughters. They were rounded up in December 1969 and, after an extraordinary trial, most of the members of the family were sentenced to death, later reduced to life imprisonment. Manson will never be released.

See Anatoly Onoprienko p. 279

CORONA, JUAN (1971)

Corona was born in Mexico but moved to California in the 1950s. Both he and his brother, Nativadad, were homosexual with homicidal tendencies. Nativadad had attacked a man in a café in 1970 with a machete. The true scope of their crimes – for which Juan would subsequently receive 25 life sentences – began before May 1971. Juan had been working as a contract labourer in an orchard in California. The orchard-owner discovered a fresh grave and contacted the authorities; it contained the body of

Kenneth Whittaker, who had been stabbed and his skull torn open with a sharp object, possibly a machete. After nine days of intensive searching, investigators discovered 25 graves; in each of these they found the heavily mutilated bodies of migrant workers, alcoholics and drifters, none of whom had been reported missing. All showed signs of homosexual rape. Juan had foolishly left receipts containing his signature in two of the graves. Nonetheless, it took the jury 45 hours to convict him on all murder counts. Juan's defence lawyers had tried to place the blame upon Natividad.

See Patrick Wayne Kearney p. 265

◀ *LEFT: Juan Corona arrives at Yuba City courthouse in 1971.*

SEARL, TOMMY (1972)

In March 1972 the body of Cynthia Kohls was found in Kalamazoo, Michigan; she had been raped and stabbed. In July the corpses of Cornelia Davault and Nancy Harte were found, and a month later the body of Jennifer Curran was discovered. Tommy Searl was arrested and a boy in his company became the prosecution witness, telling the court that Searl had raped, strangled, stabbed or suffocated the women. He was sentenced to life imprisonment.

See Gary Leon Ridgway p. 276

MULLIN, HERB (1972–73)

Herb Mullin came from a religious background and appears to have become mentally unbalanced following the death of his best friend, Dean Richardson, in a car accident in July 1965. Mullin created a shrine to Dean in his bedroom, broke off his engagement, claimed he was homosexual and declared he was a conscientious objector when he was called up in 1969. Hallucinogenic drugs fuelled his paranoid schizophrenia. Mullin committed his first murder in October 1972, beating a tramp to death with a baseball bat. Eleven days later he stabbed a college student and disembowelled her, leaving her body for the vultures. In January 1973 he shot five people, and a further four the following month. He was soon captured and found guilty of 10 murders; he will be eligible for parole in 2025.

See William McDonald p. 255

BUNDY, THEODORE (TED) ROBERT (1972–78)

Bundy was a highly educated man, handsome and attractive to women. In the period up to 1972, there were a series of killings of young women in the Washington State area, which abruptly stopped when Bundy moved to the University of Utah in Salt Lake. A new epidemic of murders broke out there.

In 1977 Bundy was arrested for the kidnapping of Carol DaRonch and was then linked to the earlier killing of Caryn Campbell. Bundy was extradited to Colorado to face the Campbell murder charge, but he escaped in June. He was quickly recaptured, but escaped again six months later and carried out another series of murders, rapes and robberies in Florida.

Bundy was to remain at large until February 1978, when he was picked up by chance for a minor traffic offence. It was then,

▶ RIGHT: Ted Bundy, who eventually confessed to 28 murders.

under interrogation, that he admitted to over 100 killings. At his subsequent trial, Bundy was sentenced to death, but made repeated appeals and assisted the FBI in constructing psychological profiles of serial killers. Psychological profiles of Bundy himself revealed few clues as to why he became a serial killer. In his own words, 'sometimes I feel like a vampire'. He was executed on 24 January 1989.

See Richard Ramirez p. 29

BONIN, WILLIAM AND VERNON BUTTS (1972–80)

William Bonin and Vernon Butts murdered 41 young men between 1972 and 1980, raping then strangling and, in some cases, mutilating their bodies. The series of murders, known as the 'Freeway Killings', took place across Southern California. The police linked the convicted rapist Bonin with the attacks and put him under surveillance, catching him in the act in June 1980. He implicated Vernon Butts and later James Monro and Gregory Miley. Butts committed suicide in prison in January 1981; Miley provided evidence against Bonin, who was convicted of the rape, torture and murder of 10 of his victims and executed by lethal injection on 23 February 1996. Bonin's and Butts' victims had mainly been young, male hitchhikers. Bonin said 'I'd still be killing, I couldn't stop killing'.

See Patrick Wayne Kearney p.265

MCCAFFERTY, ARCHIBALD BEATTIE (1973)

Scottish-born McCafferty was released from prison in April 1997 after serving 23 years for what became known as the Kill Seven murders in Australia. In 1973 he murdered his newly born son, Craig, and leading a teenage gang in August 1973 murdered George Anson, a newspaper

▸ RIGHT: Four of the six women killed by 'Son of Sam' David Berkowitz.

seller. Three days later they murdered Ronald Cox and the following day a driving instructor, Evangelos Kollias. One of the gang, Rick Webster, terrified that he would become one of McCafferty's victims, turned himself in and McCafferty was arrested. He was made out to be a Manson-like figure, undoubtedly a dangerous and manipulative individual. Four of the gang were found guilty of murder and sentenced to between four and 18 years. McCafferty, who claimed he had been impelled by voices to kill seven people, was given three life terms.

See Charles Manson p. 259

BERKOWITZ, DAVID (1975–77)

Adopted at birth by a Jewish couple, Nat and Pearl Berkowitz, David was something of a loner as a child. The death of his adopted mother affected him badly and he made his first bungled attempt at murdering a woman on 24 December 1975. Seven months later he bought a handgun and approached a car containing two women. He fired through the windscreen, killing Donna Laurie and wounding Jodi Valenti. He then

set out on nightly hunts for new victims. His second successful attack came on 23 October 1976, when he mistakenly shot Carl DeNaro, a long-haired male, but just a month later he shot Donna DeMasi and Joanne Lomino dead while they were seated on their porch. Christine Freund fell victim on 30 January 1977 and, in March, Virginia Voskerichian, then Valentina Suriani and Alexander Esau in April, when Berkowitz wrote a note to the police, signing himself 'Son of Sam'. He killed again on 31 July 1977, but this time was to be his last. He was arrested and, after psychiatric tests, considered fit to stand trial, where he pleaded guilty. He received 547 years and served his sentence in Attica Prison, in the Catskill Mountains, New York.

See Forensic Handwriting p. 176

KEARNEY, PATRICK WAYNE (1975–77)

Patrick Kearney and his lover David D. Hill killed and dismembered at least 28 male victims between 1975 and 1977. The two men were army veterans and lived in a meticulously kept bachelor apartment in Redondo Beach, California. With Kearney taking the lead, they committed a series of killings known as the 'Trash-Bag Murders', as the dismembered corpses were found dumped along Californian highways in black bin bags. The couple surrendered in July 1977 after seeing a wanted poster of themselves and knowing that they would inevitably be caught. Hill was released due to lack of evidence, but Kearney was sentenced to multiple life imprisonment. He explained that the killings excited him and made him feel dominant.

See Juan Corona p. 259

SUTCLIFFE, PETER (1976–81)

At the time, the infamous 'Yorkshire Ripper' case was the largest manhunt ever launched in Britain – some 250,000 people were interviewed and over 30,000 statements made. For over five years, the Yorkshire Ripper preyed on lone women; many of whom were prostitutes. On several occasions, former grave digger Peter Sutcliffe had been interviewed, but he had not been directly linked to the brutal attacks and murders. Sutcliffe would later admit to 20 attacks, using a hammer to incapacitate his victims before he stabbed and mutilated them. Thirteen women died from the assaults. Hoax letters and an audio tape supposedly from the Ripper confused the police and for a time directed them away from Sutcliffe.

It was pure chance, rather than investigative techniques, which led to

◀ *LEFT: Detectives discover yet another Yorkshire Ripper victim.*

Sutcliffe's capture on 2 January 1981. A routine police check on a parked car at night revealed Peter Williams, Sutcliffe's cover name. He confessed to the murders under questioning and claimed he had been told by God to rid the streets of prostitutes. On 22 May 1981 he was found guilty of 13 murders and sentenced to a minimum of 30 years imprisonment.
See Jack the Ripper p. 288

SOBHRAJ, CHARLES (1976–82)

Charles Sobhraj, of Indian and Vietnamese parentage, began his criminal career in India in the early 1970s. At first, he was involved in robbery, smuggling and black-market activities. He served prison sentences in India, Iran and Greece. By 1976, he was wanted in connection with eight murders in Turkey, Thailand and India. His chosen method was to target hippies and other western tourists, drug them, rob them, murder them – either with a knife or a pistol – and then burn their bodies. In 1982 he was sentenced to life for a Calcutta murder, but drugged his guards and spent several weeks on the run. He was then confined to the Tihar Prison; should he ever be released there are outstanding murder charges in Nepal and Thailand awaiting him.
See John Eric Armstrong p. 281

GARY, CARLTON (1977–78)

Gary Carlton was responsible for a series of rapes and murders of elderly women; he became known as the 'Stocking Strangler' due to his method of murder. His murderous career began in September 1977 and continued until April 1978. Carlton was identified by a witness and, as he had already served a prison sentence for the rape of an elderly woman in New York, the police in Columbus, Georgia, were convinced they had the right man. He disappeared until May 1984, when he was finally picked up in Atlanta and charged with the murder, rape and robbery of three women. He was found guilty of murder and sentenced to death; he remains on death row in Jackson, Georgia. There continues to be a lingering doubt as to whether he committed all the Stocking Strangler killings.

See Kenneth Bianchi and Angelo Buono p. 267

BIANCHI, KENNETH AND ANGELO BUONO (1977–79)

The Hillside Strangler was, in fact, two men – cousins Kenneth Bianchi and Angelo Buono. Between 1977 and 1979, seven abductions, rapes and murders took place in Los Angeles that were later linked to the men. Bianchi had been interviewed following this spate of murders, but no proof was found of his involvement. When the bodies of Diane Wilder and Karen Mandic were discovered in Bellingham, Washington in January 1979, his name came up again. The police found forensic evidence, Mandic's telephone number and other incriminating evidence in Bianchi's home. He implicated Buono after he had been arrested and interrogated; it was confirmed that they had carried out the murders together. Buono was convicted of just one of the murders and sentenced to life imprisonment, while Bianchi received multiple life sentences and was imprisoned in Washington.

See Albert De Salvo p. 256

▶ *RIGHT: Roger Boren, deputy Attorney General of California, during Angelo Buono's trial.*

FRANKLIN, JOSEPH PAUL (1977–80)

Joseph Franklin was a neo-Nazi who targeted mixed race couples between 1977 and 1980. His first victims were Alphonse Manning and his white partner, Toni Schwenn, who he shot to death in Madison, Wisconsin. He claimed another couple in Oklahoma City in October 1979, but lack of evidence meant that he never faced charges for these two murders. Although linked to two murders in Indianapolis and two more in Cincinnati in 1980, Franklin again got away with these killings. In August he shot and killed African-Americans David Martin and Ted Fields, who were jogging in a park with white women in Salt Lake City. In March 1981 he was sentenced to four life sentences for these two murders and in February 1986 another two for the murders of Manning and Schwenn.
See David Berkowitz p. 263

COTTINGHAM, RICHARD (1977–81)

In 1981 Richard Cottingham, a Blue Cross worker in New York, was sentenced to 197 years for 15 murders, although it is believed that his reign of terror may have claimed as many as 19 lives. He targeted prostitutes, claiming that they needed to be punished as they were without morals. Cottingham was linked to the murders through fingerprints found on handcuffs left on the corpses of two of his prostitute victims. In many respects, Cottingham's savage mutilation of his victims was reminiscent of Jack the Ripper – many of the victims had been horribly dismembered. Cottingham's is a strange case as he undoubtedly had homosexual tendencies, yet he had clearly had sex with all of his victims before slaughtering them.
See Jack the Ripper p. 288

▶ *LEFT: John Wayne Gacy Jr after the wedding to his second wife, Carole Hoff, in 1972,*

GACY JR, JOHN WAYNE (1978)

This Chicago-born murderer lured boys into his home, raped and strangled them, then buried their bodies around his swimming pool and under his house, pouring lime over them to assist decomposition. Gacy, who suffered from blackouts after a childhood head injury, murdered 36 youths. His arrest in 1978 came as the result of an assignation with Robert Priest, whose mother reported him missing, informing the police of Robert's meeting with Gacy; they searched his house and discovered a trap door leading to the mass graves. Gacy, who had visited hospitals as 'Pogo the Clown', confessed, but did not testify at his trial. On 13 March 1980, he was sentenced to death and was executed by lethal injection.
See William Bonin and Vernon Butts p. 262

GALLEGO, GERALD AND CHARLENE WILLIAMS-GALLEGO (1978–80)

In rare cases, murder runs in the family. Gerald Gallego's father had been executed in Mississippi for the murder of a prison guard, but Gerald

eclipsed his father's notoriety. Together with his seventh wife, Charlene, he embarked on a series of kidnappings, rapes and murders – targetting female hitchhikers – throughout California and Nevada, claiming at least 10 lives. After an intensive manhunt, Gerald and Charlene surrendered to the police in Omaha, Nebraska, and were extradited to California. There, Gerald was convicted of the murders and sentenced to death. The couple were then again extradited, to Nevada, with Charlene making a full confession, as she had done in California. Gerald was found guilty and sentenced to death by means of a lethal injection, whilst Charlene was given 16 years imprisonment.

See Paul Bernardo and Carla Homolka p. 280

NILSEN, DENNIS (1978–83)

Civil servant Dennis Nilsen turned two of his homes, in London and Cricklewood, into slaughter houses in which he claimed at least 29 lives between 1978 and 1983. Nilsen, a homosexual, picked up young men in central London and murdered them, then dismembered their bodies. His primary problem was the disposal of the corpses, which he either kept in bags in his home, hidden under floorboards, or attempted to flush down the lavatory. When manholes

◀ *LEFT: The pot and stove used by Dennis Nilsen to boil the severed heads of his victims.*

were checked to discover the source of a foul stench in at his Cranley Gardens home in February 1983, lumps of human flesh were discovered. At first he denied knowledge of the bodies, but under questioning later he made a full confession, detailing at length all his murders. Over the course of 11 days, Nilsen dictated some 30 hours of confessions, describing how he had picked up mainly vagrants and extracted sexual favours from them in exchange for food and shelter. His abiding desire, having established a relationship of sorts with the men, was that they should never leave him. Nilsen stood trial in October 1983 and was found both sane and guilty of the six specimen murder charges and two attempted murders. He was sentenced to life imprisonment.

See Ted Bundy p. 261

▶ RIGHT: Dennis Nilsen is driven away after being convicted of six murders in 1983.

CHIKATILO, ANDREI ROMANOVICH (1978–90)

Between 1978 and 1990 the 'Rostov Ripper', or the 'Forest-Strip Killer', claimed at least 55 young lives in Russia. The Ripper, Andrei Chickatilo, was a schoolteacher and grandfather who preyed on the homeless and solitary children. He would lure them into woodland, cut out their tongues, gouge out their eyes and perforate their eardrums before raping, mutilating and cannibalising the victims.

Chikatilo had been picked up in connection with the crimes in both 1979 and in 1984. On the second occasion he had been blood-tested, but his group did not match samples found at the murder scenes. In some rare cases, blood, semen or saliva from the same individual can be from different serological groups. Chikatilo was finally arrested after surveillance in November 1990 and in October 1992 he was sentenced to death.

See Serology p. 169

▶ *RIGHT: Arrest photos of Andrei Romanovich Chikatilo against a map of the Rostov area.*

DAHMER, JEFFREY (1978–91)

Jeffrey Dahmer, the 'Milwaukee Cannibal', is undoubtedly one of the most terrifying and gruesome of all serial killers. Between 1978 and 1991, Dahmer may have murdered as many as 17 young men. He was a depraved psychopath, cannibal and necrophile, who already had convictions for child molesting. He would invite young men back to his apartment, drug them, handcuff them and then either strangle or stab them to death. In other instances he would carry out

◀ *LEFT: Jeffrey Dahmer appears in Milwaukee County Circuit Court in 1991.*

his own medical experiments, including attempts to lobotomise his victims, or drill holes in their skull and pour in acid. Once the victim was dead he would dismember the corpse and keep parts of their bodies either pickled or frozen as trophies.

When Dahmer was arrested in July 1991, following a lead from Tracy Edwards, a young man who had managed to escape from Dahmer, the police made innumerable horrific discoveries in his apartment. There were photographs of dismembered bodies, human skulls in the refrigerator, pickled body parts and clear signs that Dahmer had eaten parts of the bodies. Dahmer was sentenced to 957 years, but he was battered to death by a fellow inmate during a prison riot in November 1994.

See Juan Corona p.259

SHIPMAN, HAROLD (1978–98)

Doctor Harold Shipman was Britain's most prolific serial killer. Opinions differ as to how many of his patients the deadly doctor despatched with drug overdoses, but it may have been in excess of 300. To some extent the enquiries are still ongoing and Shipman has been officially linked with the murders of 215 of his patients who died in his care between 1978 and 1998. The minimum number is 236; several other cases of premature death may never be positively identified as Shipman killings. The huge disparity of deaths of his patients compared to those of other doctors in similar circumstances first began to sound alarm bells to his colleagues and later to the police. The enquiries were not well-conducted and the police missed early opportunities to bring Shipman's crimes to light, thus allowing him to continue to murder. Shipman had made amateur attempts to cover his tracks by doctoring medical records and lying about the medical condition of many of his patients. His trial

began in October 1999, and in January 2000 he was found guilty of 15 specimen murder charges and sentenced to life imprisonment for each conviction.

See John Bodkin Adams p. 149

BISHOP, ARTHUR (1979–83)

Arthur Bishop was a Mormon and homicidal paedophile who claimed the lives of five children. In the 1970s Bishop had been a missionary in the Philippines, but following his paedophile activities had been

◄ LEFT: *A local in Hyde, Greater Manchester, reads of former GP Harold Shipman's crimes.*

excommunicated by the church in 1974. He claimed his first murder victim in October 1979 and his second in November 1980. The following year, Bishop disappeared after embezzling $9,000 from his former employer. Bishop struck again in October 1981; there was then a two-year gap before his next victim in June 1983. In July he killed for the last time, whilst under suspicion of another embezzlement charge. The police arrested him for fraud and interrogated him regarding the murders. He confessed and was executed by lethal injection in June 1988.

See Lethal Injection p. 183

BLACK, ROBERT (1982–90)

From 1982 until 1990, thousands of police hours were expended on tracking down a balding, bearded kidnapper, sex offender and murderer. Robert Black's luck ran out in July 1990 when he attempted to abduct a six-year-old girl from Stow on the Scottish border. He was arrested when a sharp-eyed witness who had reported the kidnapping spotted the van for a second time.

▶ RIGHT: *Robert Black is led away after the verdict at Newcastle Crown Court.*

Black worked as a delivery van driver and the police could place him in and around the scenes of all the offences through petrol bills and cash withdrawals. Black was charged with the murder, kidnapping and illegal dumping of the bodies of Susan Maxwell (1982), Caroline Hogg (1982) and Sarah Harper (1986). On 19 May 1994, the jury found him guilty on all charges and he was jailed for a minimum of 35 years.

See Gary Leon Ridgway p. 276

RIDGWAY, GARY LEON (1983–2001)

On 30 November 2001, Gary Ridgway was arrested for the notorious Green River Killings. He had become a suspect as early as 1983 and in 1987 had given samples that would later link him, via DNA, to the crimes. In the 1980s the Green River Killer may have murdered up to 50 people in Seattle, Tacoma, Washington and, perhaps, Portland in Oregon. The majority of the victims were prostitutes or runaway teenagers who had been picked up around the Pacific Highway South. They had all been strangled and dumped near the Green River in the state of Washington. Twenty years later, Ridgway was finally arrested and, after much legal wrangling, the trial preliminaries began in August 2003. The full trial is not expected to begin until 2004.

See Robert Black p. 275

RAMIREZ, RICHARD (1985)

Throughout 1985, Richard Ramirez terrorised Los Angeles and became known as the 'Night Stalker'. Ramirez would enter a home and shoot the male member of the family, then move on to rape and either beat or shoot the female and any children. Ramirez had a previous criminal record for theft and burglary, and when his stolen car number plate was

▶ RIGHT: *Richard Ramirez displays a pentagram in a Los Angeles courtroom.*

given to the police by a witness, his fingerprints were found in the abandoned vehicle. After a large police hunt, he was recognised while attempting to steal a car. He confessed to the crimes but pleaded not guilty at his trial. Nonetheless he was found guilty of 13 murders, plus other crimes, and Ramirez remains on death row.

See Ted Bundy p. 261

WUORNOS, AILEEN (1989–90)

Between November 1989 and June 1990, the roadside prostitute Aileen 'Lee' Wuornos claimed the lives of seven of her clients, usually white, middle-aged men. Wuornos showed the hallmarks of a serial killer:

Today's Execution is brought to you by the Committee to Re-elect Jeb Bush.

CHOOSE LIFE

abandoned by a teenage mother, ill-treated by an alcoholic grandfather, an early pregnancy herself, drink, drugs and a move into prostitution to support her habits. Wuornos drifted around the US until 1976; she would later claim that she had been raped and beaten by clients on at least 12 occasions. Finally she settled at Daytona Beach, Florida. Unable to establish long-term relationships with men, she attempted to commit suicide on several occasions.

By 1986 she had formed a tempestuous lesbian relationship with Tyria Moore, although she still earned her living as a highway prostitute. Wuornos was tired of being brutalised and ripped off by her clients and now packed a pistol. She killed first in November 1989, then six more times before Moore was picked up and turned against her. In January and May 1992, Wuornos was found guilty of four of the seven killings connected with her, and she was sentenced to death.
See Charlotte Bryant p. 86

ONOPRIENKO, ANATOLY (1989–96)

On 16 April 1996 Anatoly Onoprienko was arrested at his girlfriend's home in the Ukraine, thus ending the career of the killer known as the 'Terminator', who may have claimed as many as 52 lives. Initially he admitted to eight killings between 1989 and 1995. In 1996 alone it is believed that he slaughtered eight entire families. His motives are confused, although certainly he robbed his victims; he would gun down adults and batter children to death, his preferred weapon was a shotgun. During his trial he never expressed any regrets and openly confessed many of the killings. In March 1997 the Ukrainian court sentenced him to death, although to date there is still a moratorium on executions. Onoprienko himself wishes to be

◀ *LEFT: Death penalty protesters pictured before the execution of Aileen Wuornos.*

killed, warning that if he were ever released he would kill until killed.
See Andre Romanovich Chikatilo p. 271

BERNARDO, PAUL AND CARLA HOMOLKA (1990–92)

Husband and wife serial killers Paul and Carla Bernado were known as Ken and Barbie by their neighbours in Canada, but they were responsible for 43 sexual attacks and a string of murders, many of which they filmed. Possibly motivated by the fact that Carla was not a virgin when they married, Paul demanded his wife's assistance in taking the virginity of her younger sister, Tammy. In a botched attempt to anaesthetise her so that Paul could rape her, Tammy choked on her own vomit. Carla began to procure women for Paul's unbridled sexual appetite. The couple killed three people in all and became Canada's most notorious modern-day criminals. DNA from the string of rapes linked Bernardo to the killings, and when police found the couple's tapes it was enough to sentence them both to life imprisonment.
See Gerald Gallego and Charlene Williams-Gallego p. 269

GEORGES, GUY (1991–97)

Between 1991 and 1997, the vagrant Guy Georges tortured, raped and murdered seven women in the area around the Bastille in Paris. Georges would ingratiate himself with his intended victim, gaining an invitation to their homes, where he would torture and rape them and slit their throats. Georges' DNA had been on file for three years before he was arrested. He had been questioned about three rapes and murders that had been committed between 1991 and 1994. When he came to trial in March 2001, he was described as a narcissistic psychopath, but initially denied the charges. On 5 April he confessed and was sentenced to life imprisonment with no parole for at least 22 years.
See DNA Testing p. 167

ARMSTRONG, JOHN ERIC (1992–2000)

John Eric Armstrong, one of the most travelled serial killers in criminal history, was a member of the US Navy. Between 1992 and 1999, he was responsible for prostitute murders in countries as far afield as Hong Kong, Israel, Korea, Singapore and Thailand, as well as in his homeland of the United States. Following a prostitute murder in Detroit, Armstrong himself called the police; they were sceptical of the 'law-abiding' citizen's explanations and began keeping him under surveillance. The police found the bodies of the victims near railway tracks in Detroit and, working on a serial-killer profile, realised Armstrong would return to bury another body there. Armstrong returned on 12 April 2000 and, since then, police have been trying to link his confessions to a string of murders across the world.

See Charles Sobhraj p. 266

RESENDEZ, ANGEL (1997–99)

Resendez became known as the 'Railway Killer', because his crimes took place near railroad tracks in three states in America. He became the subject of an international manhunt for the murder of nine women, who he had beaten, stabbed and sexually assaulted. Resendez gave himself up in El Paso, Texas.

Resendez, who was known throughout much of the manhunt by his alias of Rafael Ramirez, claimed his first victim in 1997 and systematically used the railroad to move in and out of areas, to avoid detection and to be close to potential victims, until June 1999. Resendez finally turned himself in and was convicted of seven killings. He was sentenced to death but still remains in prison as he gradually exhausts the appeal process.

See Juan Corona p. 259

UNSOLVED MURDERS

CHRISTINA COCHRAN (1843)

Christina Cochran married John Gilmour in Ayrshire in 1843. Within six weeks, he was dead. He was buried, but Christina's flight to America caused suspicion; she was intercepted and her husband's body was exhumed. Tests revealed that he had died from arsenic poisoning. Witnesses suggested Christina had bought the poison herself or had sent a maid to buy it for her. The evidence in court was contradictory and inconclusive. Christina was found not guilty and it was suggested that John may have accidentally poisoned himself. They returned a verdict of not proven; Cochran spent the next 62 years of her life an unattached widow.

See Madeline Smith p. 284

SMITH, MADELINE (1856)

In 1856, Madeline Smith, the daughter of a wealthy Glasgow architect, met and fell in love with Channel Islander Emile L'Angelier. However, her father convinced her to marry William Minnock, a man better placed in society, and Madeline asked L'Angelier to return her love letters. L'Angelier made it clear that if he could not have Madeline he would make sure he ruined her. When his body was found on 22 March 1857, a post-mortem revealed arsenic in his stomach. The police arrested Madeline on 31 March; investigations revealed that she had purchased arsenic from various chemists. However, L'Angelier was known to be

something of a hypochondriac and he took various dangerous poisons, believing they improved his physical health, which became the key to the defence case.

As it was, the letters themselves ruined Madeline's reputation. Her implied lack of morals – relating to her affair with L'Angelier – inferred that she was capable of murder. Despite this, Madeline was fortunate to have a very eloquent defence counsel, who undermined all the circumstantial evidence linking her to the poisoning. The jury returned a not-proven verdict, but Madeline, ruined, fled to New York, dying there on 12 April 1928.

See Florence Bravo p. 285

THE ODD CASE OF EDMUND POOK (1871)

In 1871, epileptic Edmund Pook from Greenwich began a relationship with the household domestic servant, Jane Clouson. When she was violently murdered on 26 April she was found to be two months pregnant. Bloodstains were discovered on Edmund's coat and he was identified as having purchased a hammer, believed to be the murder weapon. Despite all this, Edmund was found not guilty.

See The Bootlace Murders p. 290

BRAVO, FLORENCE (1876)

After separating from her first husband, Florence maintained a long-term relationship with her close friend Dr Gully, but in 1875 she married Charles Bravo. On 18 April 1876 Charles was struck down by what was believed to be arsenic poisoning, and his death resulted in two inquests and much gossip. It transpired that arsenic was not the poison in question but that it

◄ *LEFT: A newspaper artist's impression of the Edmund Pook case.*

was antimony, a drug used in Florence's stables. The inquests were sure that Charles had been murdered but there was insufficient evidence to bring charges against anyone. Theories abounded; Gully's reputation was ruined and Florence died an alcoholic in September 1873.

See Adelaide Bartlett p. 287

◄ *LEFT: Charles Bravo poisoned by an unknown hand in 1876.*

THE WILLIAM SAUNDERS CASE (1877)

On 25 March 1877 the body of William Saunders was found near Penge Cricket Club; he had been kicked to death and thrown into a pond. He had last been seen quarrelling with James Dempsey, who was engaged to Saunders' daughter by a previous marriage. Dempsey, Saunders' wife and her eldest son, Alfred Inman, were all suspected of having murdered William. However, no charges were ever made and the police even failed to check their clothing.

See The Death of William Lyddon p. 288

THE MURDER OF GEORGINA MOORE (1882)

In 1882 the court and newspapers were more interested in Stephen Moore's love life than who killed his eight-year-old daughter, Georgina. Her body had been found near the home of one of Stephen's former lovers – Esther Pay – in Yarnley, Kent. She was suspected of having killed Georgina in revenge for being abandoned by him. The jury believed she had no motive and cleared her.

See Jeannie Ewan Donald p. 83

BARTLETT, ADELAIDE (1886)

French-born Adelaide married Edwin Bartlett in 1875. Edwin was rather a strange character, something of a hypochondriac – he had all his teeth sawn off at the roots and was perhaps suffering from syphilis – and he showed little interest in sleeping with his wife, although they did have a child that was sadly stillborn.

In 1885 Edwin engaged George Dyson, a man of education, to tutor his wife. Dyson and Adelaide began an affair. On 27 December Dyson bought chloroform so that Adelaide could use it on Edwin should he make sexual advances towards her. However, her husband had fallen ill a few days before and was already bedridden. On 1 January 1886 he died; the post-mortem the following day revealed chloroform in his stomach. Adelaide was arrested and charged with his murder, but no one could explain how the chloroform had got into his stomach. She was acquitted and disappeared from public view; she may have returned to France or emigrated to America.

See Florence Bravo p. 285

JACK THE RIPPER (1888)

In the autumn of 1888 the most notorious murderer in British history stalked the East End streets of London, mutilating then killing at least five prostitutes. The savage attacks, increasing in ferocity over the few short weeks, terrorised London and the police seemed unable to find a credible suspect or protect the street women. Mary Ann

> ▸ RIGHT: Adelaide Bartlett, who was acquitted after an inconclusive trial.

287

Nicholls (43) was the first acknowledged victim, she was lashed across the throat and repeatedly stabbed on August 31. Annie Chapman (47) had many of her organs removed on September 8; the attack on Elizabeth Stride (45) may have been interrupted on September 30, but the same night the Ripper mutilated Catharine Eddowes (46). The last and most vicious dismemberment took place on November 9, when the Ripper claimed his last victim, Mary Kelly (25).

During the killing spree, the police and newspapers were taunted with letters puporting to having been written by the Ripper. One even contained Eddowes' kidney, part of which the Ripper claimed to have fried and eaten. The police were inundated with theories and potential suspects but as suddenly as the killings had begun they abruptly ended. Writers still speculate as to the identity of the Ripper.

See The Zodiac Killer p. 203

THE DEATH OF WILLIAM LYDDON (1890)

William Lyddon lived with his half-brother and stepmother at his doctor's practice in Faversham, Kent. By 1890 William was addicted to morphine and Charles, his half-brother, used this addiction to control him.

◀ *LEFT:* Cover of the Penny Illustrated Paper *showing one of Jack the Ripper's victims.*

They frequently fought, but always Charles had the upper hand. On several occasions, police were called to the house to break up the fights. Throughout October of that year William's health and state of mind deteriorated; his brother even barred him from sleeping in his own bed. By 25 November William was dead from a morphine overdose.

Statements from the household servants brought about the trial of Charles and his mother, but the jury took only two minutes to pronounce them not guilty. If they were not murderers, they were surely guilty of supreme neglect.

See The Trial of Alfred John Monson p. 289

THE TRIAL OF ALFRED JOHN MONSON (1893)

The trial of Alfred Monson, accused of murdering Cecil Hambrough, was a tale of fraud, money-lending and deceit. The killing occurred on the Ardlamont Estate in Argyllshire on 10 August 1893. Monson, having taken out insurance on Cecil's life, faked Cecil's suicide to cash in the insurance. Cecil's father, a near-bankrupt landowner, had become embroiled with Monson and a money-lender called Tottenham, and the financial dealings became more complex since Cecil had assigned payments in the event of his death to Monson's wife. The jury heard that on the day before Cecil's death, Monson had tried to drown him; the prosecution was largely due to insistence from the insurance companies. Circumstantially there were motives, but certain peculiarities of the Scottish court produced a verdict of not proven.

See Madeline Smith p. 284

▶ RIGHT: *The trial of Alfred John Monson, accused of murdering Cecil Hambrough.*

THE BOOTLACE MURDERS (1900)

In September 1900 Herbert Bennett arranged for his wife and child to visit Great Yarmouth, so that he could indulge in his affair with a young parlour-maid named Alice Meadows. On the night of 22 September, Bennett's wife was murdered on South Denes, Great Yarmouth; she had been strangled with a bootlace. Both Bennett and his wife had been involved in frauds and other moneymaking schemes, and she had booked into the lodgings under an assumed name. What damned Bennett at the trial was the fact that he had in his possession a gold chain that his wife had been wearing on the day she died. He was hanged in 1901, but in 1912 there was a near-identical murder on the same beach and doubts were raised as to his guilt.

See Christina Cochran p. 284

THE LUARD TRAGEDY (1908)

Retired Major-General Charles Luard returned to his home at Ightham in Kent on 24 August 1908, to find his wife dying from gunshot wounds; her purse and rings had been stolen. There was an unfair press vendetta against Charles, but the inquest exonerated him. Luard was consumed with grief and threw himself in front of a train. Convicted murderer John Dickman was linked to the crime; he was hanged for another murder in 1910.

See Florence Bravo p. 285

THE WELDON ATHERSTONE CASE (1910)

The body of actor Weldon Atherstone was discovered in an empty basement flat in Battersea, two floors below the apartment of his mistress, Elizabeth Earl, in 1910. Atherstone was carrying a cosh in his back pocket and was wearing slippers; his boots were found inside the empty flat and he had been shot in the head. Nobody, including Miss Earl, could shed any light on the death of the musichall star.

See The Death of Marilyn Monroe p. 298

THE AXE-MAN OF NEW ORLEANS (1911–19)

Between 1911 and 1919 there was a series of violent murders; it appeared that robbery was not the motive and the weapon used was often the property of the victim. What was particularly bizarre in the case of these killings was the accusations of some of the victims who survived. On 28 June 1918, Louis Besumer and Harriet Lowe were attacked by the axe-man; Lowe was killed but before she died, she denounced Besumer. On the 10th March 1919, however, the axe-man struck again, injuring Charles and Rosie Cortimiglia and killing Mary, their daughter. Rosie denounced her neighbours, one of whom was sentenced to death and the other given life imprisonment. But the axe-man struck again in September and October. The last victim's wife shot Joseph Mumfre, claiming he was the axe-man. There were no more murders but also no proof against Mumfre.

See The Moonlight Murders p. 297

THE MURDER OF MABEL MAYER (1927)

On 2 July 1927, 15-year-old Mabel Mayer from Oakland, California, was murdered close to her home. Her wristwatch had stopped at 10:06 and the body showed signs that she had been brutally beaten with a floorboard. The police hunted for a man witnesses described as being nearly 6 feet tall, between 35 and 40 years and well-built, with a dark complexion and long, matted hair. They linked the murder with a street robbery committed by a similar-looking man the previous Monday.

Despite a police cordon and a degree of paranoia in Oakland for several weeks, the murderer of Mabel, known as 'Sunshine' to her friends and family, was never caught, neither was the man who had struck a few days earlier.

See The Valerie Percy Murder p. 301

THE JULIA WALLACE CASE (1931)

William Herbert Wallace returned home on the night of 19 January 1931 to find his wife, Julia, dead. Her head had been smashed with a poker, and a mackintosh, heavily stained with blood, had been partly burned. William, a Prudential Assurance agent in Liverpool, had gone out to meet

▶ RIGHT: *The entry behind the Wallaces' home (left) and the back yard of the property (right). Postcard sent from Julia Wallace to her neighbour, Mrs Johnston (centre).*

▶ *RIGHT: Elvira Barney, who was found not guilty of her husband's murder in 1932.*

a Mr Qualtrough, but the address did not exist and Qualtrough never appeared. The police charged William with Julia's murder and in a heavily biased trial in April 1931 he was found guilty and sentenced to death. The sentence was quashed by the Lord Chief Justice the following month, making legal history.

Wallace returned to work, but to his dying day he was plagued with gossip, innuendo and ill-health, dying prematurely on 26 February 1933. Further enquiries have uncovered no additional evidence.

See The Bootlace Murders p. 290

BARNEY, ELVIRA (1932)

On 31 May 1932 Elvira Barney, a wealthy socialite living in Knightsbridge, reported the shooting of her lover, Michael Stephen. The couple had been seen arguing and Barney explained that she had intended to commit suicide, but the gun had accidentally gone off, killing Stephen. She was found not guilty in court but just four years later she committed suicide in a Parisian hotel.

See The Luard Tragedy p. 291

THE CASE OF THE POISON PARTRIDGES (1933)

On 21 June 1933 a brace of partridges were delivered to Lieutenant Hubert Chevis on Blackdown Camp near Aldershot; the partridges were laced with strychnine. Chevis had one mouthful and realised something was wrong, but it was too late – he died the following day. On the day of his son's funeral, Sir William Chevis received a telegram saying 'Hooray, hooray, hooray'; it was signed 'Hartigan'. There were no arrests.

See Florence Bravo p. 285

THE BRIGHTON TRUNK MURDER (1933)

Tony Mancini lived at various addresses in Brighton with former dancer Violet Kaye. She earned her living from prostitution and Mancini was a waiter in a café. The couple had a public argument on 10 May 1933 when Violet accused Mancini of having affairs. Afterwards, Violet disappeared, Mancini claiming she had gone to work in Paris. Shortly afterwards, Mancini moved lodgings, taking with him a heavy trunk. On 17 June a headless and legless body was found in a trunk at Brighton railway station; the victim was never identified, but amongst the suspects interviewed was Mancini. He panicked and fled to London, where he was arrested following the police discovery of Violet's decomposing body in the trunk at his Brighton lodgings.

Although the two Brighton trunk murders may not have been related, Mancini had been undone by the investigations of the first murder. Mancini claimed he had found Violet's body on their bed when he had returned home and had panicked, claiming that as a convicted thief, the police would have automatically assumed his guilt. The jury returned a verdict of not guilty, but in a newspaper statement in 1976 Mancini admitted murdering Violet; the first trunk murder was never solved.

See Bela Kiss p. 143

THE CLEVELAND TORSO KILLER (1935–38)

In September 1935 the heavily mutilated bodies of two decapitated men were discovered, and police initially suspected that they were dealing with a homosexual killer. However the next two bodies they found were female. Over the next three years, 12 victims were claimed. The famous detective Elliot Ness was brought in to lead investigations and in August 1938 he rounded up vagrants and burned down the area where the bodies had been found; the murders stopped. His suspects were Frank Dolezal and a man known as Sundheim, but in April 1939 Dolezal committed suicide. Sundheim was committed to a mental institution, where he died; no clear link was established.

See The Ice Box Murders p. 300

THE SIR HARRY OAKES CASE (1943)

The body of American-born Canadian citizen Sir Harry Oakes, a multi-millionaire, was found in his home in Nassau in the Bahamas on 8 July 1943. His body had been battered and burned. The Duke of Windsor was then the governor of the islands and called in two detectives from the Miami Police Department to investigate. As a result, Oakes' son-in-law, Alfred de Marigny, was charged and tried for the murder.

▸ RIGHT: Brighton railway station as it would have looked at the time of the Brighton Trunk Murder.

295

LEFT: Alfred de Marigny is escorted by police, accused of the murder of Sir Harry Oakes.

The case was horribly mishandled and he was acquitted. Indeed, the precise nature of the weapon that had caused the fatal wounds was never established, nor were the feathers scattered around the body explained. Several attempts were made to reopen the case, but to no avail, and no further light has ever been shed on the crime.

See The Murder of Karin Cookie Kupcinet p. 299

THE CHARLES WALTON CASE (1945)

On 14 February 1945, 74-year-old Charles Walton headed off towards Meon Hill on Potter's Farm in Lower Quinton, Warwickshire, to do some hedge-cutting; he never returned home. His family called the police and that night they found his body. His throat had been slashed with his own scythe, which had been left sticking out of his neck. Cut into the skin of his neck and chest was a cross.

The case was not easy to solve and celebrated detective Robert Fabian was called in to investigate. He discovered that the death had the hallmarks of a ritual killing related to witchcraft. The one lead he had was that an Italian prisoner of war working in a nearby camp was seen washing his hands in a ditch. He also had bloodstains on his coat, but he refused to answer any questions. This later turned out to be rabbit's blood.

Fabian claimed he knew who had committed the murder; it was Albert Potter, to whom Walton had lent a considerable amount of money. Potter simply could not pay it back and killed the old man, faking the witchcraft connection. However, he was never brought to trial.

See The Trial of Alfred John Monson p. 289

THE MOONLIGHT MURDERS (1946)

On the night of 22 February 1946, Mary Jeanne Larey and Jimmy Hollis narrowly survived an attack by a 'phantom-like' murderer in Texarkana, on the Texas-Arkansas border. One month later, Richard Griffin and Polly Ann Moore were found murdered; she had also been raped. On 13 April Betty Jo Booker and Jerry Atkins were murdered in a similar fashion. Three hundred suspects were brought in for questioning, but on 3 May the phantom struck again, killing Virgil Starks and seriously wounding his wife Katy in their home.

   The police finally focussed on a man called Youell Swinney. After his arrest, the killings ceased for good. Swinney was tried and sentenced to life in 1947, but in 1974 his conviction was overturned and due to a legal loophole he was released. Technically the case still remains unsolved.

See The Axe-Man of New Orleans p. 291

THE MURDER OF STANLEY SETTY (1949)

Brian Donald Hume, discharged from the RAF, set up an electrical business in Golders Green, London. In 1949 he met car-dealer Stanley Setty, who was last seen alive in October whilst carrying £1,000 in cash in his pocket. Shortly

▶ RIGHT: *Sydney Tiffin indicates the place where he found the dismembered torso of Stanley Setty.*

afterwards, his headless body was found rolled in a carpet in the marshes near Southend-on-Sea; his body appeared to have been thrown out of an aircraft. Hume had hired a plane from Elstree airfield and was arrested; in January 1950 he faced two trials, the first was abandoned when the judge became ill and the second when the jury failed to reach a verdict. Ultimately, Hume admitted being an accessory after the fact to murder and was jailed for 12 years; he blamed the killing on three other men.

See The Murder of John Franklin Andrews p. 309

THE DEATH OF MARILYN MONROE (1962)

On 4 August 1962 the body of the world's most glamorous film star was found on her bed in her Los Angeles home. She had died from a massive dose of Nembutal and chloral-hydrate. Officially, the inquest delivered a verdict of probable suicide. The truth may have been far more sinister and indeed the favourite conspiracy theory is that Marilyn was murdered by lethal injection because she knew too much following her affairs with both President John F. Kennedy and his brother, the US attorney general Robert Kennedy.

Marilyn had been born Norma Jean Baker in 1926 and had been through some difficult times. She had married Joe DiMaggio in 1954 and Arthur Miller, the playwright, in 1956, in addition to her much publicised affairs with the Kennedys. There had been accidental overdoses in the past, as the simple Los Angeles girl struggled to cope with her fame. Robert Kennedy admitted he had been at Marilyn's home on the afternoon of her death and that a doctor who had accompanied him had injected the actress with a tranquilliser. Details about the rest of the day, and exactly how she died, remain unclear.

See The Karyn Cookie Kupcinet Case p. 299

THE KARYN COOKIE KUPCINET CASE (1963)

On the evening of 30 November 1963, the naked body of an actress known as Cookie was found in her West Hollywood apartment. She had last been seen alive three days before. What is particularly bizarre is that she made a distraught phone call to a telephone operator, claiming that President Kennedy was about to be assassinated, 20 minutes before he was. Conspiracy theorists believe that she was the victim of a clean-up squad that went around killing potential witnesses. She had called from a phone box rather than her home, possibly believing that her call could be traced. Whether her death was linked to the assassination is still not known. Her father knew Jack Ruby in the 1940s, but had no connection with him in 1963.

See Jack Ruby p. 24

JACK THE STRIPPER (1964–65)

A string of six near-identical killings, known as the Hammersmith Nudes Case, occurred between February 1964 and February 1965. They were the

◄ *LEFT: Marilyn Monroe, whose suspicious death has never been resolved.*

first modern UK crimes to be recognised as serial killings. The bodies of six naked prostitutes – Hannah Tailford, Irene Lockwood, Helen Barthelemey, Mary Fleming, Margaret McGowan and Bridie O'Hara – were found in and around the Hammersmith area. Most of the women had severe bruising to the jaw and their front teeth were missing. It later transpired that the women had been forced to strip and then engage in violent oral sex.

There was a breakthrough of sorts when it was established that the women had all been abducted between 11 p.m. and 1 a.m. and that their bodies had been dumped between 5 a.m. and 6 a.m. The focus of investigations switched to night-shift workers. Microscopic flakes of paint were found on Barthelemey's and Flemings' bodies, narrowing the search to car-spraying workers. All businesses nearby were inspected and a list of suspects drawn up, but no arrest or charge was ever made. In the investigating officer's memoirs, a 45-year-old night security guard was identified as Jack the Stripper; he committed suicide during the investigation of the case. *See* Jack the Ripper p. 287

THE ICEBOX MURDERS (1965)

On the night of 23 June 1965, two elderly residents in Houston, Texas were discovered mutilated, dissected and placed in the refrigerator of their own home. Fred and Edwina Rogers had been killed three days before. The authorities' attention focused on Charles Frederick Rogers, their son, who was rarely in the house, yet had a room upstairs. They found a semi-automatic pistol in his room, but could not find any fingerprints. There were bloodstains on the floor in Charles's room and on 24 June the police began searching for him. His whereabouts have never been established. In 1992, a book claimed that Charles was a CIA operative who had been employed to assassinate Kennedy. Whatever the tenuous links, the truth disappeared in 1965. *See* The Cleveland Torso Killer p. 295

VALERIE PERCY MURDER (1966)

On the night of 18 September 1966 in Kenilworth, Illinois, a murderer broke into the mansion home of Valerie Percy's father, who was campaigning for the US Senate. Valerie was brutally murdered for no apparent reason; she was found bludgeoned and stabbed to death. Police theorised that the murderer knew the Percy estate; the family dog had not barked and her father, Senator Charles Percy, was probably the intended victim.

See The Sir Harry Oakes Case p. 295

THE MONSTER OF FLORENCE (1968–85)

The mystery of the 'Monster of Florence' began in August 1968 with the murder of Barbara Locci, a 32-year-old married woman, and her lover Antonio Lo Bianco. The police interviewed Stefano Mele, Barbara's husband; he listed all her lovers, including Francesco Vinci and Vinci's brothers Giovanni and Salvatore. Mele then confessed that he and Salvatore Vinci had killed the couple. Two years later, he was sentenced to 14 years and pronouned insane.

On 14 September 1974, the bodies of Stefania Pettini and Pasquale Gentilcore were found. On 6 June 1981, the bodies of

▶ *RIGHT: A 1960s chest freezer, similar to the one used in the Texas Icebox Murders.*

301

Carmela De Nuccio and her 30-year-old lover, Giovanni Foggi, were discovered. The killer struck again on 23 October 1981, claiming Susanna Cambi and her boyfriend, Stefano Baldi.

On 19 June 1982 the killer struck yet again, murdering Antonella Migliorini and her boyfriend Paolo Mainardi, who survived. Two West German boys perished on 9 September 1983, a young couple on 29 July 1984 and finally on 8 September 1985, Jean-Michel Kraveichvili and Nadine Mauriot were murdered. What linked the cases was a .22 Beretta revolver and a surgical knife used to mutilate the bodies. Pietro Pacciani was convicted in 1994, but the verdict was overturned.

See The Californian Serial Killer p. 307

THE ZODIAC KILLER (1969–74)

In the late-1960s and early 1970s the Zodiac Killer, who chose his victims based on their astrological signs, killed at least five and claimed responsibility for 17 murders. The Zodiac Killer was a sexual sadist, who tortured his victims before murdering them.

On 4 July 1969, Darlene Ferrin was shot five times and her boyfriend, Mike Mageau, although also shot four times, survived and saw the killer. In 1992 he positively identified Arthur Leigh Allen, a convicted child molester from Vallejo, California who had been investigated by the police in the early 1980s and had always been a suspect. Allen died that

◀ *LEFT: Florence, Italy – the scene of a seventeen-year murder spree by the 'Monster of Florence'.*

THE NEW HAVEN MURDERS (1975–90)

Between 1975 and 1990 a dozen young women, mainly prostitutes, were killed around New Haven, Connecticut. Seven of them may have been victims of the same killer, who strangled or stabbed them. The investigating team received a call from Florida linking the killings with some older, unsolved murders and naming Roosevelt Bowden. In 1978 Bowden had killed his daughter, but he was released from prison in 1986, and killing again in 1988. He was sentenced to death, but died from AIDS in April 1994.

Five of the New Haven murders (1975–78) occurred before Bowden was in prison and two (1986) after he had been released. The three in August and September 1978 occurred whilst he was in prison.

See The Southside Slayer p. 309

THE CALIFORNIAN SERIAL KILLER (1979–86)

Between 1979 and 1986, 10 connected murders took place across four Californian coastal communities. Three Californian counties and four different law-enforcement teams managed to link at least six of the crimes through DNA evidence found at the scenes. In the other four cases, whilst lacking DNA evidence, the same methods of killing suggest a link. Authorities believe the rapist killer may have been responsible for up to 50 rape attacks and 12 murders.

See The Monster of Florence p. 301

PICKTON, ROBERT (1983–2002)

In July 2003 Robert Pickton, a former pig farmer from British Columbia, was formally charged with 15 counts of murder. He had been finally linked to a series of 63 disappearances of drug addicts and prostitutes in the Vancouver area, over a period of nearly 20 years. The police mounted

a raid on his home on 6 February 2002 and retrieved sufficient evidence to charge Pickton with two murders. In October 2002 he was charged with an additional 13 murders. Investigations are ongoing and there may be additional charges as the police uncover more evidence regarding the series of prostitute murders that had formerly been unsolved.

At the height of the investigations, over 50 anthropologists were deployed at his farm, sifting through soil and trying to uncover the remains of bodies. It is believed that after murdering the women, Pickton disposed of their bodies in a wood-pulping machine, then mixed their body-parts with pig feed. Police found women's clothing that may link Pickton directly to the disappearances. Many of the victims appear to have been Native American women.

See The Juarez Serial Killer p. 312

◀ *LEFT: Former pig farmer Robert Pickton, charged with the murder of 15 women.*

THE SOUTHSIDE SLAYER (1984–87)

Between 1984 and 1987 at least 12 and possibly as many as 20 African-American drug-addicted prostitutes were murdered in the Los Angeles area. In 1993, despite the police denying the existence of a serial killer, they arrested an African-American policeman, who later proved to be unconnected with the crimes. The victims were subjected to torture with a knife, before being strangled or stabbed to death. Some think that two convicted killers could be responsible for the murders, whilst others believe that it is the work of a lone man.

The Southside Slayer has been inactive since 1987, so there have been no further leads and it now appears that the scale of investigation has been reduced; it is likely that the culprit will never be apprehended.

See Robert Pickton p. 307

THE MURDER OF JOHN FRANKLIN ANDREWS (1986)

In November 1986 the mutilated body of John Franklin

▶ *RIGHT: Ada Wilson holds a picture of her murdered sister, thought to be one of Robert Pickton's victims.*

Andrews was discovered near Litchfield, Connecticut; his legs, head and genitals were never found. Investigations suggest that he was a serial-killer victim who had struck in New York and Florida. One of the last letters Andrews sent his family included the name and address of a long-haul lorry driver from Arkansas; he was interviewed and cleared; the case remains unsolved.

See The Murder of Stanley Setty p. 297

THE TAMMY ZYWICKI CASE (1992)

Tammy Zywicki was last seen alive on 23 August 1992, when she left Illinois, heading for university. Her body was found on 1 September in the Missouri countryside; she had been sexually assaulted and stabbed repeatedly. Witnesses suggested the killer was white, between 35 and 40 and over 6 feet tall, with dark, bushy hair. One suspect, Lonnie Bierbodt, was cleared. There is still a $150,000 reward for information leading to an arrest.

See The Murder of Nan Toder p. 313

BROWN'S CHICKEN AND SEAFOOD KILLINGS (1993)

Seven employees at Brown's chicken and seafood restaurant in Palatine, Illinois, were murdered on the night of 8 January 1993. The police made the grisly discovery several hours after closing time; the bodies were found in two walk-in refrigerators in the kitchen area. The only tangible evidence was some bullet fragments and the fact that the safe had been robbed; the electricity had also been turned off. Police never found the perpetrators.

See The Ice Box Murders p. 313

◀ *LEFT: The Southside Slayer preyed on prostitutes, with as many as twenty victims in total.*

◀ *LEFT: A Bushmaster XM-15 rifle, the type of gun used by the Suffolk County sniper.*

SUFFOLK COUNTY SERIAL SNIPER (1994)

On 22 July 1994 a man was shot whilst eating in a restaurant in Commack, Suffolk County, New York. Three days later, the sniper tried to kill a petrol-station attendant and on 3 August a worker in a fast-food restaurant was wounded. Through careful criminal profiling and despite the lack of physical evidence, police were able to arrest a man who was later sentenced to 35 years.

See John Allen Muhammad and John Lee Malvo p. 249

THE JUAREZ SERIAL KILLER (1993–PRESENT)

Since 1993 around 260 young women, predominantly slim, with long hair and brown eyes, have disappeared from the Mexican border town of Juarez. Local residents believe that the true number is closer to 400.

Officially, the authorities put the figure at 76 – all have been raped, had their hands tied, their hair cut or had their breasts mutilated. Some have had their heads crushed or driven over by a car. Most of the women were killed on their return from work. Over time, the killings have become more brutal.

In November 2002, eight bodies were found and the police arrested two bus drivers, who confessed to raping and killing the eight women and three others. These were two men amongst the dozens arrested over the years, and every time the killings continued. The two new suspects later denied involvement and claimed that the police had tortured them into making the confessions. As in the past, the new arrests do not seem to have stopped the killings. Two more bodies have shown up since the bus drivers were arrested in November. The state attorney general's office denies the torture allegations and continues to insist the men are guilty.

See Robert Pickton p. 307

THE MURDER OF NAN TODER (1996)

In April 2003, the parents of Nan Toder from North Miami Beach, Florida, accepted damages of $4.6 million from the employers of the man who killed their daughter. Nan Toder was 33 when Christopher Richee, the hotel's maintenance manager, strangled her and beat her over the head. He is serving a life sentence. The case remained unsolved until Richee was arrested and tried for the killing in November 2002.

See The Tammy Zywicki Case p. 311

THE MURDER OF JAIDYN LESKIE (1998)

Toddler Jaidyn Leskie's body was found in a dam near Moe in Australia on 1 January 1998, after he disappeared in mysterious circumstances. His mother's former boyfriend, Greg Domaszewicz, who was babysitting Jaidyn when he disappeared, was charged with the murder, but was acquitted by a Supreme Court jury in December 1998.

The deputy state coroner closed the case in 2001, after holding a closed-door inquiry and producing a two-page report outlining the previously known facts about the death. Nonetheless, police detectives attached to his office continued to investigate the circumstances of the toddler's death, taking new statements from witnesses involved, as well as new DNA and other forensic tests. In July 2003, it was announced that there will be a new public enquiry.

See The Murder of Georgina Moore p. 286

BIBLIOGRAPHY

Abbott, Geoffrey. *Rack, Rope and Red-Hot Pincers*. London: Headline, 1993.

Canwell, Diane. *Women Who Shocked the Nation*. Derby: Breedon Books, 2002.

Crockett, Art. *Serial Murders from the Files of True Detective*. New York: Pinnacle, 1990.

Crockett, Art. *Spree Killers from the Files of True Detective*. New York: Pinnacle, 1991.

Dawnie, R. Angus. *Murder in London*. London: Arthur Barker, 1973.

Fido, Martin. *The Chronicle of Crime*. London: Carlton Books, 2000.

Franklin, Charles. *World-Famous Acquittals*. London: Odhams Books, 1970.

Gaute, J. H. H. and Robin Odel. *The Murderers' Who's Who*. London: Harrap, 1979.

Gaute, J. H. H. and Robin Odel. *Murder Whereabouts*. London: Harrap, 1986.

Goodman, Jonathan. *The Country House Murders*. London: W. H. Allen & Co., 1987.

Hancock, Robert. *Ruth Ellis*. London: Weidenfeld and Nicolson, 1963.

Harris, Melvin. *The True Face of Jack the Ripper*. London: Michael O'Mara Books, 1994.

Honeycomb, Gordon. *The Murders of the Black Museum*. London: Hutchinson, 1982.

Honeycomb, Gordon. *More Murders of the Black Museum*. London: Hutchinson, 1993.

Jones, Frank. *Murderous Women*. London: Headline, 1991.

Jones, Richard Glynn. *The Giant Book of True Crime*. London: Robinson, 1992.

Kray, Reg and Ron. *Our Story*. London: Pan Macmillan, 1989.

Lane, Brian. *Chronicle of 20th Century Murder*. London: Virgin, 1995.

Lane, Brian and Wilfred Gregg. *The Encyclopedia of Serial Killers*. London: Headline, 1992.

Levin, Jack and James Alan Fox. *Mass Murder*. New York: Plenum Press, 1986.

Leyton, Elliott. *Hunting Humans*. New York: Pocket Books, 1988.

Linedecker, Clifford L. *Thrill Killers*. New York: Paperjacks, 1988.

Linedecker, Clifford L. *Serial Thrill Killers*. New York: Knightsbridge, 1990.

Lucas, Norman. *The Child Killers*. London: Barker, 1970.

Lucas, Norman. *The Sex Killers*. London: W. H. Allen, 1974.

Lustgarten, Edgar. *The Woman in the Case*. London: Andre Deutsche, 1965.

Mandelsburg, Rose G. *Torture Killers from the Files of True Detective*. New York: Pinnacle, 1991.

Mortimer, John. *Famous Trials*. London: Penguin, 1986.

Nash, J. Robert. *Encyclopedia of World Crime (6 Volumes)*. Wilmett: Crime Books Inc., 1990.

Norris, Joel. *Serial Killers*. New York: Dolphin Doubleday, 1988.

Piper, Leonard. *Murder by Gaslight*. London: Michael O'Mara Books, 1991.

Richardson, Charlie. *My Manor*. London: Sidgwick and Jackson, 1991.

Robins, Joyce. *Lady Killers*. London: Premier, 1993.

Roughead, William. *Classic Crimes*. London: Pan, 1962.

Scott, Sir Harold. *The Concise Encyclopedia of Crime and Criminals*. London: Hawthorn, 1961.

Sparrow, Gerald. *Vintage Edwardian Murder*. London: Arthur Barker, 1971.

Stagg, Colin and David Kessler. *Who Really Killed Rachel?* London: Aspire, 1999.

Steiger, Brad. *The Mass Murderer*. New York: Award Books, 1967.

Sutherland, Jonathan. *Unsolved Victorian Murder*. Derby: Breedon Books, 2002.

Wilkes, Roger. *Unsolved Crimes*. London: Robinson, 1999.

Williams, Emlyn. *Beyond Belief*. London: Pan Books, 1968.

Wilson, Colin. *The Mammoth Book of True Crime*. London: Robinson, 1988.

Wilson, Colin. *The Mammoth Book of True Crime 2*. London: Robinson, 1990.

Wilson, Colin. *Murder in the 1930s*. London: Robinson, 1992.

Wilson, Colin and Damon. *Murder in the 1940s*. New York: Carroll and Graf Publishers Inc., 1993.

BIOGRAPHIES & CREDITS

Jon Sutherland is a full-time writer and author of over eighty books. His most recent titles include *Unsolved Victorian Murders*, *African Americans At War*, and *Elite Forces of World War Two*. Jon is currently working on a series of educational reference glossaries for Business Studies graduates, a Zulu military history book and a series of interactive war books. Jon lives in Suffolk with his partner Diane Canwell and his two children.

Diane Canwell is also a full-time writer and author of over fifty books. Her most recent titles include *Women Who Shocked The Nation*, *Leisure and Tourism GCSE* and *Vikings*. Diane is also working on a series of glossary texts in Business related topics, several Business Administration books and a major history book called *Women in the American Civil War*. Diane lives in Suffolk with her partner Jon Sutherland.

Introduction

Barry Pritchard served for over 30 years with the Wiltshire Constabulary, mainly in CID and drugs units. From 1976–78 he was a member of Operation Julie, a team which investigated the worldwide production of LSD. He worked on a number of high-profile crimes for the force and with the regional crime squad. Barry retired in 1998 having been Superintendent Operations, Salisbury, for nine years.

PICTURE CREDITS

Getty Images:
60, 126, 308; Sean Gallup: 37; John Chapple: 51; Bernard Kane: 61; Spencer Tirey: 62; Craig Strong: 64; Mike Simons: 69; Chris Morton: 212; Chris Livingston: 278; Don MacKinnon: 309

Mary Evans Picture Library:
12, 15, 18, 40, 41, 42, 72, 73, 75, 82, 86, 238

Science Photo Library:
Volker Steger, Peter Arnold Inc.: 170; Volker Steger: 174

All other pictures courtesy of **Topham Picturepoint**, and collections from AP, The British Library/HIP, Fotomas, Image Works, Novosti, PA, Photonews, PressNet, Star Images, UPP, UPPA Ltd.

INDEX